THE SHERLOCK HOLMES ULTIMATE SMOKING COMPANION

By Kelvin I Jones

And with additional essays and stories by
Roger Johnson, Al Shaw, Wendy Heyman - Marsaw, James C
O'Leary, John L Hicks, R.D. Sherbrooke – Walter and David
Marcum

CUNNING CRIME BOOKS

"You know my method. It is founded on the observance of trifles."

Sherlock Holmes, The Boscombe Valley Mystery
"The pipe draws wisdom from the lips of the philosopher and shuts up the mouths of the foolish."

Thomas Makepeace Thackeray
"With Pipe and Book at close of day, Oh, what is sweeter, mortal, say?"

Richard Le Gallienne, poet of the 1890's.

"Have you not reason, then, to be ashamed and to forbear this filthy novelty, so basely grounded, so foolishly received and so grossly mistaken in the right use thereof. In your abuse thereof sinning against God harming yourselves both in person and goods, and raking also thereby the marks and notes of vanity upon you by the custom thereof making yourselves to be wondered at by all foreign civil nations and by all strangers that come among you to be scorned and held in contempt; a custom loathsome to the eye, hateful to the nose, harmful to the brain, dangerous to the lungs, and in the black stinking fume thereof nearest resembling the horrible stygian smoke of the pit that is bottomless."

— King James I of England - VI of Scotland

CONTENTS

PREFACE BY ROGER JOHNSON

"Nobody comes whose talk is half as good to me as silence. I fly out of the way of everybody and would much rather smoke a pipe of wholesome tobacco than talk to anyone in London just now. Nay, their talk is often rather an offence to me, and I murmur to myself: Why open one's lips for such a purpose?" – Thomas Carlisle, 'The Witch's Weed: A Smokers' Anthology,' 1890.

"The air was heavy with tobacco smoke"[1]

Holmes and Watson both smoked tobacco and so, it seems, did most of the men they encountered, heroes, villains and victims alike. I can't immediately think of any who expressed an objection to the habit, and only poor old Percy Phelps comes to mind as one who would say, "I never smoke myself." It was as well for Sherlock Holmes, since tobacco, its ash and the accoutrements of smoking provided so many of the clues that he recognised but others ignored.

It's the pipe that we associate most with the detective and the doctor – especially the former, and especially the bent briar that is never mentioned in Watson's chronicles or depicted in the original illustrations; it was introduced, for sound practical reasons, by the actor William Gillette, when he launched his play *Sherlock Holmes* in 1899. Nevertheless, both men also smoked cigars and cigarettes. Holmes's cigar plays an essential part in Gillette's play, helping the detective and Miss Alice Faulkner to escape from a potentially deadly situation, and a staggering number of chain-smoked cigarettes provides a vital clue in the case of "The Golden Pince-Nez".

We tend to forget these aspects of self-poisoning when we think of Sherlock Holmes today, but that wasn't always the case. Even before *Sherlock Holmes: A Drama in Four Acts* was first performed, a new edition of *The Scottish Students' Songbook* [2] included a ditty called "Sherlock Holmes", written and composed by Claude Ralston, an Edinburgh lawyer. This is the chorus:

> With his lips hard set and his cigarette,
>
> As his fingers thro' his hair he combs;
>
> He's never yet been baffled,
>
> And he'll send 'em to the scaffold
>
> By the score, will Sherlock Holmes.

Holmes's monograph *Upon the Distinction Between the Ashes of the Various Tobaccos* is lost to us. So we can't know for certain what sort of epigraph he might have chosen. Not, I suspect, that composed by Arthur Conan Doyle's friend Jerome K Jerome for his book *Idle Thoughts of an Idle Fellow*, which concludes:

'To the friend who never tells me of my faults, never wants to borrow money, and never talks about himself —

To the companion of my idle hours, the soother of my sorrows, the confidant of my joys and hopes —

My oldest and strongest pipe,

This little volume is gratefully and affectionately dedicated.'

No, it's too sentimental for Holmes. And although he didn't lack wit, he couldn't have opted for Oscar Wilde's remark: "A cigarette is the perfect type of a perfect pleasure. It is exquisite, and it leaves one unsatisfied. What more can one want?"[3]

But there is one observation that's indisputably appropriate for Sherlock Holmes. It was written by another of Conan Doyle's literary friends, Rudyard Kipling:

"A woman is only a woman, but a good cigar is a smoke."[4]

Roger Johnson, BSI, ASH

Editor: The Sherlock Holmes Journal.

1. Not the sometimes poisonous atmosphere at 221B Baker Street, but Charles Augustus Milverton's study at

Appledore Towers, Hampstead.

2. Published by Bayley & Ferguson (London & Glasgow), 1897.

3. Holmes's monograph is first mentioned in *The Sign of the Four*, which recounts events that occurred in 1887 or 1888; Wilde's witticism is taken from *The Picture of Dorian Gray*, first published in the July 1890 issue of *Lippincott's Monthly Magazine*.

4. From his poem "The Betrothed", first published in the Indian newspapers the *Pioneer Mail* and the *Civil and Military Gazette* (under the title "The Meditation of William Kirkland") in November 1888.

ORIGINAL PREFACE TO THE 1981 EDITION

Victorian epithet:
'Fill the bowl, you jolly sour,
And burn all sorrow to a coal.'

It is an autumn night. Outside, the rain lashes against the windows with persistent fury and the dank streets are awash. Only a solitary streetlamp pierces the unremitting gloom. London huddles under the relentless fury of the storm.

But inside, behind the heavy velvet curtains of an upstairs room in Baker Street a more tranquil scene unfolds before us. The room, though small and cluttered, welcomes us with its blazing fire and comfortable upholstered chairs. A hiss of gas combines with the familiar smell of an oil lamp to produce a sense of domestic warmth. Portraits of Victorian celebrities hang from the ornate walls and before the fire is a luxuriant bearskin rug. And into that rug descend the slippered feet of a lean but impeccably dressed gentleman. His keen eyes glitter in the soft gaslight. On his lap he has unfolded a medieval palimpsest which he is studying with such undeflected concentration that he barely notices the acrid wreaths of blue tobacco smoke, spiralling upwards towards the ceiling.

For two hours he has been sitting here, motionless, like a spider at the centre of its web, pondering the intricacies of these arcane markings. And so, the comfortable room has become a dense fog-enveloped oven, more deadly perhaps than the great Grimpen Mire. Long since has his companion, Dr Watson, retired to the sanctuary of the upstairs bedroom where he is allowed to breathe freely, and where his visibility is permitted to extend beyond a yard . . .

A somewhat irreverent glimpse of the Baker Street ménage, you may feel. And to some extent I must agree. Yet, like all lampoons, the truth is somehow very near at hand behind the obvious absurdity. It is quite true that scarcely a depiction of Sherlock Holmes appears before the public without some mention of his pipe, be it the meerschaum of apocryphal origin or the more accurate clay version. The smokescreens in the chambers of 221B are as much a part of the Holmesian totality as the pea-soup fogs, from whose depths the unkindly criminal springs.

Yet how accurate is our traditional view of that world? Would it disturb many of us to know that Holmes smoked as many cigarettes as he had recourse to his tobacco? Would it shock us to consider for a moment that the habit may have had its origins in a profound neurosis?

These are deep waters, my dear Watson. Yet let us set the record straight. Why not? To the man who cried "Give me data!" it would have seemed unnatural to do otherwise . . .

THE BEFORE BREAKFAST PIPE

A - THE HABIT

"Don't you smoke? Then you will excuse me if I light my pipe".
~ILLU (115)

"Tobacco smoke is the one element in which, by our European
manners, men can sit silent together without embarrassment
and where no man is bound to speak one word more than he has
actually and veritably got to say..." - Thomas Carlyle.

If we have a picture of Baker Street and its unforgettable sitting-room, that picture is surely incomplete without the acrid fumes of tobacco, the pipe-rack and the tobacco stuffed into the toe-end of a Persian slipper. And the image of Sherlock Holmes himself is quite without credence if we do not grant him the indulgence of a pipe. (A)

So all-pervasive is the tobacco aroma that curls its way around the tiny sitting-room at 221B that we must only assume Mrs Hudson to have been a long-suffering and intrepid woman. Apart from the clutter of papers and bric-a-brac on the mantlepiece and working surfaces, (107) the walls and ceiling must have been stained to a dark brown and the daily debris of Holmes own "plugs and dottles" would surely be tolerated only by the strongest of stomachs. Perhaps the fire started by Moriarty's henchmen (B) provided her with the perfect opportunity for a general cleansing and redecoration of these famous rooms.

In our very first encounter with the detective, the compliant Watson is given an unequivocal warning:

"You don't mind the smell of strong tobacco, I hope?"

"I always smoke 'ship's' myself", I answered." (I)

It was indeed fortunate that Watson was already a slave of the tobacco weed or his patience would have been sorely tested.

What were the origins of Holmes' and Watson's addiction? And where did both men pick up the habit?

In Holmes' case, there was a compulsive need to smoke. Late on in his association with Watson, he attempted to justify this compulsion.

"You have not, I hope, learned to despise my pipe and my lamentable tobacco? It has to take the place of food these days".

"But why not eat?"

"Because the faculties become refined when you starve them". (119)

Whilst the cocaine formed a means of escape from the dreary world of hum-drum criminality, the tobacco acted as a strop to Holmes' razor-sharp brain. It is a wonder that Holmes survived so long, considering the continual onslaught to his digestive and respiratory organs. It is well-known that cocaine acts as a stimulant to the mental processes. A combination of both cocaine and tobacco must have achieved considerable results, producing a rarefied mental state. Clearly, Holmes picked up the habit as a young man, for in *The Musgrave Ritual*, an early case, dating from his student days, we find him smoking cigarettes:

"Reginald Musgrave sat down opposite to me and lit the cigarette which I had pushed towards him". (59)

Did the pipe come later? Were the cigarettes the start of a lifelong habit? If we assume Holmes had a public school education, then the practice of consuming "snouts" covertly behind the games hut is not an unlikely possibility. By the period of *A Study in Scarlet* he had progressed to the full complement of pipe, cigarettes and cigars. (5) There is the possibility that, once contracted, the habit served to assist an already nervous sensibility, prone to neurotic fits of melancholia. (C)

With Watson, we are on less speculative ground. As an army doctor, it is no wonder that he smoked. The navy provided duty-free tobacco in large quantities and we have his own word for it that he smoked "ship's", (I) a rough, coarse cut tobacco popular amongst sailors of the period. (D)

The frequency of tobacco consumption may be assessed by a careful reckoning of its many instances in the canon. Holmes smokes cigarettes on no less than fourteen separate occasions. He has recourse to cigars twelve times and the pipe features a staggering fifty-four times. In addition, he takes snuff, but this may have been a passing fancy. (32) Mycroft, his brother, also indulged (68) and it may be from him that the habit was contracted. These statistics mean nothing in themselves. But when we come to examine Holmes' consumption in detail, we realise that his recourse to the drug was both unremitting and dangerous.

In *The Man With The Twisted Lip*, for example, we begin the narrative by finding the detective in an eastern-style opium den in Upper Swandam Lane. Holmes remarks to Watson, with some amusement:

"I suppose that you imagine that I have added opium-smoking to cocaine injections and all the other little weaknesses . . . " (41)

On the drive down to Kent, Holmes shakes himself and "(lights) up his pipe". (42)

No sooner has he arrived, than he takes off his coat, puts on a "large blue dressing-gown" and then proceeds to construct a "sort of eastern divan". This he sits on, Buddha-like, and once installed, smokes his way through an entire ounce of shag tobacco.

However, this is not an isolated case. In *The Hound Of The Baskervilles* he begins by smoking a number of cigarettes. On leaving the rooms at Baker Street, Watson is asked to instruct Bradley's, the tobacconist, (E) to send up "a pound of the strongest shag tobacco". (21) On returning, Watson imagines that "a fire had broken out", so dense with smoke is the sitting-room. The conversation that follows is not without its humorous side:

"Caught cold, Watson?" said he.

"No, it's this poisonous atmosphere".

"I suppose it is pretty thick, now that you mention it". (22)

Holmes then admits to Watson he has "consumed an incredible amount of tobacco". (23)

This pipe binge is equalled only, perhaps, by the example described for us in *The Golden Pince-Nez*. At Yoxley Old Place, near Chatham, Holmes and Watson meet Professor Coram who is a chain smoker of alarming rapidity. He offers Holmes an Egyptian cigarette one of many which he has supplied, tailor-made, from "Ionides of Alexandria".(86) Watson soon observes that Holmes is smoking them with an extraordinary rapidity, to such an extent that the professor is led to observe, "why you are even a quicker smoker than myself". His reply is indicative of a lifelong passion for the weed:

"I am a connoisseur", said he, taking another cigarette from the box - his fourth - and lighting it from the stub of that which he had finished. (88)

Of course, in this instance, it was Holmes' specific intention to litter the carpet with cigarette ash I order to trace the footprint of young Willoughby Smith's murderer. But note that he refers to the cigarettes in question as "excellent", proof positive of his position as a devotee.

The frequency of Holmes' recourse to the pipe is also indicated by Watson's references to a pipe in relation to specific mealtimes and parts of the day. In The Hound we find him pushing away his "untasted breakfast" and lighting "the unsavoury pipe which was the companion of his deepest meditations".(27) In *The Engineer's Thumb* we find him lounging about in the sitting-room, "smoking his before-breakfast pipe".(48) In *Charles Augustus Milverton*, we discover Holmes and Watson "smoking our morning pipe", (82) after breakfast. In *Wisteria Lodge* Holmes speaks of a chaotic case "over an evening pipe" (100) whilst in *The Cardboard Box* we find both partners chatting "over our cigars".(102) Finally, in *The Three Garridebs*, Holmes knocks out the ashes of his "after-breakfast pipe" and then slowly refills it. The conclusion we must inevitably draw from all this is that

Holmes began at any time between the hours of 7 and 9 am, paused for breakfast, then resumed with two or possibly more. Maybe he then reverted to cigars or cigarettes, but he most certainly ended the day sharing a pipe with his roommate. The actual number of cigarettes consumed in a typical morning must have been considerable (twenty or thirty at least) since Watson carefully records in *The Norwood Builder* that "The carpet round his chair was littered with cigarette ends, and with the early editions of the morning papers".(77)

If Holmes found that "a concentrated atmosphere helps a concentration of thought", (24) it helps to explain why he showed a reluctance to surrender the habit. Even well into his later years we find him still puffing away:

"A half-smoked, sodden cigar hung from the corner of his mouth, and as he sat down, he struck a match and relit it." (G)

Clearly the warnings issued by the members of the medical profession (and we must remember that the good doctor was one) went unheeded by the detective. Yet by the 1880's the connection between heavy smoking and diseases of the respiratory system had been clearly established. A study, completed in 1859, demonstrated that of 68 patients in a hospital at Montpelier, France, who had cancer of the lips, tongue, tonsils and other parts of the mouth, all used tobacco and 66 of them smoked short-stemmed clay pipes.

Holmes' own attitude to Watson's own tobacco habits is interesting" since it provides us with a good insight into his personality. It is evident that he was not without some guilty feelings upon the subject - feelings which he projected onto the long-suffering doctor. Perhaps his rough treatment of Watson harked back to the early days when Watson had the effrontery to describe the detective as a "self-poisoner by cocaine and tobacco". (40)

Ensconced in an Oxfordshire inn, Holmes remarks to Watson:

"Mrs Merrilow does not object to tobacco, Watson, if you wish to indulge your filthy habits". (130)

Some commentators have detected a slight worsening of the

relationship between the two men in later years. It is apt therefore, that Watson should apply this simile in *The Creeping Man*:

"As an institution I was like the . . . shag tobacco . . ."(126)

Mention of Watson's own tobacco consumption is much scantier. A pipe is referred to on seven occasions, a cigar only once and cigarettes twice. His consumption may well have been more moderate than that of Holmes, especially since he was a married man. Yet in *The Priory School* there is an indication that he occasionally chain-smoked:

"Holmes sat down on a boulder and rested his chin in his hands. I had smoked two cigarettes before he moved." (81)

B - THE APPARATUS

"I came to the mantlepiece. A litter of pipes, tobacco-pouches, syringes, penknives, revolver cartridges and other debris was scattered over it".

~DYIN (107)

"When all things were made, none was made better than this:
To be a lone man's companion, A bachelor's friend,
A hungry man's food, A sad man's cordial,
A wakeful man's sleep, And a chilly man's sleep."

~Charles Kingsley

It comes as something of a surprise to the student of the Holmes stories that, although we are inundated with references to the consumption of tobacco in a variety of forms, there is specific mention of only three pipes smoked by Holmes. In *A Study in Scarlet*, the first of these stories, Holmes does not appear to smoke a pipe. He merely refers to his consumption of "strong tobacco"(I) and later, he offers a cigarette to a visitor. (Watson, on the other hand, talks about "puffing at my pipe".)

The Sign of Four, the second of the recorded cases (although not chronologically (H)) is the first narrative to mention an "old briar-root pipe". (6) Afterwards, reference is made only to a "pipe". We hear nothing further of the briar until we come *to The Man with The Twisted Lip* where it crops up again as "an old brier pipe". (I) Thereafter the briar vanishes into obscurity.

The briar (brier) had been introduced into this country in 1859 and by Holmes' day had established an immense popularity. Its particularly hard properties make it ideal for a sturdy pipe. The root of the White Heath (Erica Arborea), a native of France and Corsica, is the origin of the briar.

Holmes demonstrated a particular predilection for the briar in *The Yellow Face* (55,56,57) where an amber-stemmed briar forms the basis of his deductions. The pipe in question had a long stem but it was the amber which drew complimentary remarks from Holmes. Most briars of the period had their stems made from horn or vulcanite. Amber was expensive. For instance, an amber cigarette holder, advertised in the Army and Navy Stores Catalogue of 1907 which came complete in a silver case, cost as much as 32 shillings. Holmes, who made a study of pipes, remarked that "nothing has more individuality (than a pipe) save, perhaps, watches and boot-laces". (56) Elsewhere, he observes:

"I wonder how many real amber mouthpieces there are in London. Some people think a fly in it is a sign. Why, it is quite a branch of the trade, the putting of sham flies into the sham amber". (55)

The yellowish, translucent fossil resin, found chiefly along the southern shores of the Baltic, was much prized by collectors and manufacturers alike, but the entombed insects which it often contained were a sign of its authenticity. It was this aspect that the manufacturers of artificial amber mouthpieces strove to imitate.

We are not told the exact shape or even type of briar that Holmes owned but possibly it may have possessed an amber mouthpiece.

(80) Briars came in a bewildering variety of shapes and we must not assume that his own pipe was the curved variety so often depicted. In fact, the great majority of briars were straight pipes with short stems. Most of them had a silver band with a hallmark indented. The "dry-smoker" variety with a detachable bowl was very popular at this period. Briars with vulcanite or horn stems ranged in price between 2 shillings and 3 shillings. An amber-stemmed briar cost as much as 4 shillings. The pipe which held Holmes' attention cost seven shillings and sixpence, (56) which only indicates that it was in the luxury range. It is not surprising, therefore, that the pipe had been mended twice "with silver bands". (56) Grosvenor mixture, selling at eightpence an ounce, (56) was one of the more expensive mixtures.

The second of the pipes to be specifically mentioned by Watson was the "long cherrywood which was wont to replace his clay when he was in a disputatious rather than a meditative mood". (50) Like the briar, this makes an exceptionally brief appearance, but its long curved stem and comparatively small bowl would undoubtedly have proved impractical on expeditions.

Of all the pipes in the canon, it is the clay pipe which receives most attention. This was clearly Holmes' favourite counsellor and is variously described as "the unsavoury pipe", (27) the "old and oily clay pipe", (33) the "black clay pipe", (34, 36) "clay pipe"(47) and "the oldest and foulest of his pipes". (131)

Of all the various types popular in the Victorian period, the clay pipe cuts across class divisions. It had the advantage of being cheap and easily mass-produced. If broken, it was easily replaceable. It came in a variety of sizes and types and the designs which appeared on the bowls are today an important feature among collectors. The "churchwarden" variety, still popular today, was just one of many. (L)

There was a period after the mid-century when the clay pipe waned in its popularity, owing to the 1859 report, already mentioned (sic). It was thought then that the high incidence of lung disease was directly attributable to clay-pipe smoking. Now, of course, we know it to be the tar by-product of tobacco.

By the 1880's the manufacture of clay pipes had again risen and within the metropolis there were a vast number of firms producing them. Holmes no doubt obtained his pipe from either F A Albert of Devonshire Street or the much larger Triplex Pipe Manufacturing Company of Cecil Court, Charing Cross Road (1895). Both firms produced clay pipes of distinction in their day.

Holmes favoured a type of tobacco known as "shag". The pedigree of this particular type dates back to George 111 (J) and is a preparation of tobacco rather than a specific leaf type. Any strong tobacco cut into fine shreds can be classed as "shag", (K) so Watson's description is hardly specific. "Golden Archer's", a Virginia shag of the period, sold at 2s and 11 d per 1 lb, but judging by the "acrid fumes"(22) produced by Holmes in an afternoon's sitting, one must imagine it to have been a deal stronger.

Watson appears to have switched from the coarse "ship's" tobacco (I) some time before he met Miss Mary Morstan. For instance, in *The Crooked Man* Holmes remarks to him:

"Hum! You still smoke the Arcadia mixture of your bachelor days, then. There's no mistaking that fluffy ash upon your coat."(61)

Arcadia, or Arcadia Mixture was mixture made by Surbrug's and was an American Cut Tobacco. Unlike the cheap shag of Holmes' liking, this was an expensive brand with a high leaf content, selling at lls and 3d per 1 lb. Watson evidently graduated to expensive tastes.

There is no record of Watson's own pipe, but I fancy that, as a military man, he would plump for a short-stemmed straight briar, reflecting his no-nonsense steady, reliable character. "The Bridge Player's Pipe" with a silver mounted vulcanite stem offered by Army and Navy at 2s and 6d fits just such a description.

The other two brand names which crop up in the Canon are Cavendish and Bird's-eye. Cavendish occurs in *Silver Blaze* where it figures alongside other oddments:

"We all filed into the front room and sat round the central table, while the Inspector unlocked a square tin box and laid a small heap of things before us. There was a box of vestas . . . an A D P briar-root pipe, a pouch of sealskin with half an ounce of long-cut

Cavendish..."(54)

The A D P pipe was an Alfred Dunhill Pipe and the vestas were unlike the vestas of our own period, being longer and more sulphurous. (Their manufacture involved a high incidence of disease among workers (M)). Cavendish was a medium price pipe tobacco which sold at 4s 6d per lb.

Bird's Eye, which features in Holmes' remarks in *The Sign Of Four*, (7) was a popular type available in three qualities. The high grade sold at 4s 9d, the coarse cut at 5s 7d and the "First Quality" at 4s 9d. A number of manufactures produced it, Archer's, Franklyn's (Bristol) Wile's and Lambert & Butler's amongst them.

As we know, Holmes kept his tobacco in the toe-end of a Persian slipper. (58, 69) Such a custom indicates his high rate of consumption, for the tobacco, being exposed to air, would undoubtedly dry quickly. But he also owned more than one pouch. (107, 111) Sealskin pouches feature in more than one of the stories (54) but as to the make of Holmes' own pouch, there is insufficient evidence. Pouches were also available in rubber and leather at that period and have changed little in appearance over the years. A pouch could be picked up for under 2s.

The pipe rack, which gains mention only once, (46) could either have been wall-mounted or it may have stood upright on a shelf. These were invariably richly ornamented and were produced in oak, mahogany or alloys. A standard pipe rack, carrying seven pipes, cost as much as 5 shillings.

The cigarette case which Holmes left behind at The Reichenbach Falls with a message to Watson attached to it was made of silver.(73) These were often engraved with the owner's initials and could cost anything up to 50s - an extravagant memento to leave on the edge of a precipice!

A visitor to 221B Baker Street would have discovered the cigars in the coal scuttle.(58) This seemed a rather bizarre custom to Dr Watson who thought fit to mention it in *The Musgrave Ritual* but in fact it was not an uncommon practice at the time.(N) The modern coal scuttle with its bucket-like shape was but one of many that graced the hearth sides of late Victorian England and the type which Holmes most probably used was a rectangular box affair, lined with a tight-shutting lid, japanned black and with brass mounts.

Holmes' choice in cigars is unstated but one would imagine the Havana range to have served his liking. These were by no means cheap even then, a bundle of British made cheroots costing 17s and 6d (five in a bundle). The Indian cigars (which feature in Holmes' monograph on tobacco), were much cheaper (at 1s and 8d per 5) but considerably inferior. His taste in cigarettes was that of a "connoisseur" and he showed a liking for Professor Coram's Egyptian blend. The Alexandrian Variety which he smoked in *The Golden Pince-Nez,* (Hadges Nessim), retailed at 2 shillings per 25 or 7s 9d per 100.

C - THE MONOGRAPH

"I have made a special study of cigar-ashes . . ."(3)

This would have been a splendid affair, probably privately printed in London. The "coloured plates"(6) illustrating the different ashes of the tobaccos would have been difficult and expensive to produce. Holmes had already "extended (his) practice to the continent"(7) and was clearly a pioneer in the field of criminal investigation on a par with Bertillon. The monograph (mentioned twice, both in *A Study In Scarlet* (3) and *The Sign of Four* (7) has apparently not survived the test of time. It is a pity, since this is an area of investigation which presents problems of analysis. Holmes claimed that he could "tell at a glance the ash of any known brand either of cigar or of tobacco", an astonishing assertion, considering the sheer number of brands then available. To distinguish between cigarette, pipe and cigar ash is, of course, an easy matter, since their method of manufacture differs widely. But it is not generally thought possible to distinguish the ashes of cigars or cigarettes from each other by mere observation. Tobacco is high in ash content and ranges from 15% to 25% of the leaf on a water-free basis. Flue-cured tobacco is rich in sugar, the cigarette grades having 15% to 20% more.

Holmes points out that "there is as much difference between the black ash of a Trichinopoly and the white fluff of bird's-eye as there is between a cabbage and a potato". This is something of a truism since the Trichinopoly was a cigar and the bird's-eye a common pipe tobacco. In fact, Trichinopoly is the name of a district and city in the Madras presidency whence the cigar originates. Like the "Lunkah" which occurs in the same paragraph, (7) these would undoubtedly have featured in Holmes' monograph. The lunkah was a strong cheroot. (0) The word itself is derived from the Hindi "lanka", a local term for the islands of the Godevery Delta in which the tobacco is grown.

Holmes' familiarity with the cigars of the Indian continent could be an indication of a deeper connection than the superficial evidence of Dr Watson's chronicles suggests. I have suggested elsewhere (P) that in the *Wanderjahre* the tenets of Lamaic Buddhism did much to alter his own personal philosophy. But could it be that he had, some time in his youth, perhaps touring with Holmes pere, seen and experienced the domain of the British Raj at close quarters? (Q)

To return to the central problem of the distinction between various tobacco ashes, it must be observed that the only satisfactory means of analysis involves dissolving the ash in a solution of hydrochloric acid. However, Holmes' short resume about his monograph points more to a visual distinction. (R)

The question of the monograph must, it seems, remain unresolved. It is only a pity that we shall never be permitted to see that priceless publication.

D. A NOTE ON NICOTINE

"I believe . . . he is a first-class chemist ."

~Stamford, STUD

"If I cannot smoke in heaven, then I shall not go."
~Mark Twain.

At the time of Watson's first meeting with Holmes, the latter was studying at St Bart's Hospital on a free-lance basis ("he has never taken out any systematic medical classes" - STUD) and had just discovered "the most practical medico-legal discovery for years . . . an infallible test for bloodstains". Holmes admits to Watson that he dabbles "with poisons a great deal" and Stamford earlier comments, "I could imagine his giving a friend a little pinch of the latest vegetable alkaloid... simply . . . to have an accurate idea of its effects".

(STUD)

This youthful preoccupation with vegetable alkaloids was, I believe, not merely objective. There were both personal and scientific reasons why Holmes took an interest in alkaloids.

The compounds obtained from vegetable alkaloids (morphine, nicotine, quinine, caffeine, etc) produce some of the strongest poisons known to man. Holmes, with his wayward knowledge, had clearly spent time at Bart's investigating a fascinating branch of learning where the gaps were still to be filled by subsequent pharmacologists.

Holmes admitted that drugs were a way of assisting his mental faculties. "My mind is like a racing engine", he claimed, "tearing itself to pieces . . ." Cocaine, nicotine and morphine provided the perfect answer. Cocaine is an "upper", morphine a "downer", and nicotine is also a depressant. With these drugs at his disposal, he could regulate his own metabolism, pushing it beyond its normal bounds. Instances of extraordinary activity contrast sharply with those of great languor. Compare these two passages, for example:

"See the foxhound with hanging ears and drooping tail ... and compare it with the same hound as, with gleaming eyes and straining muscles, it runs upon a breast-high scent - such was the change in Holmes since the morning".

"Holmes had spent several days in bed, as was his habit from time to time..."

And in SIGN, Watson reminds us:

"He was bright, eager and in excellent spirits, a mood which in his case alternated with fits of the blackest depression".

What Holmes was aiming for was that "equanimity of feeling" first described as a reaction to the drug opium. As De Quincey observed:

"Whereas wine disorders the mental faculties, opium... introduces amongst them the most exquisite order, legislation and harmony... it communicates serenity and equipoise to all the faculties... "

De Quincey abjured the use of alcohol. We note also that Holmes was no great user of the drug. On the other hand, he over-indulged his taste for nicotine. The reason is fairly obvious, although it has only recently been pointed out. In the brain, nervous impulses are transmitted from one cell to another because of the release at nerve endings of what is known as neuro-transmitters. Nicotine imitates this action. Tests on animals have confirmed the opinion of heavy smokers that smoking may prevent drowsiness and facilitate mental concentration.

Holmes undoubtedly wanted rapid results from his alkaloids. The cocaine would certainly have given him that for its effect is instantaneous. Morphine, on the other hand, has a much slower reaction.

Holmes, in his study of alkaloids, made use of himself in these experiments as a guinea pig but clearly developed an addiction for the "hard" drugs.

But the question remains - exactly how did he get onto the drugs in the first place? The answer, I believe, lies in the early period of his life about which we know so little.

In his youth or late adolescence, Sherlock Holmes suffered from a particularly painful malady that required the use of morphine (this was probably administered in its more popular form, laudanum). I base this assertion on clear indications in the Canon. Holmes, it appears, was his own worst enemy. His "iron constitution" was frequently pushed to the limits by his own reckless attitude to work. In *The Reigate Squires* we learn that he had been working for a period "extending over two months ... he had never worked less than fifteen hours a day."

It has also been suggested that Holmes may have been slightly consumptive as a youth. The lean figure, coupled with a pale ascetic countenance, would seem to confirm this view.

But in conclusion, I do not think it was consumption which led him to the morphine bottle and those long hours spent at St Bart's, investigating the properties of obscure alkaloids. It was probably something quite serious, a disorder of the abdominal organs which incommoded him for much of his life.

Morphine was vital in keeping Holmes' grip on his professional career whilst suffering this encumbrance. The drug is of course a spinal stimulant, obliterating pain more effectively than any other known rival and supplying a dreamless sleep.

Much of Holmes' behaviour can be explained by recourse to this theory of an abdominal disability; the inability to sleep or keep regular hours, the irregular eating habits, the irritability and intolerance of others. All these symptoms point to some long-standing disease which dogged the detective throughout his years in practice. The morphine supplied a dual-edged solution, for in his middle years, Holmes discovered that he had become a hopeless addict, suffering the accompanying displeasures of constipation, loss of energy, heavy dependence, etc.

It was left to his best and wisest friend, Dr John H Watson, to supply an antidote and "wean" him from that terrible route downwards to the realms of Morpheus.

The last link in the chain is provided for us in EMPT where, in Holmes' own words, he "spent some months in a research into coal tar derivatives". This research was carried out in the French town of Montpelier in 1894. What was it that Holmes was after? One commentator has suggested that he was probing for the discovery of plastics, but chronologically this would not have been possible.

The coal-tar derivatives consist of a number of aromatic carbon compounds. They are: benzene (used in the manufacture of plastics), napthalene, anthracene, phenol (an antiseptic), tolanine, aniline and pyridine. It is the last of these derivatives which, I believe, gives us an insight into Holmes' motivation for his research. For pyridine is a colourless liquid base got from the dry distillation of coal-tar. There is also a derivative of pyridine and that is nicotinic acid. Now this chemical is a white crystalline substance formed by the oxidation of nicotine. Moreover, it is a vitamin of the "B" group and has been found vital to the treatment of pellagra, a deficiency disease characterized by cracking of the skin. In unchecked cases, the disease can often end in insanity.

Did Holmes suffer from this disease and was he looking for a cure? I believe so, for one of the unfortunate results of long-term drug addiction is a corresponding loss of vitamin balance in the body. When the dietary requirements of the body are disturbed over a long period, a disease like pellagra is more than possible.

Holmes, then, in the midst of his career, faced an acute crisis. The morphine had at last wreaked its havoc upon him but armed with his natural talent for analysis and his profound knowledge of chemistry, he triumphed by the discovery of the efficacious properties of nicotinic acid. Once again, he was able to face the world and rid it of the "second most dangerous man in London".

NOTES

(Letters refer to footnotes, numbers to the quotations listed in the appendix.)

(A) That Holmes never smoked a meerschaum is one of those curious facts which may astound the general public. The meerschaum was the hallmark of the screen actor, Basil Rathbone, originator of the apocryphal phrase, "Elementary, my dear Watson'.

(B) *The Final Problem.*

(C) Holmes' personality is clearly that of the phallic-narcissistic type, described by Wilhelm Reich, MD, in his *Character Analysis*.

(D) "Ship's" is listed in Eric Partridge's *A Dictionary of Slang* as "a rough coarse tobacco". It was also a term applied to cocoa in naval circles.

(E) Bradleys of Oxford Street was famous in its day as a supplier of tobacco. A full description of the firm may be found in Michael Harrison's *In The Footsteps Of Sherlock Holmes*.

(F) An excellent illustration to accompany the text occurs in *Sherlock Holmes In Portrait And Profile* by Walter Klinefelter. The drawing originally appeared in The Courier-Journal, Louisville. Holmes, reduced to stupefaction, sits wreathed in a fog of tobacco smoke.

(G) *His Last Bow.*

(H) See W S Baring-Gould, *Sherlock Holmes.*

(I) The variant spelling is listed in the OED.

(J) It is first mentioned in an act of parliament of 1789 as "short cut, shag tobacco".

(K) OED.

(L) Some of the many types listed in 'London Clay Tobacco Pipes' (*Journal of the Archaeological Association, Vol XXXII, 1969*) are: Rose and Thistle; Masonic emblems; Irish emblems; The Heart In The Hand; The Spread Eagle; The Crowned Shield.

(M) This has since formed the basis of a musical, entitled *The Match Girls*.

(N) As W S Baring-Gould pointed out (*The Annotated Sherlock*

Holmes), Sir James M Barrie kept both his cigars and his telephone in a coal scuttle. I agree with Frank A Water's view that it "was a square box made of wood".

(O) A cheroot is a cigar truncated at both ends, the ends being cut off square as distinct from an ordinary cigar, which has one end pointed. Originally it meant a cigar made in southern India or Manilla.

(P) 'The Great Return,' SHJ, Winter 79.

(Q) This may seem a far shot on the face of it. But Holmes' familiarity with the caste system, his knowledge of the Andaman islanders (SIGN) and his involvement with the unchronicled case of The Giant Rat Of Sumatra are all indicative of some earlier contact.

(R) At the Exhibition on Sherlock Holmes, held in London in 1951, two types of cheroot of the period were exhibited along with ashes and a means of identifying each. The results, for those interested, were published in the Catalogue of the exhibition, but I have reproduced them below:

CIGAR TYPE 23 - Cassandra Cheroots

Ash is completely burned in furnace. One gram of this ash is dissolver in 25 cubic centimetres of normal hydrochloric acid solution. This solution is made up to 250 cubic centimetres and 25 cubic centimetre portions are titrated with decinormal caustic soda solution using methyl orange as indicator. On average 13.5 cubic centimetres of alkali is required. this means that 11.5 (i.e. 25 - 13.5) cubic centimetres of normal acid is required to dissolve one gram of this particular ash.

A similar test, applied to a Bahadur Burma Cheroot, required 14.2 cubic centimetres of acid to dissolve one gram of ash.

THE EVENING PIPE

"Little tube of mighty power,
Charmer of an idle hour."

– Isaac Browne, 'A Pipe of Tobacco.'

For the benefit of those eager to follow the course of Holmes' and Watson's "self-poisoning by... tobacco", I have listed a hundred and: thirty-two quotations relating to pipes, cigars and tobacco. These follow the order of the stories listed in the collected editions published years ago by John Murray and Jonathan Cape. Story titles conform to the standard abbreviations, accepted by most Sherlockians. The key is printed in full in Jack Tracy's *The Encyclopaedia Sherlockiana*. (NEL, 1977).

"You don't mind the smell of strong tobacco, I hope?"

"I always smoke 'ship's' myself", I answered.

STUD 1

"He was more than six feet high, was in the prime of life, had small feet for his height, wore coarse, square-toed boots and smoked a Trichinopoly cigar."

STUD 2

"Is there anything else that puzzles you?"

"The finger-nails and the Trichinopoly", I suggested.

"I gathered up some scattered ash from the floor. It was dark in colour and flakey - such an ash as is only made by a Trichinopoly. I have made a special study of cigar-ashes - in fact, I have written a monograph upon the subject. I flatter myself that I can distinguish at a glance the ash of any known brand either of cigar or of tobacco . . ."

STUD 3

"I had no idea how long he might be, but I sat stolidly puffing at my pipe and skipping over the pages of Henri Murger's Vie de Boheme."

STUD 4

Sherlock Holmes gave a sigh of relief and relaxed into a smile.

"Take a seat, and try one of these cigars", he said.

STUD 5

"My practice has extended recently to the Continent", said Holmes, after a while, filling up his old briar-root pipe.

STUD 6

"Yes, I have been guilty of several monographs. Here, for example, is one. 'Upon the Distinction Between the Ashes of the Various Tobaccos.' In it I enumerate a hundred and forty forms of cigar, cigarette and pipe tobacco, with coloured plates illustrating the difference in the ash. It is a point which is continually turning up in criminal trials and which is sometime of supreme importance as a clue. If you can say definitely, for example, that some murder had been done by a man who was smoking an Indian lunkah, it obviously narrows your field of search. To the trained eye there is as much difference between the black ash of a Trichinopoly and the white fluff of bird's-eye as there is between a cabbage and a potato."

SIGN7

He had lit his pipe again and was leaning back with drooping eyelids.

SIGN 8

"I trust that you have no objection to tobacco smoke, to the balsamic odour of the Eastern tobacco.

SIGN 9

"If the launch is above the water, they will find her", said Holmes, as he rose from the table and lit his pipe.

SIGN10

"I am going to smoke and to think over this queer business to which my fair client has introduced us."

SIGN11

My companion's book and pipe lay by his chair, but he had disappeared.

SIGN 12

"I have been working in that get-up all day", said he, lighting his cigar.

SIGN 13

"Well, Jonathan Small", said Holmes, lighting a cigar, "I am sorry that it has come to this."

SIGN 14

"Well, and there is the end of our little drama", I remarked, after we had sat some time smoking in silence.

SIGN 15

"Really, Watson, you excel yourself", said Holmes, pushing back his chair and lighting a cigarette.

HOUN 16

I laughed incredulously as Sherlock Holmes leaned back in his settee and blew little wavering rings of smoke up to the ceiling.

HOUN 17

"I observe from your forefinger that you make your own cigarettes. Have no hesitation in lighting one."

The man drew out paper and tobacco and twirled the one up in the other with surprising dexterity.

HOUN 18

(Sherlock Holmes) . . . yawned and tossed the end of his cigarette into the fire. HOUN 19

" . . . Sir Charles had evidently stood there for five or ten minutes."

"How do you know that?"

"Because the ash had twice dropped from his cigar."

"Excellent! This is a colleague, Watson, after our own heart."

HOUN 20

"When you pass Bradley's, would you ask him to send up a pound of the strongest shag tobacco?"

HOUN 21

My first impression as I opened the door was that a fire had broken out, for the room was so filled with smoke that the light of the lamp upon the table was blurred by it. As I entered, however, my fears were set at rest, for it was the acrid fumes of strong, coarse tobacco which took me by the throat and set me coughing. Through the haze I had a vague vision of Holmes in his dressing-gown coiled up in an armchair with his black clay pipe between his lips . . .

"Caught cold, Watson?" said he.

"No, it's this poisonous atmosphere."

"I suppose it is pretty thick, now that you mention it."

HOUN 22

"My body has remained in this armchair; and has, I regret to observe, consumed in my absence two large pots of coffee and an incredible amount of tobacco."

HOUN 23

"It is a singular thing, but I find that a concentrated atmosphere helps a concentration of thought."

HOUN 24

Throwing aside my cigarette, I closed my hand upon the butt of my revolver, and, walking swiftly up to the door, I looked in

HOUN 25

"If you seriously desire to deceive me you must change your tobacconist; for when I see the stub of a cigarette marked Bradley, Oxford Street, I know that my friend Watson is in the neighbourhood."

HOUN 26

Sherlock Holmes had pushed away his untasted breakfast and lit the unsavoury pipe which was the companion of his deepest meditations.

VALL 27

Finally, he lit his pipe and, sitting in the ingle-nook of the old village inn, he talked slowly and at random about his case . . .

VALL 28

"There is an appalling directness about your questions, Watson", said Holmes, shaking his pipe at me.

VALL 29

With hardly a word spoken, but with a kindly eye, he waved me to an armchair, threw across his case of cigars, and indicated a spirit case and a gasogene in the corner.

SCAN 30

"Quite so", he answered, lighting a cigarette, and throwing himself down into an armchair.

SCAN 31

"Take a pinch of snuff, Doctor, and acknowledge that I have scored over you in your example."

IDEN 32

... he took down from the rack the old and oily clay pipe, which was to him as a counsellor, arid, having lit it he leaned back in his chair, with the thick blue cloud wreaths spinning up from him, and a look of infinite languor in his face.

IDEN 33

I left him then, still puffing at his black clay pipe . . .

IDEN 34

"What are you going to do, then?" I asked.

"To smoke", he answered. "It is quite a three-pipe problem, and I beg that you won't speak to me for fifty minutes."

He curled himself up in his chair, with his thin knees drawn up to his hawk-like nose, and there he sat with his eyes closed and his black clay pipe thrusting out like the bill of some strange bird.

REDH 35

"There is Mortimer's, the tobacconist . . ."

REDH 36

"I have a case full of cigarettes here which need smoking, and the sofa is very much superior to the usual country hotel abomination."

BOSC 37

"He had even smoked there. I found the ash of a cigar, which my special knowledge of tobacco ashes enabled me to pronounce as an Indian cigar. I have, as you know, devoted some attention to this, and written a little monograph on the ashes of 140 different varieties of pipe, cigar and cigarette tobacco. Having found the ash, I then looked round and discovered the stump among the moss where he had tossed it. It was an Indian cigar, of the variety which are rolled in Rotterdam."

"And the cigar-holder?"

"I could see that the end had not been in his mouth. Therefore, he used a holder. The tip had been cut off, not bitten off, but the cut was not a clean one, so I deduced a blunt penknife."

BOSC 38

Sherlock Holmes sat for some time in silence with his head sunk forward, and his eyes bent upon the red glow of the fire. Then he lit his pipe, and leaning back in his chair he watched the blue smoke rings as they chased each other up to the ceiling.

FIVE 39

"... and (you were) self-poisoner by cocaine and tobacco."

FIVE 40

"I suppose, Watson," said he, "that you imagine that I have added opium-smoking to cocaine injections and all the other little weaknesses.

TWIS 41

We had driven several miles ... when he shook himself . . . and lit up his pipe...

TWIS 42

He took off his coat and waistcoat, put on a large blue dressing-gown, and then wandered about the room collecting pillows from his bed, and cushions from the sofa and armchairs. With these he constructed a sort of Eastern divan, upon which he perched himself cross legged, with an ounce of shag tobacco and a box of matches laid out in front of him. In the dim light of the lamp I saw him sitting there, an old brier pipe between his lips, his eyes fixed vacantly upon the corner of the ceiling, the blue smoke curling up from him, silent, motionless, with the light shining upon his strong-set aquiline features.

TWIS 43

I found the summer sun shining into the apartment. The pipe was still between his lips, the smoke still curled upwards, and the room was full of a dense tobacco haze, but nothing remained of the heap of shag which I had seen upon the previous night.

TWIS 44

"I reached this (result)," said my friend, "by sitting upon five pillows and consuming an ounce of shag."

TWIS 45

He (Holmes) was lounging upon the sofa in a purple dressing-gown, a pipe-rack within his reach upon the right, and a pile of crumpled morning papers . . . near at hand.

BLUE 46

"After all, Watson," said Holmes, reaching up his hand for his clay pipe, "I am not retained by the police to supply their deficiencies."

BLUE 47

Sherlock Holmes was, as I expected, lounging about his sitting-room in his dressing-gown, reading the agony column of The Times, and smoking his before-breakfast pipe, which was composed of all the plugs and dottles left from his smokes of the day before, all carefully dried and collected on the corner of the mantlepiece.

ENGR 48

"Good afternoon, Lestrade. You will find an extra tumbler upon the sideboard, and there are cigars in the box."

NOBL 49

"You have erred, perhaps," he observed, taking up a glowing cinder with the tongs, and lighting with it the long cherrywood pipe which was wont to replace his clay when he was in a disputatious rather than a meditative mood. COPP 50

. . he had sat puffing at his long pipe and gazing down into the fire . . .

COPP 51

We had left Reading far behind us before he thrust the last of (the papers) under the seat and offered me his cigar case. SILV 52

I lay back against the cushions, puffing at my cigar... SILV 53

We all filed into the front room and sat round the central table while the Inspector unlocked a square tin box and laid a small heap of things before us. There was a box of vestas, an ADP briar-root pipe, a pouch of sealskin with half an ounce of long-cut Cavendish...

SILV 54

"Halloa! That's not your pipe on the table!... A nice old briar, with a good long stem of what the tobacconists call amber. I wonder how many real amber mouthpieces there are in London. Some people think a fly in it is a sign. Why, it is quite a branch of trade, the putting of sham flies into the sham amber."

YELL 55

"...I should put the original cost of the pipe at seven-and-six pence. Now it has, as you see, been twice mended; once in the wooden stem and once in the amber. Each of these mends, done, as you observe, with silver bands, must have cost more than the pipe did originally. The man must value the pipe highly when he prefers to patch it up rather than buy a new one with the same money."

"Anything else?" I asked, for. Holmes was turning the pipe about in his hand and staring at it in his peculiar, pensive way.

He held it up and tapped on it with his long, thin forefinger as a professor might who was lecturing on a bone.

"Pipes are occasionally of extraordinary interest," said he. "Nothing has more individuality save, perhaps, watches and bootlaces. The indications here, however, are neither very marked nor very important. The owner is obviously a muscular man, left-handed, with an excellent set of teeth, careless in habits, and with no need to practice economy."

"You think a man must be well-to-do if he smokes a seven-shilling pipe?" said I.

"This is Grosvenor mixture at eightpence an ounce," Holmes answered, knocking a little out on his palm. "As he might get an excellent smoke for half the price, he has no need to practise economy."

"And the other points?"

"He has been in the habit of lighting his pipe at lamps and gas-jets. You can see that it is quite charred all down one side. Of course, a match could not have done that. Why should a man hold a match to the side of his pipe? But you cannot light it at a lamp without getting the bowl charred. And it is on the right side of the pipe. From that, I gather that he is a left-handed man... Then he has bitten through his amber. It takes a muscular, energetic fellow and one with a good set of teeth to do that..."

YELL 56

(Holmes) spread out the documents upon his knees. Then he lit his pipe and sat for some time smoking and turning them over.

GLOR 57

"When I find a man who keeps his cigars in the coal-scuttle, his tobacco in the toe-end of a Persian slipper... then I begin to give myself virtuous airs."

MUSG 58

Reginald Musgrave sat down opposite to me, and lit the cigarette, which I had pushed towards him.

MUSG 59

I was seated by my own hearth smoking a last pipe and nodding over a novel...

CR00 60

"Hum! You still smoke the Arcadia mixture of your bachelor days, then. There's no mistaking that fluffy ash upon your coat."

CR00 61

"... I'll smoke a pipe with you with pleasure."

I handed him my pouch, and he seated himself opposite to me, and smoked for some time in silence.

CR00 62

"Having gathered these facts, Watson, I smoked several pipes over them."

CR00 63

Sherlock Holmes sat down and lit his pipe.

RESI 64

(Sherlock Holmes' face) was as impassive as ever, but his lids had drooped more heavily over his eyes, and his smoke curled up more thickly from his pipe to emphasise each curious episode in the doctor's tale.

RESI 65

"Here are four cigar-ends that I have picked out of the fireplace."

"Hum!" said Holmes. "Have you got his cigar-holder?"

"No, I have seen none."

"His cigar-case, then?"

"Yes, it was in his coat-pocket."

Holmes opened it and smelled the single cigar, which it contained.

"Oh, this is a Havana, and these others are cigars of the peculiar sort which are imported by the Dutch from their East Indian Colonies. They are usually wrapped in straw, you know, and are thinner for their length than any other brand." He picked up the four ends and examined them with his pocket lens.

"Two of these have been smoked from a holder and two without," said tie. "Two have been cut by a not very sharp knife, and two have had the ends bitten off by a set of excellent teeth."

RESI 66

"... It was then that these cigars were smoked. The older man sat in that wicker chair; it was he who used the cigar-holder. The younger man sat over yonder; he knocked his ash off against the chest of drawers."

RESI 67

Mycroft took snuff from a tortoiseshell box...

RESI 68

"I shall be at your service in one instance, Watson. You will find tobacco in the Persian slipper."

NAVA 69

"Ah, a scent of tobacco would have been worth a great deal to us in such an investigation."

NAVA 70

(Sherlock Holmes) rose, lit his pipe, and settled himself down into his chair.

NAVA 71

"Might I trouble you for a match?"

He drew in the smoke of his cigarette as if the soothing influence was grateful to him.

FINA 72

... Something bright caught my eye... the silver cigarette case which he used to carry.

FINA 73

He sat opposite to me and lit a cigarette in his old nonchalant manner.

EMPT 74

"And now, Watson, if you can endure the draught from a broken window, I think that half an hour in my study over a cigar may afford you some profitable amusement."

EMPT 75

"Have a cigarette, Mr McFarlane," said he, pushing his case across.

"I am sure that with your symptoms my friend Dr Watson here would prescribe a sedative."

NORW 76

The carpet round his chair was littered with cigarette ends, and with the early editions of the morning papers.

NORW 77

"I never saw either of them until two months ago, and I have never been in Africa in my life, so you can put that in your pipe and smoke it, Mr Busybody Holmes!"

SOLI 78

Holmes rose and tossed the end of his cigarette into the grate.

"I have been very obtuse, Watson," said he.

SOLI 79

(Holmes) had obtained a large ordnance map of the neighbourhood, and this he brought into my room, where he laid it out on the bed, and, having balanced the lamp in the middle of it, he began to smoke over it and occasionally to point out objects of interest with the reeking amber of his pipe.

PRIO 80

Holmes sat down on a boulder and rested his chin in his hands. I had smoked two cigarettes before he moved.

PRIO 81

We had breakfasted and were smoking our morning pipe, on the day after the remarkable experience which I have recorded.

CHAS 82

On this particular evening Lestrade had spoken of the weather and the newspapers. Then he had fallen silent, puffing thoughtfully at his cigar

SIXN 83

"With your eternal tobacco, Watson, and your irregularity at meals, I expect that you will get notice to quit, and that I shall share your downfall."

3STU 84

Holmes lit his cigar and leaned back in his chair.

GOLD 85

A cigarette glowed amid the tangle of white hair, and the air of the room was fetid with stale tobacco smoke. As he held out his hand to Holmes, I perceived that it also was stained yellow with nicotine.

"A smoker, Mr Holmes?" said he, speaking well-chosen English with a curious little mincing accent.

"Pray take a cigarette. And you, sir? I can recommend them, for I have them especially prepared by Ionides of Alexandria. He sends me a thousand at a time, and I grieve to say that I have to arrange for a fresh supply every fortnight. Bad, sir, very bad; but an old man has few pleasures. Tobacco and my work - that is all that is left to me."

Homes had lit a cigarette and was shooting little darting glances all over the room.

"Tobacco and my work, but now only tobacco," the old man exclaimed.

GOLD 86

Holmes was pacing up and down one side of the room whilst the old professor was talking. I observed that he was smoking with extraordinary rapidity. It was evident that he shared our host's liking for the fresh Alexandrian cigarettes.

GOLD 87

"Dear me, Mr Holmes; why, you are even a quicker smoker than I am myself.' Holmes smiled.

"I am a connoisseur," said he, taking another cigarette from the box - his fourth - and lighting it from the stub of that which he had finished.

GOLD 88

Holmes...continued to walk up and down for some time, lost in thought and consuming cigarette after cigarette.

GOLD 89

"Have you a clue?" I asked at last.

"It depends upon those cigarettes that I smoked," said he. "It is possible that I am utterly mistaken. The cigarettes will show me."

GOLD 90

"His health - well, I don't know that it's better nor worse for the smoking."

"Ah," said Holmes, "but it kills the appetite."

GOLD 91

"... the carpet was a dun colour, which lends itself very well to examination. I therefore smoked a great number of those excellent cigarettes, and I dropped the ash all over the space in front of the suspected bookcase."

GOLD 92

"...by upsetting the cigarette box, I obtained a very excellent view of the floor, and was able to see quite clearly, from the traces upon the cigarette ash, that the prisoner had, in our absence, come out from her retreat."

GOLD 93

...when his needs were satisfied and his pipe alight he was ready to take that half-comic and wholly philosophic view which was natural to him when his affairs were going awry.

MISS94

He had lit his pipe and held his slippered feet to the cheerful blaze of the fire.

ABBE 95

"Give him a cigar," said Homes. "Bite on that, Captain Croker, and don't let your nerves run away with you."

ABBE 96

Holmes lit his pipe in silence and sat for some time lost in the deepest thought.

SECO 97

(Holmes) ran out and ran in, smoked incessantly, played snatches on his violin, sank into reveries, devoured sandwiches at irregular hours...

SECO 98

... he stood in front of the fire afterwards with a thoughtful face, smoking his pipe, and casting an occasional glance at the message Holmes smoked hard, with his brows drawn over his keen eyes...

WIST 99

"A chaotic case, my dear Watson," said Holmes, over an evening pipe. WIST 100

"I'll be back in a moment, when I have changed my dressing-gown and filled my cigar-case."

CARD 101

"The case," said Sherlock Holmes... as we chatted over our cigars that night in our rooms at Baker Street, "is one where... we have been compelled to reason backwards from effects to causes."

CARD 102

"Well, well, Mrs Warren, let us hear about it then. You don't object to tobacco, I take it? Thank you, Watson - the matches!"

REDC 103

Holmes shrugged his shoulders.

"There is nothing here," said he. "The matches have, of course, been used to light cigarettes. That is obvious from the shortness of the burnt end. Half the match is consumed in lighting a pipe or cigar. But dear me! This cigarette stub is certainly remarkable. The gentleman was bearded and moustached, you say?"

"Yes, sir."

"I don't understand that. I should say that only a clean-shaven man could have smoked this. Why, Watson, even your modest moustache would have been singed."

"A holder?" I suggested.

"No, no; the end is matted."

REDC 104

Holmes sat up at attention, his pipe half way to his lips.

BRUC 105

"Have you had something to eat? Then join me in a coffee and curacao. Try one of the proprietor's cigars. They are less poisonous than one would expect."

BRUC 106

I came to the mantlepiece. A litter of pipes, tobacco-pouches, syringes, penknives, revolver cartridges, and other debris was scattered over it.

DYIN 107

"Is there any other little service that I can do you, my friend?"

"A match and a cigarette."

DYIN 108

... Holmes took his pipe from his lips and sat up in his chair like an old hound who hears the view-holloa.

DEVI 109

During this time (the next two days) Holmes spent some of his time smoking and dreaming in the cottage.

DEVI 110

Holmes lit his pipe and handed me his pouch.

"Some fumes which are not poisonous would be a welcome change," said he.

DEVI 111

A half-smoked, sodden cigar hung from the corner of his mouth, and as he sat down, he struck a match and relit it.

LAST 112

It was over a smoke in the pleasant lassitude of the drying-room that I found him less reticent... than anywhere else.

ILLU 113

"Don't you smoke? Then you will excuse me if I light my pipe."

ILLU 114

"Anything more?"

"Put my pipe on the table - and the tobacco-slipper."

ILLU 115

I lit my pipe and leaned back in my chair.

BLAN 116

"He was smoking a pipe and reading a paper."

BLAN 117

(Watson) looked round him at... the coal-scuttle, which contained of old the pipes and tobacco.

MAZA 118

"You have not, I hope, learned to despise my pipe and lamentable tobacco? It has to take the place of food these days."

"But why not eat?"

"Because the faculties become refined when you starve them."

MAZA 119

... (Holmes) had curled down with his pipe in his mouth upon the opposite chair, when our visitor arrived.

3GAB 120

Holmes raised his pipe with a languid smile.

3GAB 121

Holmes had lit his pipe, and he sat for some time with a curious smile upon his face.

3GAB 122

Holmes took the pipe from his lips.

3GAB 123

"There you have it," said Sherlock Holmes, knocking out the ashes of his after-breakfast pipe and slowly refilling it.

THOR 124

Holmes smiled languidly and reached his hand out for his pipe.

THOR 125

As an institution I was like the... shag tobacco, the old black pipe...

CREE 126

I found him huddled up in his armchair with updrawn knees, his pipe in his mouth and his brow furrowed with thought.

CREE 127

He had refilled his pipe and resumed his seat...

CREE 128

When I arrived, I found him seated in a smoke-laden atmosphere...

VEIL 129

"Mrs Merrilow does not object to tobacco, Watson, if you wish to indulge your filthy habits."

VEIL 130

Holmes sat for some time in silent thought. He had lit the oldest and foulest of his pipes.

SHOS 131

Holmes lay with his gaunt figure stretched in his deep chair, his pipe curling forth slow wreaths of acrid tobacco...

RETI 132

GLOSSARY OF CANONICAL TERMS

"I do not believe that intelligence and creative thinking are injured by smoking."

~Emile Zola

BRIAR (brier)
A corruption of the French word, bruyere. The briar root is found mainly in Mediterranean districts. Its hard, resilient qualities make it an excellent choice for pipe manufacture. According to Alfred Dunhill, a French pipe maker broke his meerschaum while on a visit to Corsica and asked a local craftsman to make him a copy from the local briar. He was so pleased with the result, he sent supplies of this root to the village of St Claude in the Jura Mountains where the peasants specialised in woodcarving. From that time onwards they devoted themselves utterly to briar-pipe making.

CAVENDISH
This really means the process of alternately heating and pressing to make the tobacco darker. Later it was applied to a type of tobacco produced in this way.

DOTTLE
An obscure word which refers to the blackened, half-burnt strands of tobacco left in the pipe at the conclusion of a smoke. Holmes had the revolting habit of drying and collecting these overnight on his mantle-piece. This has led one commentator to suggest that Holmes suffered an impecunious youth. The practice is not recommended.

HOOKAH
An Arabic water-pipe. Thaddeus Sholto smoked one. (SIGN).

PLUG

(See dottle). A term said to have come from the Southern States where settlers soaked tobacco in honey, then pushed it tightly into holes, drilled into a hickory log. Hence, "plugs". The term can also refer to a cake of pressed or twisted tobacco used mainly for chewing. In Holmes' case, the plugs were the bits of tobacco left unburnt, and therefore re-useable.

SHAG

The term can have variant meanings. In the USA it refers to a Fine Cut but is not directly connected with Roll-Your-Own tobacco as it is in Britain today. In Holmes' day the term was loosely applied to any kind of coarse cut tobacco. Holmes smoked a dark acrid variety (22).

SOME DISJECTA MEMBRA

By Roger Johnson.

(editor of The Sherlock Holmes Journal.)

REGARDING SOME IRREGULARITIES IN KELVIN I. JONES': 'THE SHERLOCK HOLMES ULTIMATE SMOKING COMPANION'

LADY BRACKNELL: Do you smoke?
ERNEST: Well, yes, I must admit I smoke.
LADY BRACKNELL: I am glad to hear it. A man should always have an occupation of some kind.

~Oscar Wilde; 'The Importance of Being Earnest.'

p. 4, para. 5 – "No sooner has he arrived than he takes off his coat, puts on a 'large blue dressing-gown' and then proceeds to construct a 'sort of eastern divan'." There's *in reality* a considerable gap between his arrival and his settling down to smoke and think.

p. 7, para. 4 – Mrs Merrilow was the proprietor of a lodging house in South Brixton, not "an Oxfordshire inn".

p.8, para. 5 – There is in fact only one reference to Holmes smoking a pipe in *A Study in Scarlet*. In chapter 2, having been told that he reminds Watson of Dupin, "Sherlock Holmes rose and lit his pipe. 'No doubt you think that you are complimenting me in comparing me to Dupin,' he observed." (correct- ed.)

p. 11, para. 3, – Clay pipes are very easily broken. The foulest of Holmes's pipes may well have been a clay, but I fancy that the oldest was probably made of a more durable material. (? – ed.)

p. 13, para. 5 – Somewhere in a back issue of the SHJ is a letter or a brief article stating that the Dunhill company's records don't show any use of the initials "ADP.

John Hall, in *140 Different Varieties: A Review of Tobacco in the Canon* (The Northern Musgraves, 1994), says: "Those who are intrigued by the more esoteric by-ways of Sherlockian scholarship may care to ponder what, if anything, the initials 'ADP' which appeared on Straker's pipe in 'Silver Blaze', may have stood for. This has proved a tough nut to crack. The obvious candidates are 'something, something Peterson' or 'Alfred Dunhill Pipe', but they have been tried and found wanting. In view of the very large number of pipe makers and sellers, in the provinces as well as London in the Victorian period, 'ADP' may well represent an actual maker or vendor, but the identity of the firm or individual concerned remains a mystery, and a modest Sherlockian fame awaits any scholar who can crack the acronym."

But see this site: http://pipesmagazine.com/forums/topic/who-was-the-pipe-maker-adp. I think we have the answer here: Adolph David Posener.

p. 13, para. 2 – I haven't come across Wile's. Should the name actually be (W.D. & H.O.) Wills? (Conceivably – ed.)

p. 15, para. 1, l. 16 – *"Tobacco is high in ash content..."* Scientifically that may make sense (I'm not a scientist), but it reads oddly, as none of the content is ash until it's been burnt.

p. 22, note A – There's certainly no mention in the canon of Holmes or anyone else smoking a meerschaum pipe, or a calabash pipe, which is usually lined with meerschaum. It's the latter that has become the cliché and may originally have been used in the movies for comic effect. Basil Rathbone, like William Gillette before him, smoked a bent briar pipe as Holmes, though a calabash is seen among his effects in *The Spider Woman*.

p. 22, note E – I have both the second edition of *In the Footsteps of Sherlock Holmes* (Cassell, 1959), and the revised edition (David & Charles, 1971), and I can't find that "full description of" Bradley's of Oxford Street." The name appears to be fictitious. The Post Office London Trades Directories show that in 1891 Mrs Ellen Bradley had a tobacconist's shop at 157 Union Street, Borough; she was still there in 1899 – but she's the only tobacconist of that name listed. John Hall, in *140 Different Varieties*, suggests that Holmes and Watson's tobacconist was actually Benson's of 296 Oxford Street, which is listed in John's 1883 edition of *Baedeker's London and its Environs* and in my

1892 edition of the same guide. (Mr Johnson is correct in this regard! KJ)

About the author

Roger Johnson surely requires no introduction to serious addicts of the lifelong obsession that is Sherlock Holmes. He joined the Sherlock Holmes Society of London when both he and the editor of this volume were in their youthful prime. For more than thirty years he wrote and distributed 'The District Messenger,' a still-flourishing bulletin that advertises everything any self-respecting fan needs to know about the world of Sherlock Holmes. In 2007 he became editor of The Sherlock Holmes Journal. In 2012 'The Sherlock Holmes Miscellany,' jointly written with his wife Jean Upton, was hailed as "the best introduction to Sherlock Holmes that I know" by Michael Cox, producer of the classic Granada TV Sherlock Holmes series.

A TWO PIPE PROBLEM

By Kelvin I. Jones

'Better to have smoked and coughed than never to have smoked at all.'

~Russian Proverb.

The year 1901 was a memorable one for my friend and colleague, Sherlock Holmes. That year saw the solution to the bizarre series of poltergeist manifestations in Cambridge, a case which encompassed the deaths of two elderly clerics and which tested my friend's powers to the utmost limit; the questionable spontaneous combustion of Mr Gervase Smith, whose charred remains were found in a deserted warehouse in the East End of London; and the unmasking of Mme Pompey, the celebrated Nottingham ectoplasm medium.

By the autumn of that year my companion was showing signs of strain and the inevitable depression which visited him after long bouts of unbroken work had come upon him, a condition he liked to refer to as "the black hound." A self - poisoner by tobacco, he now spent most of each day seeking consolation for his frequent depressions either resorting to his old, oily briers or his untipped Egyptian cigarettes, whose odour was remarkably reminiscent to cow dung.

It was because of this that I managed to persuade him to accept an invitation from my old army friend Colonel Barchester, to stay for a few days at his Norfolk home. Barchester and I had seen action together briefly in the Afghanistan War and he had met Holmes at one of the Society of Psychical Research meetings in London where Holmes had claimed vociferously that most mediums were frauds and charlatans, a position which had been hotly contested in the debate by the robust campaigner, Arthur

Conan Doyle.

"Where exactly in Norfolk?" Holmes quizzed me, between mouthfuls of pipe smoke. "Anywhere near North Walsham?" He had no doubt been recalling the untimely death of Mr Hilton Cubitt of The Dancing Men case.

"In Norwich – the old part of the city to be precise."

"Ah. Then I accept since I have nothing better to occupy me. I shall be willing to explore a city of such renowned antiquity. Besides, I have grown weary of London. It stinks to high heaven."

Holmes was right. London did smell. It was a hot July and the street outside our apartment stank of horse manure and other unspeakable detritus. Elsewhere I think I once described it as the cesspool of the Empire. I think I was not wrong.

Travelling up from Liverpool Street Station on the Great Eastern, we arrived in Norwich in the late afternoon. Declining a cab, Holmes decided we would walk the half mile along the River to Barchester's mansion. It was a sultry day and the street traders were out in force in the city. Stopping at a newsvendor's stand briefly, he purchased a copy of 'The Norwich Herald,' which he tucked under his arm.

The Colonel lived in a tall Jacobean house in the area close to Tombland. Many of the houses in this area were timber framed and from the sixteenth century, evidence of the wealthy Norwich merchants who once plied their trade here.

Despite the apparent opulence of the buildings, I was struck by the number of ragged street urchins who pestered us for money. Holmes, who had fallen into a brown muse and who had been singularly uncommunicative since we had left the station, did his utmost to ignore their requests.

The Merchant's House – Barchester's residence – was a tall, imposing building with stucco pillars, looming incongruously from between two seventeenth century weavers' cottages whose windows were set in an attic space which had once housed the looms. The exterior of the building seemed much dilapidated, evidence, I deduced, of my old friend's advancing years and infirmity. Still a tall and imposing figure, he appeared frailer than I had last seen him some five years back and now supported himself with an ornate walking stick.

"Watson, my dear old fellow. And this, of course, is the renowned Mr Sherlock Holmes," he boomed, extending a large, warty hand. "I recall our brief meeting, sir. You are both most welcome. There are cool drinks in the sitting room."

He led the way into a panelled room, furnished with Chinese lacquered chests, three comfortable but worn armchairs and a variety of stuffed, exotic animals. To my relief, long blinds shut out much of the unbearable July heat. Once Barchester's aged servant had plied us with drinks and we had exchanged pleasantries, Barchester turned to Holmes.

"Your arrival here in Norwich is most timely."

"Oh? Why?" Holmes answered in his customary abrupt manner.

Have you perused the contents of the Herald yet?" he continued, pointing to Holmes's newspaper.

"Not yet."

'Then you would not have heard of the unfortunate demise of my friend John Parry."

"Unfortunate? In what respect?' asked Holmes.

"He has died of a gunshot wound at his home in Hellesdon. I lived next door to him for many years until I finally retired and purchased this place. He and my wife often played bridge together. He was a keen fisherman, like me, and a stalwart member of the local Masonic order."

"Suicide or an accident?"

"Unlikely to be suicide. John always had a very positive attitude. He was a confirmed optimist. And he knew how to handle firearms. He and I were both members of the Norwich City Shooting Club. To be honest, Mr Holmes I am quite perplexed by what has happened. I have taken the liberty of contacting Chief Inspector Jarvis of the Norwich police. He has been so good as to preserve the crime scene for us – if indeed we are talking of a crime."

"Really, Arthur, I thought we agreed that Sherlock was here to enjoy a rest," I objected.

"Come now, Watson, a simple matter of a professional opinion is surely not going to unduly tax my cerebral cortex,' Holmes laughed. 'I shall be only too delighted to overlook the case for you, but I cannot promise you anything new."

After our short supper was concluded, we took a four wheeler and drove through tree-lined country lanes via Castle Acre to the small village of Hellesdon. We passed down a narrow lane, flanked by tall beeches and sycamores until at last we found ourselves on the edge of the village.

The car passed a duck pond and thatched pub whose customers had spilled out onto the picnic tables at its front, then turned down another narrow lane until we reached a collection of scattered farm buildings, the largest bearing a dilapidated sign with the legend 'Grove Farm.' We got out of the four wheeler and, passing a solitary constable at the door, entered a long hallway whose walls were festooned with mounted foxes' heads and framed photographs of thick set men on grouse shoots. There was a strong smell of pipe tobacco which I immediately identified as Balkan Sobranie from my own pipe smoking habit.

"In here, sir," said Inspector Jarvis, who had appeared at the living room door. "I'm delighted to meet you both, Mr Holmes, Dr Watson. Your reputation precedes you."

Holmes did not reply to this compliment but merely smiled.

The body of a large man lay spread eagled on a leather sofa. The head, or what remained of it, was at an angle and behind it were great crimson gouts of blood, spread over the sofa and the wall behind the sofa.

'This is Dr Bates, our police surgeon, Mr Homes."

A white haired man with a red face, dressed in the traditional white suit and looking rather like a large porpoise, turned to Holmes. "Not a pretty sight, is it, Mr Holmes, but shot gun fatalities never are in my experience? However, feel free to take a closer look."

Holmes leaned over the corpse, then peered closely at the thin splashes of bloodstains on the wall behind the victim. "Notice anything significant?" asked the doctor.

"The bloodstains would suggest he wasn't shot at such close range for a suicide."

"Precisely my view. The spread should be much wider if the barrel had been inserted into the mouth. I estimate that the barrel of this shotgun was some six inches from his jaw, the latter taking the initial impact. And you can't angle a shot gun at that distance unless of course you have exceptionally long arms. And this man's middle name is not Bigfoot." Holmes smiled at the joke, despite the grim nature of the scene before him.

"Victim's name is John Parry," Jarvis informed Holmes. "A local farmer and property speculator. His wife found him like this. She says she had come back from a choir meeting about an hour ago."

"Where is she now?"

"With PC Brown next door." Holmes glanced around the room and I followed his darting glances. On a small table next to the settee was a large ashtray containing a short - stemmed briar pipe – a Peterson's with a silver band. He slipped on a glove, smelt the tobacco, then handed it to me.

"What do you make of it, Watson? "

'Probably Cavendish. I can't be absolutely sure.'

"Well done, Watson. I must confess, I can't abide the stuff. "

I glanced again at the contents of the room. A bottle of Irish malt whiskey and a single glass, half full. A copy of the Pink Un and a framed photo of Parry, red-faced and corpulent, sitting on a horse in his red hunting gear. Master of the Hunt and Lord of all he surveyed. To the left of the settee was another occasional table which had been knocked over. Correspondence was strewn on the floor. Holmes knelt down, and then began to sort through it. Bills, circulars and a black edged envelope with the words 'RIP John

Parry.' He opened it. In neat copperplate handwriting, the message read: 'Vermin, your days are numbered, FF.' There was no other clue as to the author. He slipped the letter and the envelope into an evidence bag.

"Interesting. Let's have a word with Mrs Parry, shall we?"

Cynthia Parry had been crying and her long face was smeared with mascara. She sipped the tea the PC had brought her, looking like some strange, dishevelled bird cast up on a storm wracked beach. She was middle-aged and conventionally dressed in a neat black dress; and despite her lined face and dyed black hair, was not unattractive.

"I'm Sherlock Holmes, and this is my companion, Dr Watson, Mrs Parry. Do you feel up to answering a few questions?" Mrs Parry dabbed at her eyes and nodded at us. "You found Mr Parry, I believe?"

"I got in at about eight o'clock and discovered him lying there."

"You didn't notice anyone in the lane – a carriage, perhaps?"

"No. I didn't pass a single vehicle. But then I take a back road to the church – that's where we have our choir practice. Not many people use the road. Perhaps I should explain to you inspector, that John and I had decided to lead more or less separate lives. In fact, my divorce papers came through about a month ago. Because it suits me to do so, I occupy the little white bungalow on the edge of the estate. You may have glimpsed it on your way in here. I had dropped in on John just to collect my mail when I found him like this."

"I see. Tell me, can you think of anyone who might have wanted to harm your husband? A colleague perhaps?"

Now that you mention it, yes, I can."

"And who might that be?"

"John had acquired a number of opponents, some from a group of labourers in the village. He was master of the Hunt, you know."

Holmes nodded. "Go on."

Only a month ago, someone attacked some of the fox hounds. We have also had to endure a number of threatening letters."

"Letters like this one?" Holmes showed her the letter he had found in the living room.

"Where did you find this?"

By the sofa."

"It must have arrived today – I haven't seen it."

"Do you have any idea who might be behind this campaign of intimidation?"

"Yes, I do. It's a group who call themselves Foxy Friends. The organisers are a couple living not far from here, Peter and Fanny Sloane. I can give you their address if you like."

"May I ask you the reason why you decided to get a divorce, Mrs Parry?"

"John had become impossible to live with. For ten years I put up with his drinking and bouts of violence but eventually I had come to the end of my tether."

"When was this exactly?"

"About six months ago. To make matters worse, I also found that he had been having an affair with a local woman of loose principles."

"Does she have a name?"

"Alice something. I don't know her surname. She works at the Red Lion pub down in the village."

" Thank you for the information. Tell me Mrs Parry, when you entered the room and found your husband lying on the sofa, what exactly did you do? Talk me through it."

"After the initial shock of finding him like that, I moved the shot gun –"

"You moved it? How, precisely?"

"What do you mean?"

"Which part of the gun did you actually touch?"

I can't recall exactly. The barrel I guess, and the stock, yes that was it."

"What did you do then?"

"I felt for the pulse in his neck to see if he was still alive. Then, of course, I contacted the local constable."

"And you didn't touch anything else in the room?"

"Not that I recall, no."

"That is most helpful. One more thing, Mrs Parry. Did you notice if there was a smell of pipe smoke in the room?"

"I think so. Yes. John was an habitual pipe smoker."

"You didn't notice if his pipe was still smouldering?"

"I didn't bother to look. I was otherwise preoccupied."

"I can understand that, naturally. But let me return to the smell of the pipe smoke, if you will. Was it a smell you usually associate with his pipe smoking?"

Mrs Parry thought for a moment, then she said: "I can't be sure that it was, no, I can't be absolutely certain about that."

As she uttered these words, there was the sound of an altercation in the passageway outside the room. The Detective Inspector stood up and left to investigate.

"What is it?" asked Holmes on his return.

"Someone claiming to be Mr Parry's brother, sir."

Mrs Parry stood up. "That must be Richard."

"Your brother-in-law?" asked Holmes

"He was due to visit me this evening. He's just returned from a visit to America. He works for a solicitor's firm there and was due some annual leave."

"Let him in, Inspector."

A tall, swarthy faced man stood in the doorway. He was expensively dressed in a pinstriped suit, carried a small leather attaché case and spoke with a slight American accent.

"Cynthia, I'm so, so sorry. They told me what had happened. Is there anything I can do?" Mrs Parry burst into tears. Richard Parry put down the attaché case and held her hand.

"Ask PC Brown to bring us some more tea will you, Inspector?"

After Mrs Parry had recovered her composure, Homes resumed his questioning. Turning to Richard Parry, he said: "Can I ask you the purpose of your visit here, Mr Parry?"

"By all means. I had some family and business matters to attend to. I phoned John from the States two days back and told him of my intended visit this evening."

"I see. You knew about this visit, Mrs Parry?"

"I'd been looking forward to Richard coming. Richard was very kind to me and supported me through the divorce. I spent a month with him in Los Angles prior to the settlement, just to recharge my batteries."

"John wasn't an easy man to live with – and that's putting it mildly," said Richard Parry. "Frankly, I was concerned for her safety. It seemed like a good idea that she should spend some time away from the farm."

"You mentioned just now you were here on business. Can you be more specific about that, Mr Parry?"

"Certainly. The firm I work for has contacts here in East Anglia. But I also needed to talk to John about the farm. For the past few years we've been making a substantial loss on the arable."

"We?"

"John and I are – were – both owners of the family business, though admittedly I was very much the sleeping partner."

"I see. And how exactly would you describe your relationship with your brother?"

"We rubbed along together well enough for the most part. Of course, I made my views clear to him about his treatment of Cynthia."

"When do you return to America?"

"This coming Thursday."

"We shall need a contact address."

"No problem. I'm presently staying at the Green Man on Boundary Road."

When we dropped in at the dilapidated cottage on Lynn Road the following morning, we found Peter Sloane. He was alone and answered the door in a stained dressing gown. His haggard, pale face gave us a clue to the man's lifestyle and, on entering the dingy hallway, we noted that there was a strong smell of hashish.

"This had better be good," Sloane retorted. "You got me out of the bath." He led us into a tiny living room, littered with correspondence and stained, half empty teacups where an old boxer dog eyed us suspiciously from the battered sofa.

"Mind the dog," said Sloane. "He doesn't much care for strangers - especially policemen." DCI Jarvis opted for a derelict basket chair whilst Holmes stood awkwardly behind him, ready to take notes. Sloane sat beside the dog, his dressing gown falling open, revealing a pair of creased and grubby shorts.

"I heard about Parry committing suicide."

"We're not entirely certain that he did," Holmes replied. Sloane smiled.

"Whatever. He's no great loss."

"I gather there was some enmity between you and Mr and Mrs Parry."

"I know why you're here, inspector, or who these other people are, but I can tell you that your journey is a wasted one. Me and Mandy spent last night in the pub and several people can vouch for us."

"Those several people being?"

"Members of our anti-hunting league."

"*Foxy Friends?*"

"Indeed."

"Do you know anything about this?" said Holmes, holding up the letter in its evidence bag. Sloane scanned its contents.

"This isn't my handwriting."

"But you do recognise the handwriting?"

Sloane shrugged. "Not sure. No, I know nothing about it." He handed back the bag.

"Nevertheless, you and your group actively campaigned against the Hunt," said Holmes.

"Peacefully we did, yes."

"And caused damage to two of the Hunt members' dogs."

"Don't know anything about those incidents."

"And you deny that you persecuted Mr Parry and his wife?"

"Absolutely deny it. Look, whoever did for Parry had nothing whatever to do with our group. We're a protest movement, not a bunch of assassins." The dog growled menacingly. Jarvis stood up.

"Very well Mr Sloane. We will of course check out your alibi, but we may need to question your partner as well." Sloane smiled then yawned loudly.

"Be my guest, Chief Inspector."

The police surgeon's findings arrived on Jarvis's desk two days later. Holmes and I, who had returned at lunchtime from a tour of Norwich Cathedral, instantly scanned their contents. Sadly, the pathology told us little that was new. Parry had died from a single gunshot wound. The bullet had entered at a point below the jaw and exited through the cranium, death being almost instantaneous. The evidence did indeed suggest that Parry could not have fired the gun. The only prints on the gun were those of

Parry and his wife, confirming her account. Significantly perhaps, the glass and bottle had been cleaned of prints. Maybe the murderer had downed a glass of malt whiskey, then removed his prints. There was nothing else of significance and no sign of a forced entry. On Parry's desk was a telegram from his brother telling him of his intended arrival later that evening. Holmes had just finished reading the pathology report when Jarvis entered the room. "Anything new?" asked Holmes.

"I've been looking at Parry's bank statements and recent correspondence, Mr Holmes."

"And?"

"It appears that the brother was right about Parry's finances. He owed the bank £20,000 and had already remortgaged the house." Jarvis passed Holmes a large manila folder.

"What else?"

"There are a couple of notes from Mrs Parry about bills not being paid. Notice anything about the handwriting?" The inspector passed Holmes and I a small envelope containing a folded A5 note. The handwriting was quite similar in style to that of the threatening letter that had been found in Parry's living room. Holmes nodded, thoughtfully.

"Any sign of a will among Parry's effects?" asked Holmes.

"Not yet sir. Unless it's with his solicitor of course."

"What about Sloane's alibi?"

"The pub alibi checked out. He and his partner were there until closing time - according to the landlord."

"Then I think we had better pay a visit to Cynthia Parry."

It was early evening by the time we reached Cynthia Parry's bungalow, a modest two bedroomed property which stood between tall copper beeches at the edge of the estate. Holmes instructed Jarvis to park the fly at the end of the drive. "Let's walk the rest, gentlemen." he said.

Standing outside the property was another small fly. Holmes examined the vehicle. On the passenger seat was a small attaché case with the initials RP. He knocked on the front door. After about a minute Mrs Parry appeared in a dressing gown. Her grey hair was tousled, and she looked flustered. "I wonder if I could have a word, Mrs Parry?" asked Holmes.

As he sat in the lounge waiting for Cynthia Parry to reappear, Holmes carefully examined the interior, every so often scanning surfaces with the aid of his lens. The walls were painted a ghastly green and decorated with cheap Constable prints. There was a fireplace with a worn looking range and a mantelpiece with small porcelain ornaments garnered from frequent trips to France and Italy. On the table next to him, he noticed a large ashtray and a straight Peterson's briar pipe. He picked it up and smelt it, then passed it to me. My nostrils were assailed by the unmistakable odour of Balkan Sobranie.

"Any comment to make, Watson?"

Then the truth suddenly dawned on me and I cursed under my breath at my slowness of wit. Now it was clear to me. Richard Parry had lied when he said he'd just arrived at John Parry's residence those two days ago. I nodded in confirmation.

"Well done, Watson. You are improving. Inspector, do me a favour will you? Check out that fly that's standing outside and see if you can find out who owns it?"

As Jarvis left the room, Mrs Parry entered, followed by an uneasy looking Richard Parry, dressed only in a dressing gown.

"I think you two have some explaining to do," said Holmes.

Back in police headquarters in Norwich, Richard Parry had been in the interview room for only half an hour before he gave us the full story. Initially he claimed that he had visited his brother, that there had been an argument over the financial losses of the farm and that the gun had gone off by mistake after John had threatened him. But after an hour of intense questioning from Holmes and Jarvis, the truth was finally revealed.

"I was in love with Cynthia. Had been ever since we first met at John's wedding. When I was working in the States, we kept constant contact with each other."

"And she stayed with you on more than one occasion?" asked Holmes.

"Yes, she did."

"Which is where, no doubt, you became lovers?"

"You've no idea how vile John could be to her, especially after he had had a few drinks. He abused her both physically and mentally. I think the mental abuse was the worst of it. That's why I insisted that she have a break from him and why I urged her to divorce him. The problem, you see, was that she had no money of her own. She had given up work some years ago to help run the farm with him."

"You helped her financially?" asked Holmes.

He nodded.

"I kept her going, gave her a chance to be independent. Then, when the debts began to mount up, I urged her to take immediate action."

"Very well. Now tell us the real version of what happened to John. We now know from tests that there was shot gun residue both on Cynthia's hands and clothes." Richard Parry wiped the sweat from his forehead.

"Let's take this one stage at a time," said Holmes. "You lied to us about the time of your arrival at the farm."

"When the gun went off, we both panicked. Believe me, Mr Holmes, neither of us had any intention of killing John. We tried to reason with him, and I tried to persuade him to sell the farm. I told him he had a moral duty to support Cynthia. He had been drinking as usual and became aggressive. He picked up the shot gun and told me to leave. "Slope off back to the States, you little rat," was his exact phrase. I feared what he might do to Cynthia. I told him I wasn't going anywhere until he changed his mind. He cocked the gun and pointed it at me. By now he was incensed. His eyes were blazing. Cynthia thought he was going to shoot me there and then. She tried to take the gun from him, there was a struggle, and – well, you can guess the rest."

"And afterwards?"

"We both figured that I would be the number one suspect, since I am the only entitled legatee, following on from Cynthia's divorce. John didn't make a will, you see. Cynthia came up with the idea and we each concocted our alibis. I didn't mean it to end like this. Neither of us did. You surely have to believe me Mr Holmes."

The Parry Case, as the Press subsequently termed it, came to Norwich Crown Court the following January. Holmes recalled it well, for it was during the Arctic winter of 1904, and on the day when he was required to give evidence, he and I had trudged through ankle high drifts of snow to get to the courthouse.

Richard and Cynthia Parry were both found guilty of involuntary manslaughter and given suspended sentences. They married shortly afterwards, and Cynthia settled with her new husband in America. Holmes was never quite sure that he believed Richard Parry's account of what took place that evening at the farmhouse. It just did not quite tally with the black edged threatening letter which he firmly believed that Cynthia had written in an attempt to frame the Sloanes. But it was a suspicion about premeditation which could never be proved in a court of law and thus would be deemed inadmissible.

During the lunch hour of the day on which the court proceedings were concluded, Holmes sat with me on a bench overlooking the river, smoking one of his oldest briers. Stuffing the bowl with a fresh plug of shag, he struck a Swan Vesta and drew the flame slowly across the bowl as the acrid blue fumes filled the crisp air. A flotilla of frozen looking swans floated by and he threw the remains of his unappetising pasty onto the waters to appease them. The swans, not liking the pasty very much, chose to ignore the offering. How Holmes detested the British judicial system. Its wheels turned exceedingly slow and proof of guilt was often difficult to establish. But that was nothing to the dislike he felt for the long British winter. I felt in my greatcoat pocket for my silver hip flask which I offered to my companion.

"Thank you for this, Watson. The Norfolk winter is keener than I had anticipated. Getting back to the murk and grime of the great metropolis will offer us some small consolation."

And closing his eyes as if to demand unquestioning silence, he reached once more for his old brier pipe.

SOME STRAIGHT TALK ABOUT CURVED PIPES

By Al Shaw

"No man should marry a teetotaller or a man who does not smoke."

~Robert Louis Stevenson.

It is 4:00 in the morning and here I am poring over my copy of William Baring-Gould's *Annotated Sherlock Holmes*. My Rathbonean bent shaped pipe is blazing away and, as a neophyte Sherlockian, I am out of my skull with pleasure as I sit there wide-eyed drinking it all in. Suddenly my eye is drawn to the footnote on page 104, which provides me with the following gloss:

It will be noted that neither Homes nor Watson ever mentioned a pipe with a *curved* stem; indeed, Mr. John Dickson Carr has stated that the curved pipe was unknown in England until the time of the Boer War (1889). Why then has the curved pipe – a calabash or a meerschaum, for example – become a Holmesian trademark? Because Gillette, in playing the role of Holmes, found it difficult to speak his lines with a *straight* pipe between his lips...

Hogwash! I blurted out, neophyte or not. I'm no actor, but as any pipe smoker will tell you, it is equally difficult to speak with either a curved or a straight pipe stuck between your teeth, and I'm willing to bet that Gillette removed his therefrom with every line of dialogue. Nor was I too impressed with the intelligence offered about the introduction of the curved variety into Holmes's England. Further, this became the seed of a Sherlockian urban legend. The myth that Holmes only smoked a straight pipe evolved to become the secret knowledge of the cognoscenti.

We often see this put forth when someone wants to demonstrate that they are more than a fan. Bear in mind as we proceed, omission is not proof of nonexistence. True, a curved pipe may not be specifically mentioned. Neither are toiletries, socks, or underwear but we can assume Holmes owned them all.

Although Sidney Paget and certain other early illustrators of the Canon depicted the great detective using straight stemmed pipes only, even the most cursory of research reveals that Holmes had a variety of bent and curved shapes to choose form during the whole of his active career. Let us remember, Paget drew his brother as Holmes. Did his brother simply pose with his own pipe? In fact, there was such a variety by Victorian times, that it is difficult to accept the notion that Holmes limited himself to a straight little clay pipe from the 1600s, 200 years later, during the Industrial Revolution. Even the pictures – cue Calabash, generally assumed to be a Hollywood inspired innovation, was available to Holmes in its earliest manifestations. First seen by the Dutch in Africa as early as the 1650s, and little more than a gourd as used by the natives, its large cooling chamber makes an ideal receptacle for burning tobacco, shag or otherwise. By Holmes's era, some came with meerschaum lining cups, and for those too poor to afford such luxuries, clay, plaster or wood equivalents could also be had. Victorian contemporary, Mark Twain himself, smoked a calabash frequently.

In the 1700s, another odd but equally interesting shape appeared, consisting of a porcelain bowl, often hand-painted, and a bottom receptacle with a long cherrywood stem, usually sporting a bent staghorn bit. It always featured a severe bend. Speaking of cherrywood, a candidate for the "Long Cherrywood" used by Holmes in "The Copper Beeches," (which Watson tells us he substituted for his clay pipe when he was in a disputatious rather than a meditative mood) was actually a Churchwarden. A good example is the churchwarden used by Jeremy Brett when he played Holmes. It often had a cherrywood bowl and has made a comeback these days, being sold as a "Hobbit" or "Gandalf" pipe.

On the other hand, it is possible that Holmes waxed disputatious using a carved meerschaum, which were quite the vogue from 1750 to 1850, despite their high cost, and very common from the 1850s to the 1900s when the meerschaum boom brought prices down dramatically. Meerschaum is a very porous mineral which yields a cool, dry smoke, and is considered by most users to be the finest pipe material available. Although meerschaums were not always carved, almost all were bent and many were fitted with long cherrywood stems or bent bits. Of the two Jefferson Davis' pipes in museums, one is a superb curved meerschaum from 1865. Let us remember, these were Victorian times defined by elaborate designs in everyday objects. One or more meerschaums would certainly not have been out of place at 221B, given Holmes's quirkiness and taste for oddities of all kinds.

Clay pipes are mentioned in the Canon more frequently than any other variety, but about them we are told very little. In "The Red-Headed League," Watson describes one as looking like the "thrusting...bill of some strange bird," from which we may conclude it was reasonably straight in shape. But during Holmes's time there were actually a great many moulded clay shapes available also, among them intricately carved models which set the pattern for the meerschaums. These had a fat, squat, curved bowl with an amber or cherrywood stem, and with a bent bit usually made of staghorn. His old black clay was mentioned in multiple stories, but the shape was not. A curved shape clay would tend to collect tars and juices with continued use and soon become oily and/or black. Many clay pipes actually came in black. It is likely that those of Holmes' so described by Watson were of this type.

According to Alfred Dunhill, sometime during the 1800s, a French pipe maker broke his favourite meerschaum during a visit to Napoleon's birthplace in Corsica and instructed a local craftsman in the making of a duplicate. Unable to obtain any meerschaum, the craftsman decided to try instead using burl of the local briar, it being relatively light and having a pleasing grain. The experiment proved so successful that the pipe maker turned to the manufacture of briar pipes exclusively. According to anthropologists, when a new substance is introduced in the making of an article, the old shape and function remain essentially the same until improvements in the new article are deemed necessary for improved function, at which point re-design occurs. As most meerschaums at the time were bent or curved, it is not surprising that the early briars of Holmes' time took a similar shape. Another of Jefferson Davis' pipes was a curved briar, looking very much like a curved, carved fancy meerschaum, except for the material. This, like the previously mentioned Davis meerschaum pipe, was circa 1865. The Barling pipe company started in1812 and was featured in the 1851 Great Exhibition of the Works of Industry of all Nations, held in London. They were invited for their fancy curved meerschaum pipes and proceeded to also produce curved briars by that time as well, some of which survive today.

Holmes smokes a briar in *The Sign of the Four* and in "The Man with the Twisted Lip," and despite the claims of Mr. Carr, it (or they) could well have been curved. What he actually says about the matter, in his biography of Conan Doyle, is: "curved pipes [were] unknown in England until they were imported during the South African War," and it is clear from the context that he is speaking of the year 1899, not the 1889 cited by Baring-Gould. And it is likewise evident that the particular kind of pipe he refers to is the Oom Paul, so named after Paul Kruger, president of the South African Republic during the Boer War, who smoked one and popularized it. The implication is this was the first briar with a curved shape, which is simply not the case. Photographs taken of Gillette playing Holmes in 1899 show him using a full bent briar, and it is not of the Oom Paul variety. Carried to its extreme, Mr. Carr's claim is akin to suggesting that the Corncob pipe was unknown in American until it was popularized by General Douglas MacArthur in WWII.

The fact of the matter is that from the 1850s on, there were many varieties of bent briars in use, including those featuring the Wellington shape. The Welling is the most familiar to pipe smokers as the shape of the Peterson Pipe, used by Charles Peterson beginning in 1865, when he first began manufacturing pipes. He later modified it internally, thereby creating the now famous "Peterson System" and introduced it in 1890. Peterson pipes caught on rapidly, turning the shop into a veritable factory, and much of his output found its way into London shops. In 1898, while it was being sold worldwide, the "Peterson Lip" was added to the stem, creating what many considered to be the ultimate pipe. The kind that Gillette used was most likely a Peterson. Mark Twain in the 1800s was such a devotee that in

1896 Peterson made a special Mark Twain model which in 1996 was re-issued as a centennial replica in much demand by pipe collectors. This features the shape that we see most often in movies and illustrations.

At least one photo of the agent Arthur Conan Doyle, shows him smoking a curved pipe. Although bent briars may not have enjoyed their greatest popularity until the turn of the century, there were certainly many around to be had, and in Holmes's case even earlier than the period of "The Musgrave Ritual," his first recorded case. In The Sign Of Four Watson says, "Holmes was standing on the doorstep with his hands in his pockets smoking his pipe." Well, pipe smokers will tell you that if you are going to smoke a pipe with both hands in your pockets, only a curved pipe will fit the bill. In fact, given the chronology involved, Holmes could easily have enjoyed the Peterson model before over half of the recorded exploits took place. And as I have demonstrated, he had access also to a range of bent pipes other than briars as well. How many made up his collection we do not know, but he had more than one pipe rack and a mantel strewn with a "litter of pipes and tobacco pouches" to boot. Does anyone seriously suggest that someone as easily bored with the routine as Holmes would limit an accumulation of such magnitude to one mundane pipe shape? Again, hogwash!

Sources Consulted

The Sherlock Holmes Pipe Shop Ltd., Elmurst, IL; Cellini Pipe Craftsman, Chicago, IL; The Tinderbox, Inc., Vernon Hills, IL; Iwan Reis & Co., Chicago, IL; Churchills of Birmingham, Lake Forest, IL; Alfred Dunhill of London, Chicago, IL; *A Pipe Smoker's Guide* by Charles Graves; *Weber's Guide to Pipes* by Carl W. Weber; *The Book of Pipes and Tobacco,* by Carl Ehwa, Jr.; *The Annotated Sherlock Holmes* edited by William S. Baring-Gould; *In the Footsteps of Sherlock Holmes* by Michael Harrison; *The Private Life of Sherlock Holmes* by Vincent Starrett; *The Life of Sir Arthur Conan Doyle* by John Dickerson Carr; and *"The Sherlock Holmes Reference Guide"* by William D. Goodrich.

About the author

Al Shaw had always enjoyed the Sherlock Holmes stories but when his brother, Mike, started corresponding from Africa using the Dancing Men cypher for privacy, things changed, and his appreciation deepened. Upon rereading all the stories, Al's interest in Holmes was codified. He joined Hugo's Companions in 197 and served as officer in the organization until the 80's. Al is currently "Sir Hugo," the president of Hugo's Companions. He was present the first meeting (and then a member) of The Criterion Bar Association in 1972. He wrote his first Sherlockian article (published in Baker Street Miscellanea) and became a member of The Hounds of the Baskervilles (sic) in 1982. Al reflects that he was privileged to be a friend of many of the Sherlockian giants: John Nieminski, John Bennet Shaw, Ely Liebow, Fred Levin, Bob Mangler, Pauls Smedegaard, Bill Goodrich, to name a few. Al Shaw continues to write, contributing to periodicals and anthologies, and is active in multiple scions and Sherlockian activities. In 2018, he received the investiture of "Sir Hugo Baskerville" from The Baker Street Irregulars. He has collections of Sherlockiana, Tobacco Pipes, and Fountain Pens.

SHERLOCK HOLMES AND THE OBSIDIAN ENIGMA

By Kelvin I Jones

"It is the passion of all proper people that he who lives without tobacco has nothing to live for. Not only does it refresh and cleanse men' brains, but it guides their souls in the ways of virtue, and by it one learns to be a man of honour."

~Moliere, 'Don Juan'.

I had called upon my friend Mr Sherlock Holmes during an afternoon in late July when the streets were hot and comfortless and the sky without a cloud. I had not seen him for some while, my practice and my marriage having placed considerable demands on my time and energy, so that a period of some months had elapsed without our communicating. I was not surprised, therefore, to find him listless and pinched about the face, a sure sign that he had been neglecting himself and sinking ever deeper into the reclusive, drug induced introspection for which he was renowned. Nevertheless, he was clearly pleased to see me and when his landlady showed me into the large sitting room that formed both his chemical laboratory and reception room, he smiled, put down his old and most oily of briers, then offered me a glass of malt whisky and bade me draw my chair up to the hearthplace.

"My dear fellow, what on earth have you been doing with yourself? It seems an age since we last met."

"My practice is an absorbing one," I replied. "I have several patients on my books at the moment, one a schizophrenic who needs constant medical attention."

He looked at me wearily and sighed.

"I wish I could say the same of my own practice. It has indeed become dreary of late. You remember the business at Winchester?"

I nodded.

"There has been nothing of importance since then, apart from a couple of burglary cases, brought to my attention through Lestrade. And, of course, the murder at Blackheath, which we suspected was the work of my old friend, Charlie Peace."

He got up and paced the room whilst I endeavoured to console him.

"When I first began - before I had met you - things were decidedly different. You see these?"

He pointed to a row of decrepit box files above the mantlepiece.

"Records of my first three years' cases when I had taken rooms near the British Museum. I have been going through them to see what *disjecta membra* might possibly interest you. There are some remarkable examples here, matters you may one day see fit to reveal to those less sceptical members of your profession, Watson. Who knows?"

He took the first of the boxes and pulled out a sheaf of papers, tied by a red ribbon.

"Ah ... yes, there are some beauties here. I think I told you about the murder of young Stephenson, who we believe was obliterated by MacGregor Mather's agent?"

"He of the Golden Dawn?"

Holmes nodded.

"And the assassination of Deacon Atkins?"

"The Gloucester Cathedral case...."

"Indeed."

"Ah, now this really is very interesting, sensational even, particularly to the student of abnormal psychology, doctor."

He resumed his seat by the fire opposite me and, balancing the sheaves of paper on his lap, reached up to the mantlepiece and drew down the long cherrywood pipe that he favoured when in a loquacious and ruminative mood. Soon the room was filled with the acrid stench of the rough - cut tobacco which I recalled with loathing from our student days.

"It happened more than two decades ago. I had already made some reputation for myself among friends at university as an investigator, as you will know. In the year before I left Gaius College, Cambridge, I had done a small favour to a college companion by identifying the perpetrator of a number of blackmail letters. Pritchard - that was the fellow's name - knocked on my door in Montague Street one morning, telling me he had heard something of my growing reputation, and asked me if I might spare him a moment or two. Apparently, he had tracked me down from Dr Roberts, who, as you know, liked to keep a register of where we students all ended up, simply for his own satisfaction. Anyway, despite the threadbare nature of my surroundings, I invited him in and plied him with barley water, for it was a hot summer's day, much like today, and the poor fellow looked dehydrated. When he had revived sufficiently and I had shared a pipe with him, he began to tell me of his problem."

"It doesn't concern me directly, you understand."

"Then whom does it concern?"

"My uncle."

"Proceed."

"You may recall something of the work of Dr John Pritchard, the distinguished brain surgeon, for I believe he achieved some measure of fame in the field of nervous disorders."

"Indeed, I do. His treatise on nervous lesions has become something of a classic."

"Well, when my uncle retired, he was lucky enough to receive a large inheritance. He purchased a house near the village of Chilham, down in Kent. It was a large, rambling place set by a river in the back of beyond, built in the middle ages and added to since by both Flemish weavers and eighteenth - century squires. Being particularly fond of his two nephews, Jasper and I, our uncle had maintained a steady correspondence with us since he made the move. At first the letters were enthusiastic but as time went on it became apparent to me that all was not well with my uncle and that perhaps he had fallen prey to some form of monomania. Each letter I received was written in a crabbed but orderly copperplate on thick vellum, but the third of them seemed by comparison to be hurried and untidy, as if the writer were agitated. The first was dated June 1st and read as follows:

"My dear James,

Here I am at last in the house of my dreams. You must see Gretton to appreciate its beauty. It is a mansion of most elegant proportions once owned by a doctor, I am told, and set in a distinctively eighteenth century landscape, although the lands hereabouts are steeped in history, and I understand that the house itself is set upon a site of pagan significance. Such delights for a discerning bachelor who has always had to content himself with a set of dingy rooms near St Barts Hospital!

"The rooms are lofty and panelled throughout in a rich walnut. In each one there is a most original ceiling whose sculpture has been inspired by a rich and sometimes almost decadent imagination. The drawing room, for example, sports an enormous vine with ripe and abundant grapes from whose leaves naked satyrs peep and stalk each other. Half hidden in the tangled roots are mythical beasts - unicorns, mermaids and centaurs, all engaged in some form of ferocious combat - or is it amorous play? - I cannot decide which. However, it is the study which succeeds most in claiming one's admiration and attention. Here the ornate oak panelling is at once recognisable, being the work of the wood carver, Grinling Gibbons. I had seen something of his decorative stuff at Hampton Court Palace and St Paul's Cathedral where he carved the choir stalls and the great organ screen.

"How can I convey the exquisiteness of these decorations? They are based on that theme of perennial fascination among baroque artists: the last judgement. On entering the room, one is confronted by a great archway from which angels and archangels rise up, trumpeting the resurrection. Through the doorway and between the book stacks themselves one glimpses scenes of such depravity and sin the like of which would affront the more tender sensibilities. Amidst ruined buildings and overgrown glades the naked dead engage in carnal pursuits, whose nature I may not describe here for fear of offending you, dear nephew, whilst above them the heavenly hosts stretch out their arms, imploring them to rise upwards and forgo the inevitable fires of Hell. All this is depicted with such force and conviction that one might have imagined the artist to be divinely inspired. You must see it for yourself, though I would warn you against sullying the eyes of the fairer sex, should you deign to visit me - as you must - in the near future.

Your Dearest Uncle."

'Nothing very remarkable or outre about that." I remarked.

"Ah, but consider, if you will, the contents of the third letter, dated some months after. I shall read to you the most significant section of his epistle."

"In the drawing room the centrepiece is a most beautiful high window. From it I can look across the lawn to the folly at the bottom of the garden, a curious druidic temple erected by one of the previous owners. The window itself appears to be tinted, for the sunlight is strangely muted by its effect. Indeed, I have examined the glass with a lens and discovered it to be of ancient origin, similar to the medieval glass used in York Minster though not so old. It has become one of my pleasures to sit by this window on hot summer afternoons. In fact, I have become so enamoured of this spot that I have begun to take my meals in that room. By a curious stroke of luck, the builder thought fit to install a window seat.

"But enough of the window. The rest of the house demands equal attention. There is a magnificent library and five bedrooms, all of which you are invited to sample. I would be more than jubilant should you be able to spare the time to visit me here. Owing to the isolated position of Gretton I seldom entertain visitors, so the days are indeed long, though by no means unfulfilled.

Come at once!

Your Uncle John."

"Again, nothing untoward so far," I commented.

"No, but may I read to you the next letter. It dates from three weeks later."

"Proceed."

"I must confess that the house in question exceeded my wildest expectations. The solicitors, Butler, Jessup and Moran, informed me that the building had been designed by the renowned architect John Thorpe and constructed under the direction of Smythson. I think that you would find the design fascinating. There are no courts and the house is square, symmetrical, and finished with a block at each corner.

"Enclosed in the centre is a large hall which is exceptionally high in order to accommodate the clerestory type windows (themselves fitted with the most magnificent stained glass depiction of Saint George slaying the dragon - this you must see for its sheer beauty!), without which it would receive no daylight. The hall timber, too, is remarkably ornate, and typical of the late Elizabethan design, possessing many grotesque gargoyles in the pagan mode, chief of which is a large Green Man, complete with intertwined snakes, hiding among foliage.

"And now I must describe to you the interior. Beautiful plaster ceilings in all the rooms, decorated in rib and strapwork, both intricate and decorative. Flowers, leaves and fruit abound and half-concealed a number of satyrs and tiny, almost demonic shapes engaged in amorous pursuit of each other.

"But perhaps the crowning jewel is the carved stone fireplace and chimneypiece. Here the pagan influence is seen at its richest. Cusping and trefoil patterns everywhere, and amid them heraldic motifs, grotesques, masks, caryatids, obelisks, vases and balls, all a rich and wondrous swirl and a delight to the imagination.

"And beneath all this the cellars, a series of stone-vaulted spaces, damp but still serviceable, an ideal resting place for wines.

"If you think that I have been over-fulsome in my praise, my dear

James, please come down to Chilham, and I shall prove how wrong you are. It would indeed be pleasant to take dinner together, much as we were sometimes wont to do in my days at college. I still retain the meerschaum which you gave me and smoke the same revolting brand of shag tobacco. How would it be if we were to share a pipe? Besides, there is something I wish to show you: a little discovery of mine, which I am eager to share. Will you come this very weekend? I look forward to your reply.

Yours very sincerely,

Your affectionate Uncle."

"I still don't see where this is leading,' I objected, relighting my cherrywood.

"Please, be patient. There's a lot more to the story.'

"Very well, but please try to be more concise. Or provide me with some idea of why you consider these letters to be so important.'

"Very well, then. I must admit, Sherlock, that, unlike yourself, I am not by nature a lover of the railway. Under normal circumstances I would perhaps not have made this visit, but the content of my uncle's letter had intrigued me greatly. From an early age I have shared his obsession with buildings of great antiquity and distinction. The house at Chilham sounded fascinating and I could not let myself forgo the opportunity to inspect it. And there was something else that nagged at my mind: a feeling that somehow, historically, I already knew of this place. Before packing my suitcase, I checked my voluminous files but was unable to discover a reference to it.

"The hustle and bustle of London came as something of a shock to my naturally reclusive nature so that I was more than happy to hail a cab at the railway station and instruct the driver to drive to Chilham. The district in which the house was situated was a curious mixture of the old and the new and as the cab wound through narrow suburban streets of Medway, I caught glimpses among the dull yellow brick houses of great mansions with

Palladian frontages set back from the road. There were older buildings, too: Georgian villas with immense sweeping driveways, half concealed by rambling rhododendron and magnolia bushes and mock - gothic splendours with turrets and lancet windows.

"By the time we pulled into the narrow driveway that led to Grantchester House, evening was fast approaching and as we dipped down a sharp incline, I gained a view of the River Medway, the sun casting its waters into a burnished mirror. By contrast, the house itself seemed dark and somewhat forbidding. It was just as my uncle had suggested in his letter, yet there was another dimension, too: a sense almost of a personality which at the time I found to be slightly disturbing and which confirmed my suspicion that, somewhere in the past, I had encountered this great building before and known a little of its history. Some infamy had been done here, but what it was, I could not recall.'

"Cut out the poetry, James, and please *stick to the facts.*"

"The cab slid to a halt. As I got out and was in the act of paying the driver, a light came on in the entrance porch and the drive was at once illuminated, the shadows of the bushes lining the path up to the front door like hunched figures. The powerful Edison lamps threw the front of the building into relief and I became aware of a grim edifice cast from sandstone, starkly simplistic, broken only by a series of tiny oriel windows. Soon the great doors opened to reveal my uncle, dressed elegantly in a paisley smoking jacket. I was amused to think that he had probably donned this apparel for my benefit. He looked decidedly thin and I noted there was a pallor to his face, denoting sleepless nights.

"James, it's good to see you. A pleasant journey?"

"Insufferable, dear uncle. Aren't you going to invite me in?"

"Although it was a summer's evening, a cold wind had got up and I had begun to shiver. He led the way through a dim hallway where panelled oak walls displayed a series of dark oil paintings.

"Have you eaten? There's some cold chicken and salad in the great room. I prepared it specially - oh, and a bottle of claret. You see, I remember your tastes!"

"After the long journey and the intense heat of the summer sun the meal, though simply prepared, was welcome. Between us we finished the bottle of claret and retired to a couple of large oak chairs situated either side of an immense fireplace in the "great room" as my uncle termed it. Despite the rich interior of the room, there was little furniture to be seen save a worn Turkish rug, a set of occasional tables and a dark and battered trunk.

"Now then," resumed my uncle, after we had lit our pipes and finished exchanging our respective snippets of gossip, "I have something rather remarkable to show you."

"He got up and lifted a trunk onto the low table in front of me. It was an exquisite piece of craftsmanship. The leatherwork was extremely ornate with a soft kid underlayer and on top of this numerous whorls and circles sewn into a pattern. On the lid itself the initials "J.D." had been stamped and directly above, there was a face with two enormous eyes and a cruel looking, indented mouth. Around the eyes were several thin lines radiating outwards, indicating, one would suppose, a suggestion of energy. I had seen something of the sort before when examining the Roman mural at Chillingworth which was consecrated to Mithras, but never had I seen in a face such animation and sense of power. The entire effect I found somewhat disturbing, though I did not admit as much to my companion.

"Magnificent, isn't it?" he said, proudly.

"Most curious. Where exactly did you acquire it?"

"I found it, dear boy."

"*Found it?* Where?"

"In the cellars. It was not long after I had moved into the house. I'd been clearing out a great heap of rotten timber and old pots and pans - the detritus of several previous owners, I would imagine."

"Have you opened it yet?"

"No. I thought I'd wait for a second opinion. I have taken the liberty of writing to our solicitors. One of their number – Moran, the senior partner – is something of an antiquarian and is looking into the matter."

"I examined the surface of the trunk carefully and guessed from the patterning of the discoloured hinges that it was most probably of Tudor origin.

"These clasps look none too sound. If we are to open it, we shall have to be careful."

"We set to work immediately, cleaning away the rust from the hinges and adding a little lubrication here and there. At last both hinges began to shift under slight pressure and the lid came up. I took a lamp from one of the tables and we peered inside. A smell of damp vellum rose up to greet our nostrils and I moved back, momentarily overcome by the sudden pungency. There was something else, too, a suggestion of something which had long decayed, a sickly smell which I could not readily identify.

"Against the discoloured cream of the interior lay three bundles of manuscripts, all of them so brittle and badly spotted that they crumbled at our touch. In addition, there were a few tattered leather - bound volumes, mainly quarto size. Carefully, we lifted them out. Despite the poor condition of the bindings, the pages themselves were intact. Among the volumes were alchemical and magical treatises by Albertus Magnus, Paracelsus and Cornelius Agrippa, plus a Latin translation of Euclid. I gasped in astonishment.

"Clearly, whatever else J.D. might have been, he was also a scholar," I remarked. We finished emptying the trunk. My uncle was just about to replace the lid when I noticed a small fissure in the base. I told him to wait and, pushing my index finger through, found that there was a space about three inches deep.

"A false bottom. Interesting."

"The wood was rotten with age and came away easily in my hands, the leather covering separating from the sides. Beneath lay a scroll of parchment tied with a black ribbon. We removed the ribbon and unrolled it. Although the ink had faded, most of the writing, minute and spidery in form, was still discernible.

"My uncle handed me the manuscript. It read:

"....do hereby commit the secret of Gabriel (it ran) to darkness and secrecy, for the protection of thofe gentlefolk who are all of a prying and inquifitive nature. The great secrets and mysteries of eternity as transmitted to myfelf and J D. being contained in the following table of magical numbers, let them be revealed only to him who has the power and infpiration of the spirits:

73 14 49 14 31 55 8
45 8 15
l2 6 21 67 15 12 26
6 32 32 61
35 15 73 11 4
33 52 63 52 12 15 8
71 8 42
6 15 19 23 62 14
8 24 41 91 24 59
71 15 12 33 51 12 33 41
101 26 15 36
31 22 113 26 34 12 11 46
11 14 25

Dated this day,
the twenty first of March,
in the Year of Our Lord, 1605.
E. V."

"James passed me the manuscript, then stared at me for a moment before speaking.

"Well, Sherlock, what do you make of it?"

"I'd say it is a cryptogram of some sort. I have seen something of the kind before. With a little imagination and a large amount of persistence we may well unscramble it."

"I wonder who E.K. was."

"A mathematician perhaps? Who knows? I never theorise without data. It muddies the deductive faculty. Leave this with me, James."

"By now it was well past midnight. James took his leave of me to write several letters that required his attention whilst I filled my pipe with shag and concentrated my energies on the elucidation of the coded message.

"Taking a notebook from my jacket pocket, I sat down to examine the spread of numbers before me on the table. All cryptograms are based upon the principle of repetition of certain key figures.

"There are a set number of approaches involved. Once you have determined which one of these is the correct one the others will follow quickly. In this case, the number of repeated items was statistically high which indicated that the numbers themselves stood for letters. Since there are but 26 letters in the English alphabet, the probability is that they will be repeated often, even within a short sentence. The most commonly repeated of all these are the vowels, since they are fewer, the "e" being the most used.

"Following this hunch, I therefore looked for the most repeated number, which happened to be 15 (it occurred no less than 7 times.) I copied out the table again, substituting "e's for the 5s. Now it is also a fact that the most commonly used consonants in the language are T, H, S and N (although not necessarily in that order).

"I went back to my table and I discovered that the numbers most repeated besides 15 were 12 and 26. Unfortunately the pattern that emerged was not particularly helpful. It was obvious that this was a substitution cipher but with an astrological basis. What was the next thing to do? Why, to determine the positions of the definite articles, of course. It was a fair bet that the following lines contained the words THE or AND:

45 8 15
71 8 4

"Now if both lines did represent THE or AND, then the coding was variable. What did this mean? Surely that each line was governed by a key - the key in this case being the astrological symbol set at the beginning of each word. In that case the letters were variable according to the relative position of the symbol. It was time to look at an astrological chart. I went to the shelves, pulled out one of the large astrological treatises dating from the eighteenth century and examined its pages closely. Listed were twelve star signs in their relative order: ARIES, PISCES, AQUARIUS, CAPRICORN, SAGITTARIUS, SCORPIO, LIBRA, VIRGO, LEO, CANCER, GEMINI, and TAURUS.

"I looked back at the document. Could there be a clue hidden in it somewhere, a pointer, perhaps? It did not take me long to find what I was after. The letter was dated 21 March - the date ascribed to Aries, a clear indication that the numbers were arranged on a rotational basis. One other thing occurred to me: that with all of the numbers, the first digit was never higher than 12 and often as low as 1 - 5.

"It was now becoming clear to me that the first of each of the double numbers indicated the position of the star sign in relation to its group sign. What did the second number represent? Why, that must surely signify a letter within the name of the star sign itself. I therefore started with Aries and wrote out the following:

73 14 49 14 3 55 8
b enea t

"What then was B? H of course. And why 8? Because H is the eighth letter of the alphabet. I knew now the identity of the other single numbers: 6 and 4 were F and D. In no time at all I had decoded the full text, working my way round the astrological table and carefully counting the numbers in their relative positions, revealing the following message:

Beneath the stones, feet tread.

Beneath the finger heaven-pointing

Lies Gabriel's key.

"But now I had deciphered the message, there still remained

the problem of what it all meant.

"James returned the following morning, holding a telegram and looking grey and disconsolate.

"What on earth has happened?" I asked.

"My uncle John was found this morning in the conservatory by Matthews, the manservant. The police were called. At the moment, they are saying he appears to have died from unknown causes."

"You suspect otherwise, James?"

"I have an odd feeling about the whole business."

"Do you wish that I should come down to Chilham and investigate this affair?"

"I should be greatly indebted to you if you would accompany me."

"And thus, it was arranged, Watson. I was pleased to assist young James, for at the University he had been of considerable help to me in the examination of some medieval palimpsests which I had been asked to translate from the French.

"When we arrived at the small Kentish railway station, we found a trap waiting to convey us to the house. In the rear was a short, stocky man who introduced himself as Inspector Green.

"This is my friend, Mr Sherlock Holmes. He is a consultant private investigator," said James.

Green looked at me quizzically.

"That's not a role I'm familiar with."

"That is because I am the only one of a kind. I act in a private capacity for a number of people – and occasionally I also act on behalf of Scotland Yard when they encounter certain difficulties."

"Really, Mr Holmes? I was not aware that you did."

"That is what you may expect of me, Inspector. I do not advertise my services."

"Green examined me obliquely as if he were regarding some

strange bird of prey."

"What can you tell us about the circumstances pertaining to Dr Pritchard's demise?" I asked, as the fly rattled down narrow lanes and over a large bridge.

"The manservant, Matthews, discovered the body at about ten pm yesterday evening."

"Did he in any way attempt to move the body?"

Green shook his head.

"He cycled up to the constable's house in Wyndham Lane and the officer then alerted police headquarters in Strood. I arrived about two hours later – shortly before midnight, in the company of Dr Valeur, the police surgeon."

"And what were Dr Valeur's findings?"

"He could not ascertain the precise cause of death, It will require an autopsy of course. But when I received the telegram from James here asking us to delay matters, I consequently obliged. Of course, I had expected Scotland Yard…"

"Quite so, Inspector," I replied. "Inspector Lestrade sends his apologies, but at present he has a heavy case load. He asked me to make some preliminary observations. May we see the body?'

"As I spoke these words, the fly rattled over a narrow bridge and the tall, foreboding gothic towers of the Pritchard residence loomed into view. Standing before the great, oak studded door was a man in his late fifties, immaculately attired in a morning suit and bearing a black arm band.

"Matthews, this is Mr Sherlock Holmes, an old university pal of mine."

"Casting me an inquisitive look, Matthews took my case and we entered a long, gloomy hallway, lined with oil paintings, depicting classical scenes. At last, we reached the conservatory, a bright, sunny extension at the rear of the property.

"It was evident, even at first glance, that the body of Dr Pritchard was exhibiting the signs of rigour. Yet was I correct in my assumption? A closer examination with my lens contradicted my initial impression as to the cause of death. In the victim's neck was a small but distinct aperture, approximately 0.1inches in diameter. I took a small bag and, smearing the neck with a piece of cotton wool, deposited the sample into a paper bag. All the while I said nothing but was aware of James and the Inspector staring at me as I strode around the room, examining every feature of the contents. The conservatory housed a great number of artefacts, probably gathered from eastern and South American countries. Among the bric a brac of assorted swords, daggers, Buddha figures, Indian tablas and tiny Hindu god and goddess figures, at last I came across what I had been looking for: the murder weapon. I picked up the long bamboo pipe and held it aloft so that my companions could gain a clearer view of it.

"Behold, gentlemen, the weapon that slayed Dr John Pritchard!" I announced.

"What on earth is it?" demanded James.

"A blowpipe. A thing popular among the indigenous tribes of South America for despatching their enemies. A blow from this pipe will send a poisoned dart across a room at a considerable velocity. And I believe the poison is our old friend, curare. This is the first use I have seen of this resin - based poison for quite a considerable while. It is frequently mentioned in the memoirs of explorers, especially regarding the weapons employed by pigmy tribes in and around the Amazon basin."

"But who would have access to the poison or have the knowledge to administer it?" asked James.

"Clearly, someone who was familiar with the layout and contents of the house," I replied. "Apart from Matthews, how many other staff work here?"

"There's the maid, Agatha, the cook, Mrs Enderby, the gardener, Eric – but he only appears on alternate afternoons and Sundays – oh, and a young lad, Robert Saxby, who is – was – my uncle's buttons."

"Any visitors lately, apart from James here?" Inspector Green asked Matthews, who all this while had been standing expressionless, some six feet away from the scene of crime,

"None, sir."

"And you heard nothing in the night? The sound of a carriage coming or departing, for example?"

"Nothing like that sir."

"Which could indicate that the murderer may have made his way over fields from a nearby village or settlement," said James.

"How far is the nearest settlement?" I asked.

"That would be Cobham, some two miles to the south of the manor house," Green informed us.

"I should like to interview the remainder of the staff, James."

"By all means."

"I have already taken statements from them," said the inspector, "but if you think it may be of some use to the investigation, Mr Holmes."

"Indeed I do."

"After dinner, and after I had interviewed the rest of the staff, James left me alone in the house to ponder over an after-dinner pipe. I sat by the great fireplace, dipping into a curious edition of Foxe's *Book of Martyrs* whose explicit illustrations left nothing to the imagination of the reader, but after a while, I tired of its gross sensationalism and turned my attention to the trunk.

"It was a remarkable piece of handiwork. In fact, I had never seen anything quite like it. The tracery was exquisitely fashioned, and, by the style, I guessed that it might be Flemish in origin. The face on the lid I thought particularly absorbing. I had seen something similar on the roof bosses at Rheims Cathedral. Although it might be described as fanciful and grotesque in the extreme, there was something faintly disconcerting about the expression. There was a peculiar knowingness about it. I had the odd feeling through the evening that the eyes were following me as I moved about the room, a fanciful notion which I admit is laughable when thought of in the cold light of day. However, I was at that time alone in the house, apart from the servants, and although there were lamps in the four corners of the room, the wood panelling appeared to absorb much of the light, adding a depth and lustre to the face. I tried sitting in various positions in the room but wherever I moved to, I experienced an uncomfortable feeling, so that eventually I gave up my vigil and the volume that I had borrowed from the library and retired early to bed.

"The following morning when I came down to breakfast, I was about to make my customary greeting when I noticed that James was staring fixedly at a large crystalline egg in front of him. It lay on the oak table shining with a strange inner luminosity. The colours within its oval shape were uncanny. They appeared to evade the direct gaze of the observer, shifting from blue to turquoise and then purple. At first, I thought it was a trick of the light or some piece of nonsense that he had arranged for my benefit, but I soon realized that this was not the case and that the stone retained its own energy source. As I continued to watch, fascinated, the whole object became translucent, all trace of its former crystalline qualities having vanished. It was nothing more than a piece of volcanic rock really, yet somehow it had a presence, almost a personality.

"Remarkable isn't it? " he cried, jumping up and clutching the stone in the palm of his hand. "See how it glitters! I worked out where I might find it, you see. The clues were all in the cryptogram."

"Where did you get this, James?"

"Where I expected to find it of course. In the church. I discovered it in the tomb directly adjacent to the steeple. "

"You desecrated a tomb?"

"I opened the stone lid no more than six inches. It was a matter of a few seconds, nothing more."

"Whose tomb was it?"

"I can't tell. The inscription was badly worn – almost indecipherable. It had the initials 'E.K.' on it. That's about all I could make out. The stone lid shifted easily. There was nothing inside save bones – and, of course, this…isn't it just remarkable?"

"I am very sorry to say this James, for I have greatly valued our friendship in the past. However, I cannot condone what you have done; it is pure sacrilege, whatever your reasons may have been. I have decided that under the circumstances it would better if I left. I shall be catching the train back to London. I shall leave a note for Inspector Green, explaining to him what I have managed to discover about this case. In the interim, please take care."

"Why, what on earth do you mean?'

"I am referring to your father's killer. He is still at large, but I cannot tell you who he is, for as yet, I lack proof. This sorry affair is not yet concluded."

"Believe me, Watson, when I tell you that I shall always regret leaving James to his own devices. He was always something of a precipitate fellow, but I was very angered at what he had done. Of course, both he and I had separately worked out the significance of the obsidian stone he had so eagerly wrenched from the grave of Edward Kelly. You will no doubt recall that Edward Kelly was a scoundrel and self - styled magician who flourished in the 16th century. He obtained a scrying instrument known as an obsidian – a volcanic, prismatic stone from South America – which he convinced the astrologer Dr John Dee, would enable the two men to transmute base metals into gold. The two employed a young boy to sit with them in a séance and they summoned spirits to enable them to do this. The boy became so distraught he suffered an epileptic fit and subsequently died."

"And were they ever found guilty of their crime?"

"They were not. Both men went on to do other things, Dee to serve as astrologer to Queen Elizabeth the First. The fate of Kelly is unknown."

"And what of the murderer of the good doctor?"

"The tale is not quite done, Watson. On the morning following my return to London, I received an unwelcome telegram from Inspector Green, I have it here."

Holmes passed me the note. It read:

PLEASE COME AT ONCE. JAMES PRYOR FOUND DEAD
AT MANOR. YOUR ASSISTANCE APPRECIATED.

"You responded?"

"Naturally. But this time I was able to apprehend the murderer. Just before I left the manor house, you see, I carried out a detailed search of the rooms of both the manservant and the maid. On the sleeve of the manservant's shirt I discovered minute traces of curare which proved that he must have handled the substance prior to his master's death. When questioned by me and the police he revealed that he had dispatched James in a very similar manner when he had been discovered trying to secrete the obsidian stone in his pocket."

"What had he intended to do with the stone?'

"He had been under instruction by one of the family solicitors – a man called Moran, a creature, it transpired, of the vilest antecedents and background – to discover the whereabouts of the stone and procure it for a not inconsiderable sum. I discovered subsequently that this man Moran was none other than our Colonel Sebastian Moran, the old shikaree. He had been working under instruction from one Professor James Moriarty."

"And what was the upshot of all this?"

"The manservant was sentenced to hang, following his appearance at the assizes. Regrettably, Moran disappeared without trace and subsequently spent some years travelling through India. Poor James lies alongside his uncle in the church at Chilham where there is a small memorial which I paid to have mounted there. *'Those who dwell in darkness shall carry a shadow unto their grave.'* Hafiz, if I am not mistaken."

And thus saying, he rolled up the vellum scroll, then put it back carefully in the box. He reached for his burnished cherrywood, plugged the bowl with plugs and dottles, then lit it. For some long while I observed his lean, aquiline face and keen blue eyes, as the grey streams of tobacco encircled his head, until, eventually, he slumped slowly forwards in the basket chair and his eyelids closed in response to an all -consuming reverie.

THE ADVENTURE OF THE GRACE CHALICE

By Roger Johnson

"If you give up smoking, drinking and loving, you don't live any longer. It just seems like longer."

~Old music hall joke.

"Watson," said Mr Sherlock Holmes from the bow-window, where he had been standing for the past half-hour, gazing moodily down into the street, "if I mistake not, we have a client."

I was more than pleased to hear the excitement in his voice. Holmes had been restlessly unemployed for nearly a week, and neither his temper nor mine had been helped by the dull, leaden skies of March with their intermittent showers, which caused my old wound to ache abominably.

"A prosperous man," he continued. "Plump, well-dressed, purposeful and not without self-esteem. Ah, he has paid off the cab and is approaching our door. Let us hope that he brings something of interest." He turned away from the window, and at that moment we heard a determined ring upon the front-door bell. Within a minute our good landlady had shown into the room a plump man with heavy jowls and thick grey hair.

"Gentlemen," said our visitor, as the door closed softly behind Mrs Hudson, "my name is Henry Staunton."

"Indeed?" replied Holmes, calmly. "Pray take the basket-chair, Mr Staunton. Your name is, of course, familiar to me as that of a connoisseur of *objects d'art*."

"It is true, sir," said our visitor. "I am a man of somewhat retiring, and I might even say refined, tastes. I like to surround myself with elegance and beauty. I do not live extravagantly but I may perhaps call myself a patron of the arts. It is my weakness."

86

"But why have you come to Baker Street, Mr Staunton? Has some item from your collection been stolen?"

"It has, sir. It has! I shall come straight to the point, for I dislike circumlocution, as, I am sure, do you. Besides, I wish to have the matter settled without even the least delay. You must know, then, that I recently acquired from old Sir Cedric Grace the celebrated golden cup known as the Grace Chalice. I may say that it cost me a very considerable sum — a pretty penny, sir! But I do not grudge it, for the chalice is unique, quite unique. It was made for the monks of Melcarth Abbey sometime in the fifteenth century. The records say that it is made of Welsh gold, elaborately chased with biblical symbols. When the monastery was dissolved, the chalice was not among the valuables appropriated by the Crown, though Thomas Cromwell's commissioners made a thorough search. It came to light more than a century later, after the Civil War, when the Grace family acquired the property.

"Now, before depositing it with my bankers, I determined to retain the chalice at my house for a short while, so that I might study it thoroughly. Ah! I had, of course, taken out an insurance policy upon it. My house is called Holly Trees. It is not large, but it suits my needs, and the situation close to Highgate Ponds is very charming. I am a bachelor, you see, and I live a simple life. Ahem! I kept the chalice in a safe in my study, securely built into the wall, and hidden behind a looking glass. You may imagine my distress — my utter distress, sir — when, this very morning, I discovered the safe unlocked and the chalice gone!"

"You would be well advised," said I, "to give the police a description of the chalice, Mr Staunton."

Our visitor stared at me with an expression of mild reproof, and said, "I should rather not have to deal with the police, Dr Watson. I value my privacy, and I do not relish the thought of large clumsy boots tramping through my house and garden. No, I prefer to call upon the skill and discretion of Mr Sherlock Holmes." He made a little flourish with his hand, and I remembered my friend's assessment of him as a man not lacking in self-importance.

Holmes himself sat quietly, his eyes closed, and his long legs stretched out before him. "That is very good of you, Mr Staunton," said he. "You will appreciate, however, that I must have all the details, however trivial they may seem."

"Of course, sir, of course. Well, my housekeeper, Mrs Elliott, called me at seven o'clock this morning, rather earlier than usual, and she was in a most agitated state. Rather than trust to her somewhat incoherent account, I went myself directly to my study, where I found that the safe door stood open and that the study window was broken. Here, plainly, the miscreant had gained entrance. I observed also a double line of footsteps running across the bare, damp earth from the high garden wall, and returning thither."

"This case presents some curious features," remarked Sherlock Holmes, glancing intently at our client. "Are we to understand that your study overlooks bare ground?"

Staunton permitted himself a pained chuckle. "It does seem odd, sir, put like that. However, the matter is simply explained: the ground has been prepared for a new lawn, but my gardener has strained his back, and the turves have not yet been laid. A fortunate thing, as I am sure you will agree, sir! Most fortunate, for now we have the clearest clues as to the thief's means of entrance and egress. Naturally, I have left strict instructions that the footprints are to be left untouched."

"Naturally," agreed Sherlock Holmes. "Very well, Mr Staunton, I think that we had better come at once and investigate the scene of the crime. I shall just gather a few essential items of equipment. Watson, will you call a cab?"

On the short journey to Hampstead, we learned that the immediate household consisted of Mrs Elliott and a maidservant, Sarah Gilbert, who both slept at the rear of the house, as did our client. ("Mrs Elliott's two rooms occupy the second floor back. She can almost see Hampstead Heath from her sitting-room window, I believe.") The only other employee was a gardener, who rented a cottage in Bacon's Lane.

Mr Staunton kept no dog, for he disliked the creatures, and his only recreation was to play cards twice a week — for money, he admitted with candour — with a cousin, who lived at Mill Hill. "But you may dismiss any suspicion of Walter," said he, "for he would have no cause to steal from me. I should tell you that as a result of our card-playing I am in his debt for a tidy sum."

Told that the study was on the ground floor front of the house, I wondered whether a passer-by would be able to see the study window from the street but was told that was out of the question: "Oh, dear me, no! No indeed. The entire property is surrounded by a high brick wall. There is a gate, of course, but that is as high as the wall, and made of solid oak planks. As I told you, sir, I value my privacy."

"No doubt;" Holmes interjected, "there is a gate at the back of the property?"

"There is, Mr Holmes," said our client, "but it is kept locked. The only person who ever uses it is the gardener, Albert Lowry, who comes and goes that way."

At Holly Trees, we found that the wall and the gate were indeed formidable, and the ground bare right up to the front of the house, save for the stacks of turf. It was plain that, if an intruder were sufficiently quiet, neither the servants nor their master, who admitted to being a heavy sleeper, might very well have been unaware.

Holmes made a minute examination of the very clear footsteps that ran, just as we had been told, directly from the garden wall to the study window and back. The damp earth had preserved the impressions wonderfully, and since no one had had occasion to trespass upon this smooth, bare patch there were no other prints to be seen.

"Our burglar could hardly have left plainer traces if he had intended to," said my friend. "How very fortunate! Well, before the weather does take a turn for the worse, we should preserve these prints." The equipment he had brought included plaster of Paris, which he mixed with water that I fetched, directed by our client, from the scullery, the thick white liquid then being poured into both a left and a right footprint.

While the plaster set, Holmes examined the full length of the intruder's trail, both coming and going. Upon his return, as he and I carefully lifted the casts from the earth, he remarked to me, "There are two very singular features here. For instance, it would appear that our man let himself down from the wall with commendable delicacy, for there is no indication that he jumped, and we look in vain for the marks of a ladder. Hum — size eleven boots, new or recently soled. A long stride. Just so!" Turning to our client, he said, "Mr Staunton, I think we have seen all that we need to see here. Now, let us look at the place of forced entry."

It was evident that the burglar knew what he was about. The study window had been broken in a most efficient manner, the pane smeared with treacle and covered with a sheet of strong brown paper. There would have been very little noise, and the broken glass could just be pulled away to leave an opening. The thief had removed just the one pane and reached through to undo the latch. On the sill was the print of his left boot, muddy and indistinct, as one might expect, and that was all. It was time to turn our attention to the interior.

The furniture of the study, itself of much interest, held an eclectic accumulation of antiques, witness to Henry Staunton's abiding pursuit. In fact, he could not resist drawing our attention to some of his treasures: "That landscape is by Madame Vigée-Lebrun, and the portrait is the work of Godfrey Schalcken. Both are genuine. I have my doubts about the Fragonard on the far wall, but you will admit that it is very charming..."

Our immediate attention, however, was fixed upon the thick carpet, where muddy patches led from the window to the opposite wall, where the door of the safe stood open, just as our client had described it. There was little to be learned from the safe, even by such an expert as Sherlock Holmes. We could descry faint smears that might have been made by gloved fingers, and the lock was quite undamaged, indicating that it had been opened with a key.

"Let us be clear, Mr Staunton," said my friend. "Nothing was taken except the chalice?"

"Nothing except the chalice, sir. I begin to suspect that I have harboured a spy in my house, but I cannot think how that could be. The servants are certainly innocent. Both the maid and the gardener have been in my employ for at least fifteen years, and the invaluable Mrs Elliott has worked for my family since I was a young man. I trust them all, sir, trust them implicitly. Besides, I am quite sure that none of them knew of my purchase. Even the housekeeper never enters this room without my express permission."

In answer to my own question, we learned that there were two keys to the safe, the one carried at all times on our client's watch-chain and the other deposited with his bankers, Holder and Stephenson.

"Very good," said Holmes. "Now, you have cleared your servants of suspicion. Have you recently entertained any visitors?"

Staunton appeared a little flustered by the question. Eventually, with some reluctance, he confessed that, yes, there had been a visitor, who had spent two evenings at Holly Trees within the past ten days. "But you need not suspect him, Mr Holmes. The idea is quite absurd! I have told you that I am not a sociable man, but once a week I play Ecarté or Piquet with my cousin Walter Ruskin. Sometimes we meet here and sometimes at Walter's house at Mill Hill. He is a bachelor, like me, with no other close family."

The name was not unfamiliar to me. Was he, I enquired, Ruskin the gunsmith, whose premises in Jermyn Street were patronised by the nobility? "That is correct, Doctor," was the reply, "though Walter retired six months ago. He is a good fellow. We have been friends since boyhood."

To Holmes's further questions, Mr Staunton admitted that he had not only told his cousin about the Grace Chalice, but had shown it to him, and allowed him, briefly, to examine it. "Walter congratulated me," said he, "and told me that I should deposit it in a bank vault as soon as possible. I wish now that I had taken his advice!"

Holmes absorbed this information. "Your spare safe key is secure," he remarked, "but your cousin might perhaps have had the opportunity to take an impression of the key on your watch-chain. Such things can be done quickly and discreetly."

Plainly the thought distressed our client, for he seemed truly fond of his cousin. "It is no doubt possible, Mr Holmes," said he, "but I cannot believe that Walter would stoop to such a thing! Besides, he would have no cause to steal from me. As I have told you, he is my creditor, not my debtor, thanks to our weekly gaming."

"Nevertheless," said I, "we must examine every possibility. Can you give us a description of your cousin?"

"If I must, Doctor! Walter is quite as tall as Mr Holmes here, but more heavily built. He is fifty-nine years of age, with thick dark hair and a heavy moustache. His eyes are light brown — hazel, I think, is the word."

"What about his boots?" Holmes asked. "Do you know what size he takes?"

"Really, Mr Holmes! I — I am not sure... Walter is much taller than I, and his feet are larger than mine. Larger than yours too, I should say. Size ten, perhaps, or even size eleven."

"I see," said my friend. "Well, Mr Staunton, I think we have done all that we can do here — for the time being, at least. My next move must be to call upon Mr Walter Ruskin, if you will kindly give me his address. I have a curious feeling that this is one of those straightforward cases that turn out not to be quite so straightforward after all."

Shortly afterwards, Holmes and I left Holly Trees, with assurances that we should certainly pursue the case. My friend was manifestly unsatisfied with his investigation so far, and I in my turn recalled an earlier remark of his that had puzzled me.

"You suggested," said I, "that there was yet another odd feature about the footsteps in the garden. What was it?"

He looked at me in his singular, introspective fashion. "You did not notice it? Why, it was simply that at no point did the steps returning from the house overlap those made in going to the house."

While I pondered upon this, he continued, "Now, old fellow, I shall endeavour to make my way to Mill Hill. I think perhaps you should return to Baker Street. You would probably do well to have some lunch on the way. I know how grumpy you can get if you miss your lunch."

"Whereas," said I, "a problem like this is meat and drink to you. Very well, Holmes."

I returned to Baker Street to find our old friend Mr Lestrade of Scotland Yard waiting in our sitting room, positively bursting with news. "It's the Northcote case, Doctor," he explained. "You'll remember Esmond Northcote, of course?"

Indeed I did. Northcote was a smooth, elegant and dangerous man who preyed upon the weak. He was a proven card-sharp, a known blackmailer and a suspected murderer. The police had been unable to prove the murder, but Northcote was convicted of blackmail and sentenced to five years hard labour at Maidstone Prison.

"Five years?" I said. "Then he must have served his time by now. You surely haven't come just to tell us that Northcote has been released?"

"No, indeed. That's not the whole story, Dr Watson, but I think I shall save the important part until Mr Holmes returns. You don't mind if I wait here, I hope — and perhaps you wouldn't mind telling me something about the case that Mr Holmes is investigating..."

We sat companionably, chatting and smoking, until Sherlock Holmes entered the room, grim-faced, with the news that Walter Ruskin had not been seen for nearly two days. The only positive information to emerge was that Ruskin did take size eleven in boots. "Our client wished to keep this matter confidential," Holmes remarked, "but it seems that we shall have to call in the police after all." Seeming to notice our visitor for the first time, he said, "Now, Lestrade, what brings you here?"

"It's the Northcote case, Holmes," said I.

"Northcote? He was released three days ago from Maidstone Prison. What about him?"

"He disappeared from view almost immediately, Mr Holmes," said Lestrade, "but we think we've found him again. I put it like that because the man we have is dead and rather horribly mutilated."

My friend's frown gave way to an expression of intense interest. "Pray continue," said he.

The little detective was silent for a moment, then: "It's not a nice thing, sir. The man's face has been quite burned off with acid. He was killed by a savage blow to the head, and then ... Well, there's not enough of his face left to identify him, but all the rest fits. He's a big man, muscles well developed from rowing, a good head of hair. We found him this morning in Abney Park Cemetery, of all places, behind one of the tombs. I don't suppose many decent people will mourn him, but we are still bound to search for his killer. Anyway, Mr Holmes, as you took such an interest in Esmond Northcote's arrest and trial, I thought you might wish to come and see the body."

Holmes shrugged his thin shoulders and said, "Why not? There are no threads in my current investigation, or none that I can follow today. By all means let us visit the mortuary."

Lestrade gave a sigh of relief and said: "Thank you, sir. And if you would come along as well, Dr Watson, your medical knowledge might prove useful. There'll be a post - mortem, of course, but not until this evening."

If I were a squeamish man I should not have taken up medicine as a profession. I had seen many unpleasant sights during my time as an Army Surgeon, but nothing as appalling that which lay on a stone slab in the mortuary at Stoke Newington.

Even Lestrade, inured as he was, was moved to murmur, "Man's inhumanity to man! I'm no philosopher, but something like this, well, it almost makes me despair for the future of the country."

Sherlock Holmes turned to him and said sharply, "That will do, Lestrade! We must look upon the dead clay before us, not as the mutilated shell of a fellow man but merely as an object of professional study."

Abashed, Lestrade nodded and cleared his throat. "There's no doubt in my mind," he said, "that death was caused by a blow or series of blows to the back of the head."

I carefully raised the dead head and scrutinised the great bruises at the base of the skull. "Two blows at least," I observed, "with a heavy and very hard object. You can feel where the occipital and parietal bones have been shattered."

"It is a brutal business," said Holmes, "but it would not be reason enough in itself to bring us all the way from Baker Street. The complete obliteration of the facial features is decidedly unusual, however. All that can be said in mitigation is that the destruction of the victim's face was carried out after death. How long has he been dead, Doctor?"

There could be no certain answer to that question. Rigor mortis had passed, leaving the flesh elastic, but I could only say that in my opinion death had occurred between twelve and twenty-four hours earlier.

Asked about the man's clothes, Lestrade replied, "They're at the police station, Mr Holmes. You can examine them if you like, but I don't think they'll tell you much. The body was dressed only in good quality woollen long johns. No hat, no boots, no outer clothing at all, and no jewellery either."

Holmes turned his attention to the dead man's muscular arms. "Whoever killed this man was determined to eradicate his identity entirely," said he. "Esmond Northcote has disappeared from view, so you think that this is he. There is a superficial resemblance, but I think I can prove to you that you are mistaken. You see that the forearm muscles are well developed, just as the Inspector said?"

In some puzzlement, we agreed.

"Observe," said Holmes. "I take the hands in my own and close the fists... Now feel those muscles!"

The result was remarkable. Even without touching it I could see that the muscle of the right forearm indicated considerable strength, consistent with what we knew of Esmond Northcote, but that of the left astounded me. It stood out like an egg and was by far the most highly developed I had ever seen.

"Well, that rules out Northcote!" exclaimed Lestrade. "He's right-handed, and besides, his only sport was rowing, and that would tend to develop both arms equally. This man must have been left-handed, and remarkably strong."

Holmes shook his head. "No, if he had been left-handed then we should be marvelling at the muscular development of his right forearm. I know of only one activity that can cause the muscle to swell like that. It happens through years of taking the recoil of a rifle." He turned to me. "Look at the man, Doctor! Look at his tall stature, his thick dark hair, his large feet. Imagine the moustache and the light brown eyes, and now tell me who he is."

"There is only one man," I replied: "the retired gunsmith."

"Walter Ruskin," said Lestrade. "Another fugitive! But who would want to kill him, Mr Holmes? And who, in heaven's name, would want to do *that* to his body?"

"Who indeed? I must ask you to restrain your natural impatience, Lestrade. There are some further enquiries to be made, but I shall not be able to get the answers until tomorrow morning. Meanwhile, can you arrange for a constable to keep watch overnight on Mr Henry Staunton's house?"

The request was unexpected, but the Inspector rallied. "You think he's in danger, then? From the person who murdered his cousin? Very well, Mr Holmes. We'll go straight to Highgate Police Station, and I'll make sure that it's done."

"Excellent! Afterwards we shall return to Baker Street. I am sure you will not refuse another cigar, and perhaps a glass of brandy to help keep out the cold. And as we go, I shall attempt to fill in some of the details."

At three o'clock the following day, Holmes and I met Lestrade and a uniformed constable outside the locked gate of Holly Trees. Holmes nodded in response to the Inspector's greeting, and said, "Just the one constable, Lestrade?"

"There are two, Mr Holmes," was the reply. "Constable Mayne here has come with me from the station, and Constable Rowan has been inside guarding the house since the small hours. Rowan is expecting us, of course, and I hear him coming now, to unlock the gate." In a lower tone, Lestrade added, "It's like a fortress, this place!"

The approaching footsteps had stopped, and we heard the sound of the big key turning in the lock, and the slight scrape of the bolts as they were drawn back; then the gate swung quietly open. As soon as the four of us were inside, Constable Rowan secured the gate again, and we all proceeded towards the house.

At the front door, Sherlock Holmes instructed the police officers to stand back a little. With a quick glance at Lestrade and me, he gave the bell-pull a sharp tug, and we heard the resultant clang from inside the house. The door was opened, after a brief pause, by a young maidservant, but before she could ask our business, her master appeared, his face a picture of indignation, and told her that she might go.

To my friend's greeting, he snapped, "Good afternoon, fiddlesticks! I have a bone to pick with you, Mr Sherlock Holmes. I specifically told you that I did not wish to call in the police, yet almost immediately you send a uniformed clodhopper to my house. And, bless my soul, here are yet more policemen! What is the meaning of this, sir?"

Holmes remained tranquil in the face of this onslaught. "Yesterday, Mr Staunton," said he, "you commissioned me to investigate the theft of a rare and valuable mediaeval chalice. Dr Watson advised you, if you recall, at least to report your loss to the police."

"Well, sir?"

At this point I took it upon myself to suggest that we should pursue the conversation indoors, as we had some rather shocking information to convey. With a notable lack of enthusiasm, our client agreed, and Holmes, Lestrade and I followed him to the study, where he demanded to know what information could be so shocking that it required the presence of a police officer.

"You told us yesterday," said my friend, "that the only person, apart from yourself and your insurance broker, who knew that you had the Grace Chalice in this house, was your cousin, Walter Ruskin. You also told us that he was above suspicion."

Curiously, Henry Staunton's mood appeared to lighten a little. "I did, sir, I did," said he. "But the matter has been much on my mind since we spoke, and I confess that I am less certain now of my cousin's innocence. I told him about the chalice just the day after I bought it. That was nine — no, ten — days ago. We next met just six days later. That was our last evening together, and there was at least one occasion during the course of that evening when he had the opportunity to take an impression of my key. Dear me, what a wicked world it is, to be sure."

"It is, indeed," replied Holmes. "When I went over to Mill Hill, your cousin's man, Perkins, informed me that he had left his house at seven-thirty the previous evening and had not returned. As he was punctilious in his habits, the servants were becoming decidedly uneasy. Perkins suggested that I make enquiries here, Mr Staunton, or at your cousin's club. Of course, I assured him that his master was not here, and you will not be surprised to learn that he had not been seen at his club for two days. In short, it seemed that Walter Ruskin had disappeared."

Our client frowned and said, "Dear me! Well, that seems to settle the matter. Walter Ruskin, a thief! Stealing from his own cousin. Who would have thought it?"

"But you can see now that the case has become a matter for the police, Mr Staunton," I observed.

"And it is no longer a matter of burglary alone," said Holmes. "Late yesterday afternoon, Inspector Lestrade here asked us to go over to Stoke Newington to examine a body that had been discovered there. The man had been battered to death. Then his body was stripped, and the facial features disfigured beyond recognition. Nevertheless, I was able to identify the deceased as your cousin, Walter Ruskin."

That information did indeed prove shocking to Mr Henry Staunton, who was briefly lost for words. At length he stammered, "Oh! Er — oh, dear! Is — is it possible that my suspicions were mistaken?" He paused for a moment in apparently desperate thought before exclaiming, "Can there be a madman at large? Is the same person responsible for both crimes, do you suppose?"

Holmes agreed that such was indeed the case, prompting another outburst: "Then I must have police protection! Inspector, I must insist upon police protection!"

"It won't do, you know," said Holmes, calmly. "Really, it won't. We have the cabman who brought you back from Abney Park. He distinctly remembers the large leather bag that you carried. I have no doubt that it contained your cousin's clothes — and, most importantly, his boots. You had a use for those boots, I think."

"Lies! All lies!"

My friend continued as if there had been no interruption: "Your cousin had agreed to meet you by one of the tombs in the cemetery. I don't know what reason you devised for the meeting, but it was really very careless of you to leave his body so close to that particular monument. It marks the resting place of Walter Ruskin's maternal grandfather, Marcus Staunton — whose second son was, of course, your own father."

Staunton grew increasingly desperate. "Lies!" he cried again, but Holmes spoke on, relentlessly.

"I made other enquiries this morning. The results were very enlightening. It seems that in recent years you have been gambling heavily upon the stock exchange and losing heavily too. You have taken out a substantial mortgage upon this house, a mortgage which is in peril of foreclosure. The considerable debt that you owed to your more wealthy cousin must have been the final provocation, even though it is unenforceable in law.

"You resented your cousin's wealth, and I think you resented the fact that he had bequeathed it to the Royal Humane Society and not to you. The opportunity to buy the Grace Chalice suggested further opportunities to you. You made certain that your cousin, and only he, knew of your purchase, so that when the chalice was removed suspicion would inevitably fall upon him. At the same time, of course, you ensured that the money you owed him need never be paid."

Lestrade murmured, "Ingenious, really."

"Too clever by half," I replied.

Whether the others heard us, I do not know, but Holmes persisted as if we had not spoken.

"You yourself removed the precious object from the safe. I have no doubt that it is carefully hidden somewhere in the house. Your object, plainly, was to claim on the insurance while retaining possession of the chalice. You may even have intended to sell it. Such illicit transactions are not, alas, uncommon. Then, wearing your cousin's boots, which are at least three sizes larger than your own, you planted those incriminating footprints in the garden, taking long strides to give the impression of a taller man. It was unfortunate for you that the boots were new and could not be easily identified as his, but that could not be helped."

The notion of a thief climbing over that high wall was not, I thought, wholly satisfactory. But I could not think how the footprints had been managed. They led from the garden wall to the study window and back.

Holmes took pity on me. "You are looking at things back to front, Watson," said he. "Do you remember the second curious quality of those prints? The two lines of prints are close but quite separate. What burglar would ever tread so artistically?"

And then, of course, I saw. We had been told that an intruder had walked from the wall to the study window and back. Consequently, the footprints appeared to us to confirm our client's story, whereas —

"In fact," said Holmes, "the person who left those prints had walked from the study to the garden wall and back, taking great care on his return not to tread on any of the impressions made on his outward journey. Had he not stepped so carefully the fact of an inside job would have been plain to the meanest intelligence. In all probability, then, our client himself was responsible for this charade."

Staunton's protests were of no avail, though both Holmes and I had to hold him down while Lestrade slipped the handcuffs over his wrists. Then the two constables were summoned, Rowan to convey the prisoner to the police station, and Mayne to search for the precious chalice, which Holmes was certain must be hidden within the house.

"I confess," said I, when we had left the house for the colder but fresher atmosphere of the garden, "that I have rarely felt so relieved at seeing a criminal taken into custody."

Sherlock Holmes took his pipe from a pocket of his overcoat, and carefully filled it with tobacco from the pouch that he had stowed in another pocket. When he had the pipe drawing to his satisfaction, he observed, "Envy and resentment have gnawed away at his soul, I fear. He hated his cousin as only a mean man can hate a generous and contented one."

After a moment's cogitation, Lestrade remarked, "Our case will be complete if we can only find the boots, you know, but there's little chance of that, now, is there?"

Holmes smiled. "I am not so sure," said he. "For all his elaborate planning, Staunton has been singularly careless. It would not surprise me if Mayne uncovers the boots as well as the chalice."

In this, as in so much else, Holmes was correct. The precious cup had been concealed under a flagstone in the wine cellar. Walter Ruskin's boots were found among Staunton's own footwear, and they proved to match exactly the casts that Holmes had made from those clear, sharp prints in the garden of Holly Trees. A few days later came word that the Edinburgh police had apprehended Esmond Northcote and charged him with common assault. He was able to prove an alibi, and left the court a free man. No such conclusion was possible for Henry Staunton. He was hanged at Pentonville Prison, and it seems that the loyal Mrs Elliott was his only mourner.

THE ADVENTURE OF THE CUNNING MAN

By Kelvin I. Jones

"Three things are men most likely to be cheated in – a horse, a wife and a cigar."

~ Old saying.

As Sherlock Holmes dipped his cutthroat razor into the water and lathered his cheeks, a feeling of immense weariness began to overwhelm him. And then he thought of Charles Whitaker.

It had come as something of a relief when the invitation had arrived from his old friend Charles to stay with him for a short while. "It will be a respite for you, Holmes, a chance to recharge your batteries and taste rural life again."

Mrs Hudson had entered, wheeling before her a small breakfast trolley, bedecked with silver dishes. A rich aroma of fried bacon tantalised his nostrils. She smiled warmly at him, then glanced at the open Moroccan case with its hypodermic.

"Sleep well, sir?"

"Most comfortably, thank you, Mrs Hudson," he replied. Martha had aged considerably over the years but was still as sprightly as ever.

"I hope bacon and eggs are to your liking."

Not wishing to break with tradition, he smiled back at her.

"I'm sure they will do very well, Mrs Hudson."

He had recognised the expensive cream envelope that Martha had brought him on a silver dish at once, for it bore the familiar ornate watermark of his old friend Charles Whitaker. He lit his oily old brier before opening it. Soon the room was wreathed in

103

blue smoke.

"Dear Sherlock," it ran, "I was so deeply sorry to hear of dear Watson's sad passing. Bill Hunter tells me you are still in the smoke. Why do you not quit the city for heaven's sake? For my sins, alas, I am still here in Cambridge, at your old alma mater, earning my usual pittance as a lowly professor of medieval studies - though nowadays, in a strictly part time capacity. However, to come to the point: now I'm in recess, I thought you might care to take the great trek east to see me at my Norfolk residence. That is, if you have no real objection to my tiresome company. Are you aware of the importance of the Thorsford Hill Figure, by any chance? It is one of those curious enigmas which I rather fancy turning my hand to solving. You are probably aware of its reputed links with Boadicea and the Iceni. Perhaps you will let me know and wire me if you could bear the company of an old curmudgeon.

Yours ever, Charles Whitaker."

Holmes finished his breakfast, refolded the letter, then smiled. Charles Whitaker, old undergraduate ally, antiquarian, Cambridge don, clergyman and author of "British Hill Figures." The last time he had seen Charles was over a year ago at Irene Adler's funeral. His great domed head, piercing blue eyes and Semitic features often distinguished him from his contemporaries as did the striking originality of his work. A pioneer in Anglo Saxon and early medieval studies, his work included such titles as "The Maes Howe Inscriptions", "Early Christian Crosses" and "The Mythological Origins of The Weland Legend." However, his most important work of recent years, "British Hill Figures," was now regarded as the standard reference work on incised hill figures in Britain.

Holmes pushed aside his plate and reached for his old pipe again. Plugging the bowl with a fresh, aromatic supply of shag, he passed a lighted match across the rim and sat back, clouds of dense, acrid tobacco smoke spiralling above his head. The Thorsford hill figure. Where had he heard mention of that before? A feeling of annoyance welled up in him. His books were packed in a large chest in his bedroom. It would take a considerable while before he would be able to track down the reference to it. And as for the Iceni... The Boadicean revolt was a centrepiece of every child's history lessons, yet so far she had not been satisfactorily linked with any site in Norfolk. There was the iron age fort at Warham, near Wells, of course, and the post Boadicean town at Caistor built by the Romans to dominate the former Iceni tribal territory. Yet, to his knowledge, Norfolk boasted not a single Iron Age hill figure. He would send a wire to Charles and accept his invitation. His ebullient and dynamic personality would assist him in pulling himself out of the slough of despond which had for so long enveloped his spirit.

He strode into the hall, leaving behind him a trail of tobacco smoke.

"Mrs Hudson, I shall be going away for a few days. Have you seen my Bradshaw?"

Heaving his large, battered suitcase into an empty compartment, Holmes collapsed on to the faded velour seat and consoled himself by mopping his brow with a huge, spotted blue and red handkerchief. The train lurched him forwards, his knee banging against the seat opposite, his suitcase sliding to the floor. Through the open window the stale, soot - smelling effluence of the locomotive wafted in, making him cough. He stood up and shut the window, then spread eagled himself on the seat. Reaching for his old clay pipe, he primed it with a plug of dark tobacco and within a minute had filled the small compartment with the equivalent of the Great London Fog.

Since Watson's death, Holmes had lost touch. Occasionally in the newspapers, he would hear of Whitaker's exploits. There had been the case of the fraudulent medium, Madame Sophia, who had grown wealthy at the expense of numerous nouveaux riche families in Norwich; the episode of the Dunwich poltergeist, which was only resolved by the internment of certain bones which had fallen from the cliff, and, not least the terrifying case of the Cromer Black Shuck which had dominated the headlines in the Anglian Post for a week in the long, hot summer of 1919. Of course, Whitaker's expertise was not limited to the realm of the invisible. Although few of the lay public knew it, he was also an expert in the realm of osteo-archaeology and had contributed widely to the literature of the subject in various academic journals. Before the war, he had been consulted by Scotland Yard in at least three cases involving the exhumation of corpses from London cemeteries and on one occasion was called upon to give evidence in court regarding the demise of Lady Eveline Gambon. In those days, of course, he had been unknown to the general public and this facet of the case had passed unnoticed. However, it had been Holmes who had recommended him to the police.

Suddenly, the compartment door was rolled open to reveal a tall, elegant woman wearing a broad- brimmed, purple hat. For a moment she put down her suitcase, then, overcome by the overpowering smell of the pungent tobacco smoke, decided to cut her losses and retreated, coughing, pulling the door shut, her face crumpled in disdain.

Holmes breathed a sigh of relief and peered out of the soot-lined window. Already the dingy grey suburbs had begun to bleed away. A diluted sun hung overhead, dappling the brown fields and scattered woodlands. At the far edge of the horizon, a flock of birds wheeled and turned in a frenzy of movement. He reached into his waistcoat pocket for his monocle, adjusted it on the end of his nose, then opened the scuffed volume with its tattered brown covers.

"In the Roman and Gallic contexts," he read, " the horse features prominently in terms of iconography. The most important of all the horse deities in ancient Gaul was the great goddess Epona, otherwise known as "The Divine Horse". Her cult was widespread in the Celtic period, but it spread widely during the Roman occupation of Britain. She was also the principal goddess of the tribe of the Iceni. In her iconographic manifestations she is most commonly seen with a dog or bird on her knee and is seated side-saddle.

"One of her most important manifestations is that of the Celtic hill figure, which is inscribed into the hill at Uffington in Berkshire. This most probably dates from the first century BC, but some commentators believe it may be considerably earlier. The notion that this is an Epona ritual site is endorsed by a

parallel site at the Irish hill named after the goddess Macha, a goddess connected to the worship of horses. Both the Irish Macha and the Welsh goddess Rhiannon were connected with horses and both owned magical singing birds who woke the dead "and lulled the living to sleep." The horse appears to have symbolised both sexual vigour and fecundity. This is vividly demonstrated in a 12th century text by Geraldus Cambrensis ('Description of Ireland') where he describes the inauguration of an Ulster king. A white mare was brought forward and the king elect would then drop to his hands and knees, declaring himself to be a beast. The mare was then killed after his union with it. He then sat in the pot where the animal was placed and bathed in the broth and ate its flesh. Thus, he became king."

Holmes paused for a moment, balancing the open book on his knees. If the hill figure at Thorsford was indeed that of a horse, it might prove to be a direct link with the power and authority of Boadicea. He had often wondered how this diminutive figure had been able to muster such widespread support in the east and march on the capital with such devastating results. It had taken the combined forces of several legions to force her into submission. Could it be that this warrior queen was venerated as a direct representative of the Goddess Epona ?

He lay back against the compartment seat, again allowing himself to slip into a smoke induced reverie. The sunlight played on his face. An image of a beak-headed horse floated before his eyes, a face which seemed both animate and ancient. A shrill whistle pierced the rattling rhythm of the swaying locomotive as the train plunged into a tunnel, and he was marooned in sudden darkness.

In his first - class compartment, Holmes stirred, only to find that he had slept on his arm for at least forty minutes, inducing a severe jabbing pain in his left elbow. He sat up, emitting a cry of pain. The train had stopped. He pulled back the compartment door and stared out. Norwich Station. Half a carriage down he caught a glimpse of a solitary news vendor, standing on the platform. He pulled down the window and summoned him. It was the Norwich Post, bearing the bold headline: SENSATIONAL MURDER OF NORFOLK WIZARD. He returned to his compartment to find that all trace of his fellow female occupant had disappeared, leaving a faint trace of perfume behind her.

He settled down in the middle seat, his pipe alight, scouring the lead story.

"The funeral of a well- known Norfolk cunning man who was discovered dead in strange circumstances last Tuesday, took place today at Thorsford. William MacBride, a former groom at Munnington Hall, and erstwhile labourer, was found dead in his cottage four days ago, but as yet, no clue has been offered as to the cause of his death. The ancient thatched cottage which lies on the outskirts of Thorsford village had been the home of the deceased for over twenty years.

"MacBride was well known in North Norfolk for his powers as a wart charmer and wizard and was frequently visited by folk from Norwich for the purpose of having their charms renewed. He had also gained an impressive reputation for the procuring of stolen goods and was thought to have made considerable sums of money from his dubious craft.

"MacBride earned some notoriety a year ago when he was indicted under the Vagrancy Act for fortune telling and was sentenced to a month's imprisonment in Norwich jail. As we reported in yesterday's edition of the Post, according to the police, MacBride had been battered to death, his skull having been shattered by some blunt object. However, no murder weapon has been discovered. Almost every piece of furniture and personal effects in the downstairs room had been smashed and one of the downstairs windows had also been broken.

"The most singular fact was that before him on the table, completely untouched and unbroken, were four items: a bottle of whisky, a loaf of bread, a jar of berries and a copy of the Holy Book. Nothing appeared to have been stolen from the deceased's collection of belongings and his book of spells and conjurations had survived intact. Chief Inspector Alan Gould of the Norwich Police has stated that he is no nearer a solution as to the cause of MacBride's death but that his investigation will continue undaunted.

"The Reverend Lewis Trenchard, who led today's funeral service, which was attended by about fifteen people, is itself a testimony to the popularity of this eccentric Norfolk wizard. An inquest will be held in Norwich on Saturday."

Holmes folded the newspaper and stared out of the carriage window, reflecting on what he had just read. Was it not preposterous that in the age of reason, common folk still had recourse to the services of a self-proclaimed "wizard"? But perhaps he was not entirely right. He recalled Whitaker's own investigation into fraudulent mediums and the elaborate hoaxes of the spiritualist movement. One medium in particular, a large, coarse Glaswegian woman by the name of Helen Fitzsimmons, who had even impressed the writer and psychic investigator, Conan Doyle, had produced ectoplasm by the yard and fooled a professor of linguistics in her lodgings in Cann Street. It had taken the forensic skills of Whitaker and Holmes to expose her machinations, which included the ingestion of yards of muslin through her mouth and vagina. The Fitzsimmons affair had been widely reported in The Cambridge Herald and earned the medium fourteen days in jail. Such cases were not unusual, so he should not really be surprised to read of the existence of a so called "cunning man" in a rural backwater like Thorsford.

The train slowed, entered a deep cutting, then gradually climbed onto a broad plateau, rimmed by tall poplars on one side and on the other the cliffs of the Norfolk coast. To his left the sun was already low on the horizon, casting deep shadows across the adjoining woodland. Ancient oaks and birch trees loomed here, as if gathered in mute conspiracy. Holmes had forgotten the primeval power of this landscape. As a child, his parents had taken him on holiday to Cromer, that jewel of seaside towns, and his father, a keen palaeontologist, had roamed the scarred cliffs between Sheringham and Cley, dragging his infant son behind him like some diminutive mascot. But in young Holmes's mind the immensity of sea and sky had carved out a place in his imagination to which he often returned in adult years. Here in the east, the primal power of nature with its severe, snow-bound winters and icy winds, suggested a haunted landscape.

It was not just the history of the place which obsessed him.

Down the centuries, dark age queens jostled with Viking invaders, but there was more to it than that. The sheer immensity of the sky and the land pinned you down, and cut you down to size, so that you paled to insignificance. Once, during a summer vacation in their undergraduate days he had found himself with Whitaker, digging in a trench near Hunstanton at the site of an Anglo-Saxon burial. It had been near sunset and he was bent low, peering at the outlines of a skull, half buried in the sand. Without warning, the great orb of the sun had dipped westwards beneath the horizon. A darkness had slipped into the trench, so sudden and profound that he had scrambled for his paraffin lamp, filled with an irrational but compelling unease. Although he had seen nothing, the moment had haunted him down the years. What was there to explain? Nothing in particular, of course. Merely the power and eeriness of the landscape itself.

The train shunted to a stop. He picked up his suitcase, adjusted his cloth cap in the carriage mirror, then made his way out into the gangway. Through the darkness he could see the glowing gas lamps of the station platform. A figure waved to him. He smiled and waved back.

It was his old friend, Whitaker.

A few days prior to Holmes' arrival, Whitaker had just finished his morning shave and was about to visit the post office when Mrs Annis, his landlady, popped her head round the living room door only to announce that there was a visitor anxious to see him.

"Can't it wait?" he had replied rather testily.

"He seems to be in a distressed state, sir," Mrs Annis had replied assertively, fixing him with an unblinking stare.

"Very well, then Mrs Annis. Who is it, for heaven's sake?"

"George Robinson, the blacksmith."

"Show him in then. Oh, by the bye, would you pop down to the post office and get me a copy of the Times?"

"I'll have to see. Maybe later when I've finished baking," came the non-committal reply.

George Robinson was a short, squat individual of middle years with straight, jet black hair and pugnacious features. He was dressed in a shabby corduroy jacket, a pair of stained brown trousers and, somewhat incongruously, a battered brown hat.

"You'll 'ave to forgive me sir, visiting you at this short notice, but to be frank, sir, we're at the end of our tether," he began, his thoughts spewing out in an avalanche of words, his sonorous Norfolk accent booming in the oak lined room.

"Let's cut to the chase, Mr Robinson. And there's really no need to shout. What exactly has happened?"

The blacksmith sat down in a straight back chair opposite Whitaker, his ungainly form hanging uncomfortably over the edge of the seat. Whitaker noted that he was perspiring profusely, a broad band of sweat darkening his shirt front.

"It's my wife, Muriel, you see. She has this condition - a bone ache in her arms and legs. She's had it for years but recently it's got much worse."

"Go on."

"Well, about six months ago a friend of hers suggested she visit the wizard."

"The *what* - ?"

"The cunning man, William MacBride."

"And what sort of man is he?" Whitaker asked, a smile hovering about his lips. He had heard of cunning folk before. In his opinion most of them were frauds.

"There's a lot of people hereabouts who rely on him for their charms. Farmers say he can cure beasts of disease."

"And your wife visited MacBride?"

Robinson produced a large red handkerchief, wiped his glistening forehead, then blew his nose on it.

"At first he told her it would be easy to cure her of the condition. He used to give her a little packet of white powder which she had to throw into the fire and say a few words he'd written down for her."

"And she got better?"

"At first - yes, she improved a good deal. He charged her two shillings a month. But then she got worse."

"So what happened? You went back to complain?"

"I told him it wasn't working, and she should have her money back. But he told me not to interfere. He said she must finish the course, or he could not vouch for the consequences of her actions."

"So she continued?"

He nodded.

"She started to visit him more often. Recently it's increased to once a week. As a result, we've run so short of money. I've had to take on extra work to pay his bills."

There was a silence. Whitaker played with his watch fob as the big man opposite him shifted uneasily from buttock to buttock.

"So, what do you intend to do about this affair?" he asked.

"I was rather hoping that you might speak to him, put him right, in a manner of speaking."

"You believe, then, that your wife is under some sort of spell?"

"She thinks that if she doesn't finish the course of treatment some terrible calamity will befall her."

"And do you also believe that?"

"I don't know what to believe, I'm that worried about her."

Whitaker stood up.

"I can't promise you anything, Mr Robinson, but I'm willing to speak to this MacBride. We'll see what he has to say about the matter. Does your wife know you've come to see me?"

Robinson shook his head.

"I wouldn't want her to know."

"Then for now we shall keep this between ourselves."

The small thatched cottage where MacBride lived lay on the eastern edge of the village. Robinson led the way past a battered wicket gate into a small unkempt garden bordered by large laurel bushes. Over the diminutive doorway hung a rusting horseshoe. The front door, which was open, led them into a dark, musty hallway.

"Mr MacBride?" Robinson called but there was no answer. Whitaker stepped forward in front of Robinson, putting his finger to his lips, then opened the door to the dingy living room. A smoking peat fire burned fitfully in the grate, but this was one of the few signs of domestic normality in an otherwise chaotic interior. Whitaker took out a notebook and made his way round the room. For many years he had utilised his friend Holmes' methods. Observation, analysis and logical deduction were not simply words. To Whitaker and Holmes, they were all important strategies.

Books and papers lay strewn across the floor. A tall pine dresser was covered with broken china and a number of jars had spilled their contents on its shelves. In the centre of the room, spread eagled on a chair, sat William MacBride, his dark eyes staring, his face pale and bloodless, his mouth open in the rictus of death.

"Quickly. Go down to the post office and ask them to telephone for the police," Whitaker instructed the blacksmith. When Robinson had left, Whitaker looked about the room, making a mental note of its condition. There was a small safe on the wall above the fireplace which remained unopened. A cash box lay on the table, but this also appeared to be intact. There was also a half consumed bottle of whisky, along with a loaf of bread, a jar of berries and a tattered copy of the Bible, opened at the Book Of Revelations. The latter's placing struck him as somewhat odd until he recalled that cunning men would often use the Holy Writ as a tool in their divinations.

He peered at MacBride's still corpse. There was a small metal box beneath his hand. He opened the lid and found inside an Ephemerides, two books on the science of the stars and three plates of brass, which, when combined, formed an orrery.

Engraved on their surface were tables and diagrams of the planetary motions. In addition, there were several small cloth bags which, on further examination, were found to contain herbs and powders.

Whitaker closed the box and replaced it on the table. Then he made his way across the wrecked room into the hallway and out into the daylight. Bordering the cottage was a wide flowerbed and he noticed that one of the adjacent downstairs windows was broken. He peered down at the muddy earth but could see no evidence of footprints. Neither was the front door forced. The circumstances puzzled him. It occurred to him that Robinson himself might not be altogether above suspicion. Whoever had dealt the blow on MacBride's forehead must have possessed a great deal of strength. Moreover, he had opportunity as well as motive.

A sudden sound came from the heart of the laurel bushes. He turned and glimpsed the outline of a magpie, intent on some terrible act of predation. Whitaker made his way down towards the wicket gate and waited for the arrival of the police. He felt easier here, away from the oppressive gloom of the cottage with its staring, white faced corpse and the black and white, winged omen of bad luck. He shivered.

Far above him, on Thorsford Hill, the sun slipped from behind a bank of dense cloud and illumined the dark outline of the ancient hill figure. For a fleeting moment he imagined he could see it in its entirety: a rearing, dragon-like creature, its elongated head turned towards him, the eye fixed and unwavering. He felt a sudden chill and drew his greatcoat about him.

Sherlock Holmes stepped forward into the glare of the station gas lamp and extended a broad hand to greet his old colleague. Whitaker smiled and shook the offered hand vigorously. He thought that Holmes had aged since last he saw him. The formerly dark, sleek hair was now shot with grey and there were deep crows' feet around the piercing blue eyes.

"Good to see you again. It's been too long."

"Caius College at High Table, as I recall," Holmes boomed back above the noise of the departing locomotive. Momentarily they were engulfed in a cloud of acrid smoke.

They walked side by side towards the station yard, Whitaker casting sidelong glances in Holmes' direction. His old colleague looked thinner and bowed. He bore the marks of recent bereavement, it occurred to him.

"I have a fly waiting. It's not far. Good journey?"

Holmes nodded. Whitaker heaved the suitcase into the back of the vehicle, Mrs Annis' strong arms guiding it to its destination.

"Holmes, this is my housekeeper, Sophia Annis."

"Pleased to meet you sir. It'll not take long sir. There's a cold supper waiting at the rectory."

As the fly rattled along the unmade road, Whitaker pulled the tartan rug across their legs and offered his friend a tot of brandy from his hip flask.

"That is most welcome. Have you have read this edition of the Norwich Evening Post?" asked Holmes.

"I haven't set eyes on it yet - just today's Times. I imagine you're referring to William MacBride's funeral?"

"I confess I knew nothing of it before today. I rarely read the sensational press, as you know."

Whitaker took the hip flask and replaced it in his great-coat pocket.

"It was a most bizarre affair. I had the misfortune to discover the body."

"Really. And what did you glean from the scene of crime?"

"Very little I'm afraid. There was apparently no murder weapon and the cause of death seems indeterminate."

Whitaker described the circumstances of his visit to MacBride's cottage as the fly rattled between two lines of giant poplars, the freshly risen moon casting shadows on the glistening road. At last the street lamps of Thorsford village came into view and they turned up a narrow lane, past the church, heading in the direction of the rectory gates.

"What about motive?" Holmes enquired. "From what you've told me he was well known in the area."

"Even in Norwich. Yes, his notoriety was widespread."

"Enemies?"

"I have no doubt of that. I can't imagine that George Robinson was the only malcontent."

"You've spoken to the police?"

"I made a statement, of course. Not that it was of much use to them. Chief Inspector Gould of the Norwich Police is heading the investigation."

"Any leads?"

"None so far. There's a coroner's court on Tuesday. I've been asked to attend. To be honest, I'd not expected to be plunged into a maelstrom of murder and mayhem."

"Hard lines. I shall do my best to assist you then. My, this is rather grand, isn't it?"

The fly trundled to a stop and they climbed out, Holmes staring with astonishment at the imposing frontage of the rectory entrance.

Later, after brandy and cigars, the two men retired to the comfort of the study. Whitaker lounged before a blazing fire as Holmes, pipe alight, peered at the collection of ecclesiastical volumes on the dusty shelves.

"Your predecessor - Ebenezer Oakenfull."

"Yes - his reading was somewhat eclectic, I gather. Some of these titles suggest -"

"That he was more preoccupied with folklore and superstition than theology or his ecclesiastical duties?"

"Yes, I would agree wholeheartedly. There are several boxes of correspondence which I intend to go through when I get time to do it. He appears to have been conducting extensive research into the pagan history of the region. I suspect that he had intended to write a book on the subject."

Whitaker puffed at his cigar.

"Is there much to know about the subject, then?" Holmes asked.

"I gather so. It seems there is some kind of continuity from dark age practices through to the witchcraft scares of the 17th century -"

"Ah, the imposter, Matthew Hopkins."

"Yes indeed, our old friend the 'Witchfinder General' once made an appearance in these parts. A woman was burned at King's Lynn for causing her husband's death. An uncommon occurrence in those days, hanging being the preferred method of execution."

"And is there a link with the present? Have such practices really survived the age of reason?"

Whitaker laughed and replenished their glasses.

By the following Monday, it had rained heavily, and the snows began to clear, rivers of slush pouring down the riverbank and spilling over into the eastern section of the churchyard. That afternoon the phone rang and Chief Inspector Gould reminded Whitaker that he was required to give evidence at the coroner's court in Norwich. He explained that the main coach road was open and asked if he would be requiring transport. Whitaker politely declined, declaring that he had his own transport and would arrive in good time before the commencement of the proceedings.

After what seemed an interminable journey by fly through slush bound roads, Holmes and Whitaker eventually arrived at their destination in Norwich, the old knap-flinted Guildhall in the centre of the city. They entered through the south west doorway with its ornate jambs and foliaged spandrels to find themselves standing in a large room with fine stain glass windows and linenfold panelling and seats sporting curious beasts and grotesques.

The court was packed with an assortment of agricultural labouring men, tradesmen and a scattering of professional types in dark suits and heavy ulsters. First in the stand was Chief Inspector Gould. A short, stocky man with a florid face and muttonchop whiskers, he peered at his notebook through a pair of narrow rimmed spectacles, coughed nervously, then uttered his findings in a low, booming voice. Not much more could be deduced from his account apart from the details which had already appeared in 'The Norwich Evening Post.'

Next to the stand was the police surgeon, a tall, athletic young man with dark hair whose evidence was rendered somewhat comic by virtue of a slight lisp. However, his testimony was not without interest. The contents of the deceased's stomach revealed that immediately prior to his death, he had consumed a large meal and copious amounts of alcohol. The wound to his temple had caused an epidural bleed and subsequent brain damage. The fracture itself was semi-circular in shape and may have resulted from a blow from a piece of pipe, wooden stake or similar object. There was also a small subdural bleed at the back of the skull where the deceased had recoiled against the back of his chair, indicating that a person of considerable strength had administered the fatal blow. There was little trace evidence of any significance at the scene of the crime save for a considerable number of long hairs which had attached themselves to the victim's jacket. However, these appeared to be of animal, and not human origin.

Next it was the turn of Ronald Perceval Bloxham, the squire of Munnington Hall. A thin, ascetic looking individual dressed in immaculate frock coat and scarlet waistcoat, he spoke in a low, scarcely audible voice, his phrases clipped and expressionless. It transpired that MacBride had worked for Bloxham on a part-time basis as a groom and handyman. On the day in question he had spent the afternoon trimming hedges on the borders of the estate. He had been dismissed at 5pm by the head gardener for being drunk at work but was seen by Sir Ronald at 5.30pm heading down a narrow footpath in the direction of the Green Man Public House.

Next to give evidence was Henry Stanmore, landlord of the Green Man. He told the court that MacBride had sat sullenly at the bar from about 6pm until closing time. He seemed unwilling to leave the premises and was much preoccupied, spending much of the evening making notes in a small, spiral bound notebook.

Whitaker gave his evidence. He was questioned closely about the condition of the cottage and its contents which he observed on his arrival at the scene of the crime. He explained the reason for his visit to MacBride, whom he described as a man of 'dubious reputation' and gave the coroner background information regarding the nature of Mr Robinson's dilemma. The coroner questioned him closely at this point and Whitaker was able to reveal MacBride's function as a local cunning man. He commented on the large variety of abstruse astrological volumes in the deceased's collection, indicating that although MacBride was a common labourer, he appeared to be highly literate and was evidently self-taught. He also revealed that he had had an opportunity to glance at some of MacBride's correspondence which demonstrated the breadth and social variety of his clientele. Indeed, he had been surprised at some of the names in MacBride's notebooks, indicating that some clients were members of the affluent classes.

At this point in the proceedings the coroner raised his eyebrows, then coughed, but made no comment. Next to give evidence was Mrs Ada Robinson. A thin, pale-faced woman with a hooked nose and lined features, she clung to the stand, her arthritic hands the colour of ivory. In a faltering, wheezy voice, she reluctantly gave her testimony.

"You are Ada Robinson, the wife of George Robinson?"

"I am."

"And what was your relationship with the deceased?"

"I asked him for help. I had been suffering a great deal of pain."

"So you went to MacBride for help?"

"That's correct."

"And how exactly did he help you, Mrs Robinson?"

There was a pause as Mrs Robinson gazed helplessly round the courtroom. The coroner repeated his question to her.

"He gave me some bags of salts which I was told to hang round my neck."

"And you were required to do this for how long?"

"For about four months, I should say."

"And I understand that your husband, Mr George Robinson, was not entirely happy with this?"

"It was costing us a lot of money. No, he wasn't happy."

"And I understand that your husband consulted Mr Whitaker in the hope that he might intervene?"

"George said MacBride ought to give us the money back because my condition wasn't improving."

"And how did he feel about Mr MacBride? Was he angry about this?"

"Not angry, no, just concerned about me."

"I see. Thank you, Mrs Robinson. You may stand down."

The last to give evidence was George Robinson. Dressed in a baggy corduroy suit and looking distinctly apprehensive, Robinson gave his evidence in a faltering Norfolk drawl. He denied harbouring any feelings of animosity towards the deceased. Yes, he regarded MacBride as a cheat and an imposter, but he wished him no harm. At this point Robinson began to flush and shift nervously from foot to foot. The coroner thanked him for his contribution and asked him to stand down.

In summing up the evidence, the coroner opined that William MacBride had been unlawfully killed by a person or persons unknown. In conclusion he thanked the police surgeon, Whitaker and Detective Inspector Gould for their detailed observations. The session having concluded, Holmes and Whitaker emerged into the cold air of a bright October morning and made their way through slush-lined roads to their fly in Pottergate.

Holmes had never seen Munnington Hall before. He had read of its splendours, of course, but seeing it for the first time on a cold, cloudless October day, the soft autumn sun burnishing its limestone and brick facade, was an altogether surprising experience.

The hall lay at the end of a long, beech-lined driveway about a quarter of a mile in length. One either side of the drive sheep and cattle grazed on lush grass and there was an air of undisturbed tranquillity about the estate. Eventually the fly drew level with the main house, an impressive mansion built in the Dutch seventeenth century style, two and a half storeys high with mullioned gables and elaborate pediments. Whitaker bade Mrs Annis farewell and they were left alone, staring up at the great doorway with its detached, unfluted columns and heraldry.

Holmes pulled the bell pull and within a few minutes the door swung open. Facing them was a tall, aged butler dressed in an immaculate frock coat. Sallow skinned and entirely bald, he looked at Holmes closely, hovering in the doorway like some ancient bird of prey.

"Who may I say is calling, sir?"

"Mr Charles Whitaker and Mr Sherlock Holmes."

He bowed slightly, then turned, muttering: "This way please."

He led the way down a dark corridor, lined with eighteenth century paintings whose subjects, almost without exception, showed a series of studies of racehorses. They passed through a door on the left and entered a magnificent drawing room, fitted with Jacobean oak panels and a grand plaster ceiling. At the far end, dressed in a sober grey morning suit, stood Ronald Bloxham. At his side, clad in a long, diaphanous floral gauze dress, was a tall woman with long, lustrous blond hair. Her face was striking and reminded Holmes of Rossetti's painting of his wife. The eyes were large and dark, the nose Roman in shape and the lips wide and sensuous. Deep lines were etched about the eyes and mouth, suggesting some prolonged period of worry or unhappiness. Bloxham stepped forward, greeting them in a voice which was faint and sepulchral.

"Gentlemen, we are so glad you could come. This is my wife, Augusta."

Lady Bloxham extended a thin hand.

I am very pleased to meet you at last. Ronald tells me you are interested in our hill figure, Mr Whitaker?"

"Yes, I have invited Mr Holmes, an old friend of mine from my Cambridge days to examine the entire figure."

The meal was as sumptuous as the surroundings. Afterwards, over brandy, the four of them sat in the drawing room before a blazing fire as Bloxham informed his hosts about his passion for equestrian pursuits.

"I have always had a love for that noble beast," he explained, mellow with food and drink. "Horses are sacred animals, reverend. The ancients knew it. Yet in our own age we have treated them as no better than mere machines or beasts of burden. Call me extreme if you will, but I believe that the bond between man and horse is a purer and more noble thing than that between man and woman."

Holmes looked across at Augusta Bloxham. She looked slightly ill at ease.

"Did you know, Mr Holmes, that the Celts who buried their warriors alongside these noble beasts believed they would enter paradise together?"

"I have read of such burials."

"They understood more than we do."

"This man MacBride. I understand he acted as a groom for you, Sir Ronald?"

"In a part time capacity, yes. MacBride may have been something of a rake, but he had a remarkable affinity with horses.

He was a horse whisperer, you know. He had that ability to read their thoughts. It was a rare talent."

"To say nothing of his psychic abilities," interposed Augusta.

"Yes, he was also a talented medium," agreed Bloxham.

"I wasn't aware of it."

"Oh yes, he was of great assistance to us, especially after Leonard, our eldest, died at the Somme."

"I'm sorry to hear of your loss. I had the misfortune to lose several relatives in that conflict," Holmes observed. "You have my sympathy."

"Yes, MacBride was able to get through to the other side on a number of occasions. We were much comforted by that. MacBride had a strong spiritual presence. The fact that he often abused his powers is only regrettable. Now that he has passed on, we still maintain our circle, but it is not quite the same."

"You have a seance circle here in Thorsford ?""

"At our neighbour's place - Eveline Da Costa's. We meet each Sunday evening at Glamis house. You would be most welcome to join us."

But Holmes politely declined the offer. They left Munnington Hall shortly after eleven o'clock, glad of the waiting fly and Mrs Annis' presence. They drove back down the long driveway, the sky above them illuminated only by a weak, fogged moon. Mrs Annis chatted amiably as, far off towards the east, low rumbles of approaching thunder began to break the silence of the still, cold night.

Augusta Bloxham finished dressing, then sat before the long mirror at her dressing room table and applied her mascara. In the oval mirror, sad eyes peered back at her. The face, though once beautiful, was now lined and showed the effects of her deep mourning. The cheeks were thinner and the once beautiful, swan-like neck was stretched and gaunt. She finished applying the mascara and reached for her eye liner. He had once told her that she needed no makeup, that her natural beauty was all he wished to possess. Those words could never have been spoken by her husband, for where William was all fire and passion, Ronald was ice. When the news of Donald's death at the Somme had reached them, he had not shed a single tear but retreated to his study where he had remained for two whole days without food or drink. After that, he had slept in a room at the end of the corridor. It was as if she no longer existed. At first, she blamed herself for the transformation. All her efforts at talking to him about the problem had been denied. From that point onwards he had retreated into his own, inner world.

She finished using the eye liner and reached for her lipstick. "A skin as soft as swan's feathers." The phrase came back to her, his words full of passion. Her hand trembled at the memory of his strong arms and the sweet smell of his body. When she had made love to him it was as if her whole body had been on fire.

It had begun innocently enough. MacBride's reputation was well known to her as a cunning man and dispenser of aphrodisiacs. Foolishly, she had believed that Ronald's impotence was a passing phase. She had first contacted MacBride in the summer of 1915. Cautious about her reputation, she had communicated via her maid, who delivered a letter, explaining her husband's predicament. MacBride had provided a charm which she wore about her neck, but this had had little effect. Desperation had driven her to visit his small cottage in person. She had only seen MacBride as a part time groom in the stables at Munnington Hall and was then only vaguely aware of his reputation as a cunning man, though there had been stories which had circulated among her staff. MacBride had been much younger then. She was surprised, therefore, to find a tall, burly man of about thirty with dark, wild hair and close - set eyes. He had been courteous in the extreme and had plied her with whisky. In the course of that afternoon she had been interested to discover that he was of mixed ancestry. His mother was a Romany whose family had been driven east in the mid 1850's but his father (so he claimed) was of noble birth, being able to trace his ancestry back to one of the illegitimate sons of George the Third. He had held her captive with tales of his exploits and misadventures.

There was something intense and Byronic about his manner and she felt herself drawn to this dark haired man. At the conclusion of her visit he prescribed an aphrodisiac which she was instructed to place in her husband's tea. When she got home, she found herself besotted with this mysterious individual who had quite captivated her soul and when she retired that evening, she tried out some drops from the little phial which he had given her. That night she hardly slept, being consumed with a kind of sexual frenzy the like of which she had never known. She got up and went to her husband's room. But when she looked at his sleeping form and the pale, ageing face against the white pillow she knew immediately that she felt only hatred towards him.

It was Augusta who had told Sir Ronald about MacBride's psychic powers. From the outset he had been impressed. They had sat in awe as the voice of their dead son had filled the darkened room. MacBride's weekly visits to Munnington Hall had provided Augusta with an extra opportunity to hold that firm, muscular hand and to wonder at the strength that emanated from her lover's body. And all the while her husband had suspected nothing.

They met twice weekly after that. She told Ronald that she had joined a circle of ladies from Norwich whose purpose was to bestow Christian charity among the poor. In reality, however, she would be dropped by Jennings at the edge of Thorsford village and make her way to the perimeter of Wayland's Wood to MacBride's cottage. It was as if she were consumed by a kind of madness. In her day to day world she was Lady Bloxham, mistress of the manor of Munnington, wife to the squire, a demure woman of middle years. But alone with her lover, she was a wanton libertine, driving MacBride to sexual excess. It was as if something had opened up inside her, a late flowering of her libido. And so she had begun to contemplate dark deeds.

She dared not call it murder. Not to herself, anyway. She had not the courage to speak, let alone think of the word. Yet murder was what she had intended. Weary with his pale, expressionless face, driven to distraction by his lack of interest in all things save his love of horses, she knew that she must be rid of him. She wished to be with MacBride every waking hour, yet fate had meted out to her this miserable existence where, for six out of seven days each week she would live a pretence of a life. She began to pray that he might die in a riding accident or be struck down by some mysterious disease. And then it occurred to her that she might, for once, be mistress of her own fate, and lend Nature a helping hand. She told MacBride about her plan.

At first, he seemed shocked and wished to have no part in the proceedings. At last, however, relenting under pressure, he compromised and told Augusta that he would supply her only with the means. So it was that on a Thursday afternoon in late October she left MacBride's cottage, a small phial of digitalis in her purse, determined that she would bring to an end the Bloxham line. She would wear her widow's weeds for the best part of a year, she told herself, then she would elope with MacBride and take rented rooms in Norwich, perhaps even change her name by deed poll. There being no male heir, the bulk of the estate would be left to her. She would sell it in its entirety and purchase a mansion somewhere on the south coast where she and MacBride would spend the remainder of their days in comparative luxury. She had returned home to find Ronald out horse riding. She went to the living room and opened the drinks cabinet, thinking how she would do it. Would she drop the digitalis into his evening whisky when he was distracted? That way he would die in his sleep. Or maybe she would secrete it in his hip flask and he would fall from his horse. "A heart attack," they would say. "He was a man of middle years who over exerted himself." It would be a credible end. At the age of forty nine he had already suffered a mild heart attack and had been warned by his doctor to avoid strong drink.

But it was not to be.

In the early evening Ronald had returned home and broken the news to her as if it were a regrettable but predictable event. MacBride had been found in his cottage amid a scene of disorder, bludgeoned to death by persons unknown. She had not known how she had kept her composure. As the words hit home and Bloxham reached for the whisky bottle, the colour had drained from her face and she felt that her heart would burst. Bloxham had scarcely noticed her reaction. She wished in that moment that she had poisoned his glass there and then, so great was her despair.

There was a sound below of horses' hooves in the courtyard. She stood up at the dressing table and moved to the window. Bloxham was dismounting from his white stallion, Jennings the groom standing in attendance. She turned from the window, her heart closed against him, tears welling from her dark eyes.

Holmes adjusted his scarf and made his way through the ticket barrier, past busy city commuters and out into the sunshine on Riverside Road. Here and there in the cobbled streets tradesmen and bowler - hatted clerks jostled for space en route to the courts, then passed him, their faces set and earnest, intent on the day ahead. As he turned into Tombland and passed the four-gabled house with its strange figures of Samson and Hercules, a pale faced vagrant lurched towards him demanding money, but he fended him off with an outstretched hand and the thin, haggard figure melted into the shadow of an adjacent alley way.

The city had a gritty, murky feel to it. Grimed by coal smoke, and hazy with remnants of the early morning mist, the streets were lined with horse manure, decaying leaves and litter. In the midst of this murk, the Erpingham Gate loomed above him, flanked by polygonal buttresses, decorated with heraldry and standing figures under leaf canopies. The easterly wind which had dogged him all the way from the railway station and along Friths Lane was absent here, blocked by the long Gothic cloisters where he now strolled on, his solitary footfalls sounding like pistol shots in the cold, crisp air. Past the rounded Romanesque east end of the Cathedral, he took a short cut over the turf, making his way via a short path to the Bishops' Palace. Here he paused and reached for the brass bell pull, conscious of the stillness of the hour and the timelessness of the ancient building. Within, footsteps sounded on an uncarpeted staircase. The door opened, revealing a tall, bespectacled young curate with a hooked nose who stared at him inquisitively.

Mr Sherlock Holmes, to see the Bishop," he informed the owl faced sentinel.

The young door attendant smiled weakly.

"I am expected," Holmes added impatiently.

"If you would like to sit in the ante - room I shall inform the Bishop of your arrival."

Holmes waited in the oak panelled room, eyeing the marble bust of Bishop Reynold as his feet began to thaw. There was a minute's delay, then a door opened on the floor above and he heard heavy footfalls on the bare oak treads.

Bishop Bill strode towards Holmes, his corpulent torso tight beneath his purple surplice, his broad ruddy face as boyish as ever.

"Mr Holmes!" he exclaimed. "Good to see you. I got your wire. Come up to my rooms and we'll talk."

Holmes followed Bishop Hunter's ample form up the wide oak staircase. He had not changed much since their last encounter a year back in the case of Jeakes' Summoning. A few more grey hairs, perhaps, a few additional pounds added to his already spreading figure, but the ebullient, generous personality remained unaltered. If ever a man beamed beneficence it was Bishop Bill. They stepped into a dark, oak panelled study, lined with leather bound tomes ranging from ecclesiastical history to Gibbons' *Decline and Fall of The Roman Empire*.

Bishop Bill opened a desk drawer and, placing a tin of tobacco ceremoniously on the table in front of his visitor, proclaimed:

"Feel free Mr Holmes. This is a very good quality shag. Now, what is all this about Ebenezer Oakenfull?"

Holmes filled his old, oily briar and soon the study was wreathed in a fog of blue tobacco smoke.

"The letter I referred to in my wire - "

"Ah, yes."

"I have it here. I think you should read it. I found this among Oakenfull's correspondence files. I'd been going through some of his collections of books and pamphlets at the rectory and found it tucked in the flyleaf of a copy of Caesar's "Gallic Wars"."

He placed the letter in Hunter's chubby hand and the bishop scanned its contents. The untidy scrawl and long spiky loops of the 'g's and 'y's suggested to him that the author of the letter was a person of considerable strength and conviction.

"This is the last warning I shall give you," he read. *"I have repeatedly told you to stop interfering in my affairs but you have consistently ignored my previous advice. As a consequence, I have lost a great number of clients. I tell you that if you do not desist I shall have no option but to put a stop to your machinations. I do not stand in awe of your Christian God nor do I bow to your false theology. Take heed. I am on to you - WM."*

Bishop Bill passed the letter back to Holmes.

"Strong stuff," he commented. "And you believe the author was - ?"

"William MacBride."

Bishop Bill leaned back in his chair and placed his fingers in a steepled position as if he were about to utter a prayer.

"To be frank, it does not come as much of a surprise to me."

"You knew of the enmity between them?"

"I was aware of it, though I believe it was not public knowledge. Ebenezer had contacted me about the matter a few weeks before his demise. This man MacBride was a social pest."

"So I gather."

"He also had considerable influence in the district."

"I was aware of it."

"I am not sure you know the half of it, Mr Holmes. Not only did he operate as a so called "wizard" or cunning man, he had also started up a spiritualist group. His meetings drew followers from as far away as Norwich and Kings Lynn. Ebenezer had become concerned about his sphere of influence. Then of course there was his reputation as a womaniser."

"I was not aware of that."

"Oh yes, he had a particular penchant for young women. His little peccadilloes caused quite a stir in the community, I can tell you. It was even rumoured that he had affairs with some of his more exalted female clients."

"Really?"

"Yes, but we shall not name names. Better not. Especially as some of the ladies concerned are members of our congregation here at the cathedral."

There was a silence. Unabashed by the bishop's disclosures, Holmes sucked on his pipe.

"You mentioned a spiritualist group?" he enquired.

"So I did. Apparently, MacBride had some reputation as a medium. He would advertise in the local newspaper. It was something Ebenezer took great exception to. In fact, he went so far as to report MacBride to the local constabulary. As a result, MacBride was prosecuted under the Vagrancy Act. That was the start of the trouble. He never forgave him for it."

Holmes nodded. "Go on."

"Well, it developed into a feud. There was no other word for it. They exchanged letters in the local press. But that wasn't the half of it. Ebenezer even threatened to read out the names of the parishioners who patronised MacBride's sessions. In return he broke into the church and defaced the reredos. Of course, nothing could be proved. This battle went on for about a year, as I recall. Then of course Ebenezer fell ill and died."

"But how exactly did he die?"

Bishop Bill leaned forward on the table and adjusted his gold rimmed glasses on the bridge of his thin nose.

"It was terribly dramatic. He was at Sunday communion. It was coming up to Easter. Anyway, he was delivering a sermon based on the sinfulness of Sodom and Gomorrah when he was gripped by a series of violent convulsions. They took him back to the vicarage but within twelve hours he was dead."

"Heart failure?"

"No, it was food poisoning. It was a terrible end, poor fellow."

Holmes removed the briar from his lips, then relit the mixture, acrid fumes filling the study.

"It was said MacBride had a considerable number of enemies in the parish. Is that right?"

"Oh I don't doubt it. He'd even cuckolded a number of husbands in Thorsford. But on the other hand, he had his allies. Squire Bloxham, for one."

"I believe he worked for the squire as a groom?"

"That's right. He had an affinity with horses. Some even said he was something of a horse whisperer. Ebenezer always imagined there was some deeper bond between them, though he couldn't fathom precisely what it was. He was quite frequently seen at Munnington Hall. Yes, there's no doubt about it. MacBride had charisma. That was part of his appeal to the gentler sex, you see. What is it?"

He broke off abruptly, staring across at Holmes, who appeared to be lost in thought. There was a long pause before he answered.

"I have a suspicion - a hunch, call it what you will - that Ebenezer Oakenfull was murdered," he said at last. He was standing now, staring out of the window, watching the autumn leaves swirling about the quadrangle. The sky was dark and heavy with rain clouds and the air seemed ominously still as if it presaged a storm.

"Murdered by whom?"

"I believe MacBride poisoned him. I shall probably never be able to prove it, but I think it is a distinct possibility."

Bishop Bill, who had now joined him at the window, placed a reassuring hand on Holmes's shoulder.

"You may be right, Mr Holmes," he remarked. "But the

question is, who killed MacBride?"

When Holmes arrived back at the rectory, he found Charles Whitaker and Inspector Gregory waiting for him.

'I'm sorry to inform you, Mr Holmes, that Sir Ronald Bloxham is dead.'

Holmes took out his old brier and began to fill it.'

'You don't seem surprised, sir.'

'I am not.'

'The maid found him early this morning. She called the family doctor. It's thought he died of food poisoning.'

'I've called for an autopsy,' added Gould.

'Under the circumstances, that is a most wise precaution.'

Charles added that he and Holmes had received an invitation to dinner that evening from Henry Stapeley. Holmes assented, and some hours later the two men set off to one of the large houses on the edge of the village. They arrived just as it was getting dark and walked down the narrow, tree shrouded driveway.

Dressed in a dark green smoking jacket and voluminous Arabic style pantaloons, Stapeley answered the door.

"So good that you could both make it. Do come in, gentlemen."

Stapeley led the way down a narrow hallway lined with books, and they entered a low beamed living room, lit by candles and a roaring log fire. Stapeley bade them sit and took their coats into the hallway, his tall, thin form bending to avoid contact with the beams. Holmes inspected the room. A dark, eighteenth century mahogany sideboard accommodated a variety of silver ornaments, a stuffed cat and a Dutch tobacco jar. To his left, the silk - papered wall was lined with oil landscapes by members of the Norwich School.

"Admiring my Cotman, I see?" remarked Stapeley, who had

entered bearing a drinks tray.

"It's a fine piece."

"I have three others by him upstairs."

"You're a collector, then?"

"Of paintings and antiques, yes. It has been my passion for over a decade, Mr Holmes. It is also my living, of course. I understand that you are interested in prehistory, like myself?"

"I have dabbled in such matters, but it is Charles who has a deeper knowledge of the subject."

"Of course," replied Stapeley, exhibiting a toothy smile. "Charles here has told me much about the excavation and his theories about Boadicea."

"The body on the hill?"

"Exactly. It's an exciting thought, isn't it?"

"But merely a speculation, I'm sorry to say. It seems unlikely that Thorsford Hill marks the grave of the warrior queen."

"Nevertheless, the whole area seems soaked in finds from the Iceni. I have one or two pieces upstairs which form the core of my collection, including a gold torc."

Whitaker raised his eyebrows.

"Oh yes, I'd be happy to show you my collection after dinner. Anyway, let us charge our glasses, gentlemen. A toast to the treasures of the past!"

Whitaker was quiet over dinner, a sumptuous affair consisting of roast duck, roast potatoes and fresh vegetables, followed by a lemon pie. His silence was noted by Stapeley who spent much of the meal chatting to Holmes about the collections in the Ashmolean Museum. After the port had been consumed and the cigars lit, he turned to Whitaker.

"You seem rather troubled, Charles."

"Holmes and I have had rather a long day of it I'm afraid. Most of it spent with the Norfolk constabulary."

Holmes explained briefly the circumstances relating to the discovery of Ronald Bloxham's body. Stapeley leaned back in his chair, his face serious.

"The whole thing's appalling - grotesque," he said, pulling at his goatee beard agitatedly. "We had our disagreements of course. But I would never have wished that fate upon him."

"Disagreements?"

"Oh yes, they were many. Mostly involving land disputes. When I purchased this cottage several years ago, I was told I had rights over several fields and their adjoining rights of way. They abutted the perimeter of the grounds of Munnington Hall. I made it my business to exercise my rights you see. It didn't go down too well with Sir Ronald. In fact, he became rather litigious over the matter. Cost me a deal of money I can tell you. He even threatened to shoot me on one occasion. He was, in many respects, a dislikeable individual. But I would not have wished that on him. Not at all. How is Augusta taking it?"

"Not very well," said Charles.

"I feel for her, I do. She was never very happy in the relationship you know. Hardly surprising really, considering her husband's complete obsession with equestrian matters."

"Really?"

"Oh yes. It was like a religion to him. Something he shared with that strange character MacBride. They were both members of a sort of secret society you know. It was common knowledge round here - especially after MacBride made it public - more by chance than intention of course."

"Secret society? What do you mean, precisely?" asked Holmes. He leaned forward on the table, his eyes glinting in the firelight.

"Have you ever heard of something called 'The Horseman's Word?'" Stapeley asked.

"I confess I have not."

"Nor had I," Stapeley added. "I discovered it purely by chance through a friend of mine at Edinburgh University," he explained. "It was originally called "The Society of The Horseman's Word". Its origins are somewhat obscure. It seems to have been connected with freemasonry and some of the medieval guilds. But unlike freemasonry, it does not share that society's belief in the Christian creator. On the contrary, it believes in the power of Satan."

"And what has this to do with Squire Bloxham or William MacBride?" asked Holmes.

"MacBride was certainly a member and I have every reason to believe that the squire was. They use a talisman you see. I spotted it both at MacBride's cottage and at Munnington Hall. Look, I made a drawing of it."

He stood up and, plucking a scroll of paper from the bookcase, unrolled it on the dining table.

"Here it is, - a sort of cross made of riding crops, bisected with four horseshoes."

"Most curious," Whitaker said.

"I discovered from my Edinburgh colleague that members of this esoteric society all possess a great power over the horse. In short, they are horse whisperers. They have the power to stop a horse in its tracks or command it to do almost anything they wish. I have seen this in action with both men. MacBride, who was once Squire Bloxham's groom, had the ability to work a horse into a frenzy when he so desired. Bloxham relied on him to calm his stallion prior to important race meetings. I have seen much the same thing with the Squire."

"This society," enquired Holmes. "Does it have any other distinguishing marks - a creed or ideology for example?"

Stapeley pulled a small silver cigarette case from the pocket of his smoking jacket and offered the two men one of his Turkish cigarettes.

"It has its own initiation rite - according to McEwen - that's my Scottish contact, incidentally. The order is hierarchical and is divided into six grades. Each represents what they term "The

Miracle of The Bread." The grades are termed The Plough, The Seed, The Green Corn, The Yellow Corn, The Stones and finally the Resurrection, the latter being the highest. Membership is available to men aged between sixteen and fifty. Each recruit is compelled to take what is termed The Horseman's Oath. In it the initiate swears that he will conceal and never reveal any part of his horsemanship nor speak or write down the secret word of the brotherhood."

Holmes pondered for a moment. Then he said:

"Doesn't it strike you as odd that both men were part of this society and that both have met untimely ends?"

"I admit it's a coincidence. Are there any obvious suspects for the Squire's murder yet?"

"It's far too early to tell. It appears that someone - or in my opinion more than one person - broke into Munnington Hall and murdered the Squire in the early hours of this morning. Whoever it was seems to have had prior knowledge of the geography of the Hall."

"Which would indicate a local man."

"Possibly. However, I'm intrigued by what you've told me about the Horseman's Word. I should like to look further into the matter."

"I can help you there. I have some working notes on the society. I'll lend you them if you like."

When Holmes and Whitaker emerged from Bowood Cottage later that evening, they discovered that a sharp frost had descended, riming the fields and trees. They made their way down the footpath that led back to the rectory, each in silent thought. When they reached the gate that marked the crossroads, Holmes glanced up towards Thorsford Hill. The sky was flooded with moonlight which cast a silver sheen on the frozen landscape. From here he could see the great hill with its humped summit and the dark trees beyond. Below, etched in white, lay the lines of the mysterious hill figures, two laid bare and the third half buried in the turf. He thought of the events at Munnington Hall. It felt as if some dark force was present here, the dark powers which had lain here for centuries beneath the earth. They turned and walked down the yew alley. He had heard Charles say something about his plans for the following day and the completion of his scouring, but Holmes had not really been listening. He was thinking of the Horseman's Word, his hand gripping the packet of papers Stapeley had lent him. As he glanced back along the alleyway, he thought, for a brief moment, he heard the whinnying of a horse, but realised it was only the sound of the wind in the branches.

The following day dawned fair and bright, despite a keen easterly wind which perpetuated the ground frost. Whitaker was up early, and by eight o'clock had already completed his breakfast. Downstairs in the study he met Holmes. The latter, who was deeply engrossed in the papers lent him by Stapeley, had already broached his after- breakfast pipe and was wreathed in dense coils of pungent tobacco smoke.

"Up already?" Holmes enquired, glancing up from the study table.

"I want to make an early start. I have a feeling in my bones that today will be a remarkable one. What are you doing?"

"Following a hunch."

"The Horseman's Word?"

"Right."

"You really do think it had something to do with Sir Ronald's death, then?"

"It's a hunch. Nothing more. But then, in my line of business, I have often come to rely on the irrational as a source of inspiration."

"Well, good luck then. I am armed with one of Mrs Annis's sandwich boxes and a hip flask containing some excellent malt whisky."

"I shall be joining you after lunch, time permitting. I have to give a statement to Inspector Gould this morning so I'm hopeful that he'll be on time."

The hard frost of the previous night had not made Whitaker's job easy. Using a Cornish shovel, his sticks and a plumb line, he toiled away, breaking the iced sod, then clearing shovelfuls of earth from the limestone rock beneath. With the sun's heat on his back, he soon began to sweat and had to remove his thick sheepskin jacket in order to continue.

Holmes returned to the study and opened the packet of papers Stapeley had lent him the previous evening. For some while he poured over its contents, a collection of hand-written foolscap sheets entitled: "The Horseman's Word: Some Observations, by Henry Stapeley Esquire."

'A secret society with distinct pagan overtones (he read), The Horseman's Word or Society of the Horseman's Word, has existed for many centuries in both East Anglia and the far north-eastern portion of Scotland. The cult originated in the town of Huntly in Aberdeenshire and reached its peak in Scotland in the late 1870's.'

He skipped a page and his attention was caught by the following entry:

'The initiation ceremony of the Horseman's Word usually took place on Martinmas, otherwise November the First, and was held in an isolated barn. The number of people present at a ceremony had to comprise an odd, not even number. When a sufficient number had been assembled, the word was passed round for members to attend. This was often done by passing a single horsehair in an envelope to each member. Each horseman was expected to bring to the ceremony a bottle of whisky, a loaf of bread and a jar of jam or berries. This form of ceremony was also practised in certain areas of North Norfolk, although by the late 1860's this was no longer the case in Suffolk. On the night in question, the novices were each taken blindfolded into a barn. When they reached the door, the horseman brother leading them gave what was termed "The Horseman's Knock" - three taps, and with this the leader would whinny like a horse. Each novice was then questioned and had to identify himself to the 'minister' inside. The novice was required to say that he had been told by* *the Devil to attend 'by the hooks and crooks of the road.' He was then asked: "What is the tender of the oath?" to which he replied, "Hele, conceal, never reveal; neither write, nor dite, nor recite, nor cut, nor carve, nor write in sand." In other words, no member of the group would ever impart the 'Secret Word' to anyone who was not a member of the cult. The initiation would then commence with novices, still blindfold, seated round the minister with the left foot bare and left hand raised in obedience. The minister then explained to the novices that Cain had been the very first horseman and that the Devil would be invoked by reading from the Bible backwards. Then he gave each 'The Word' which, when whispered to a horse, would allow the horseman to control each horse who came within his sphere of influence.*

The proceedings were ended by the minister cracking a whip across the knuckles of each initiate. As dawn approached and before the horsemen would return to their houses, they would sing the ceremonial toast:

Here's to the horse with the four white feet,

The chestnut tail and the mane -

A star on his face and a spot on his breast,

And his master's name was Cain.'

To this account Stapeley had added a note in green ink: "Suspect Bloxham and Macbride are both members of this cult. Passed the barn Tuesday last at around ten o'clock and heard voices inside. Bloxham's stallion was leashed to a rail outside. I heard several men chanting inside something very similar to the words mentioned above. This appears to be some bizarre variation on freemasonry. MacBride, I believe, is a man of power as a man called Martin may also be, the latter having once been a blacksmith, an occupation much revered from ancient times. I have it on good authority from Jennings that the Squire holds regular meetings at this venue. I have also witnessed MacBride's power over horses. He exhibits much the same influence over women, so I am told by Jennings."

Holmes paused. A sudden noise had distracted him. He looked towards the study window and there, sprinting down the path between the tall beech trees, was the wild, dishevelled figure of Whitaker. He was gesticulating and appeared to be shouting excitedly, his hand clutching a cloth bag. Then he disappeared from view, and Holmes heard the door to the rectory open and a cry of surprise from Mrs Annis as the door to the study was flung open.

"It's gold!" Whitaker bellowed, his face suffused with joy. "I've found Boadicea's gold!"

Whitaker finished laying out the gold pieces on the white cloth and stood back to admire his bounty. On the other side of the table Holmes picked up his magnifying lens and began to scrutinise the collection.

"The torc is really magnificent," he commented, "and, judging by the detail here and the weight of the thing, would have been made for a person of wealth and status. What a pity it's been damaged."

"This clean break would indicate to me that this has been done deliberately," Whitaker replied.

"But why would that be? For what purpose?"

"As part of a ritual - an offering to the gods. You remember how in Tacitus's account, Boadicea calls upon the goddess of war, Andraste, to lend her aid in the Iceni's uprising? The tribes would have provided a sacrifice of worth. What better than a piece like this? Just look at it. It's astounding."

"The enamelled brooch. That's been fractured too."

"Yes, and also this necklace. Judging by the type of work here, I would have no hesitation in placing them at just the right period to coincide with the Celtic uprising."

Their conversation was curtailed by Mrs Annis who announced that Inspector Gould had been spotted making his way up the driveway towards the rectory. Whitaker hurriedly collected up the pieces of treasure and beat a quick retreat to the living room in order to photograph his bounty.

When he entered the study, the inspector seemed haggard and disconsolate. Holmes offered him a whisky and the two men sat either side of the fireplace, cradling their glasses.

"Inspector, I thought you might like to know I have acquired some information about Sir Ronald which may be useful to you in your investigation."

"Really?"

Holmes leaned forward and gave him the papers he had perused that morning.

"This information was given me yesterday evening by Henry Stapeley, the retired schoolmaster. He believes that both William MacBride and the Squire were members of an occult society called The Horseman's Word."

"And what exactly is that?"

"It's rather similar to Freemasonry, but has pagan or occult leanings. As you are no doubt aware, the Freemasons are a Christian oriented group, but the Horseman's Word pays lip service to the Devil. For that reason, I am dubious about its aims."

Gould perused the papers he had been given.

"It seems an odd business, if you ask me."

"It appears to be a horse cult and there are distinct degrees or grades of office. I would imagine that Sir Ronald would have attained the highest of the ranks and from what I have learned about MacBride, I guess he was equal in status. Who the other members were I have really no idea, save for Martin, the blacksmith - that is, according to Stapeley."

"You are suggesting that this information may have a bearing on Sir Ronald's death then?" Gould asked.

"I can't be certain. As you may recall, the two men were fairly close, and it strikes me as more than coincidental that both have met untimely ends. It is possible that one of the group may have had a motive for killing both of them. There is another factor to consider. Oakenfull had made an enemy of MacBride by his constant attempts to humiliate him. Bishop Hunter has given me a deal of evidence about the background to their rivalry. By the way, have you considered that Oakenfull may have died of food poisoning?"

"I was aware that he'd died suddenly, but I recall there was nothing particularly suspicious about his death," said Gould.

"I'm not so sure. What if he was indeed poisoned? Yesterday I spoke to Mrs Annis about this business. She told me something very interesting, inspector. Apparently, the day prior to his death some wild mushrooms were left on the doorstep of the rectory with a brief note."

"Was the note signed?"

"It was not."

"Did Mrs Annis keep the note?"

"No, she didn't."

"Did she eat the mushrooms herself?"

"Mrs Annis doesn't care for mushrooms but wild mushrooms were a special delicacy of Oakenfull's. He ate them on a regular basis. It was several hours after the meal that evening that he began to develop acute abdominal pains from which he never recovered."

"So what are you suggesting?"

"That Oakenfull was murdered, of course."

"As you say, Mr Holmes, these are interesting and plausible theories but at present they are entirely unproveable."

Holmes stood up.

"What worries me, inspector, is the thought that somewhere in this community we may have a murderer who has struck not once, but twice. And as things presently stand, neither of us has any proof as to who that person might be."

"Very well, then, I admit it. I am a member of the Horseman's Word."

George Robinson had flung down the scissors he had been sharpening and wiped his hands on his apron. His face, which was bathed in perspiration, was twisted into a frown.

"I'm not here to judge you, Mr Robinson," said Holmes. "It is of no consequence to me whether or not you are a member of a secret society. I am simply seeking information about two of that society's members, both of whom were known to you. Now, can we just sit down sensibly together and talk about this?"

Robinson passed a hand through his shock of wiry grey hair and subsided into a chair. He stared uneasily at Holmes.

"What do you want me to tell you?"

"How many members are there in your group?"

"Thirteen, prior to the deaths of MacBride and Squire Bloxham."

"Was there any enmity between the members of the group?"

"Not that I know of."

"And what grade did Squire Bloxham occupy in the society?"

"He was the master of our lodge. It was he who held the ceremonies of initiation."

"And how long had MacBride been a member?"

"I understood he'd been a member before he moved here from Cornwall, nigh on thirty years ago. He were the true master of the horse. Bloxham thought he knew a lot, but it were all book learning with him. MacBride was the master of the equestrian arts."

"Can you think why anyone should wish to kill Sir Ronald?"

Robinson shook his head.

"The members of our order had the utmost respect for Sir Ronald. Treated us fair, he did. With MacBride it was altogether different. He were unreliable. When the drink took him, he let things slip. That's why he came to a bad end, in my opinion."

"What do you mean?"

"He was seen twice summoning his horse in the marketplace. He used the secret word. Sir Ronald heard him do it. He were warned about it but he took no notice."

"You're suggesting that Sir Ronald may have resented him for that reason?"

"I'm not saying that. I'm just saying MacBride was a liability. He didn't know how to control himself. It was the same with women. They thought he was irresistible. Treated 'em the same way he treated the horses. Rode 'em and reined 'em in. They fell for it every time. Even made advances to our Mary, though she would have none of it. If you ask my opinion, Mr Holmes, I believe that no human being killed MacBride. It was the Devil's own work."

"Explain."

"Whatever killed MacBride was not of this world. Who in their right mind would have caused that amount of damage to the room? Why, even the windows were smashed. Why should anyone bother doing that? All those things broken, yet the table in front of him was untouched. It makes no sense."

"What are you saying, man, that the Devil himself killed MacBride?"

"I don't know what to believe. All I know is that some force entered that room and gave a great blow to his head. I am sure that no human hand could have done that. That's all I'm saying. MacBride supped with the Devil and maybe he came for him in the end."

The following morning, Mrs Annis laid the breakfast table and soon re - entered, carrying a large bowl of porridge. Within a few minutes Whitaker also came in, dressed in plus fours, hiking boots, a suede waistcoat, red shirt and cravat. Mrs Annis placed a silver platter in the middle of the table containing the morning post, then retreated. Whitaker greeted his old colleague, then, opening a buff envelope, announced:

"Ah, this may interest you, Holmes. The torc and other items about which I sent a telegram to the British Museum."

"Oh yes?"

"They have been provisionally dated at around AD 60."

"Which means ...?"

"That we have a date contemporary with the Iceni's revolt against the Romans. The treasure was probably buried on Thorsford Hill as a sacrifice to the gods. I'm more certain than ever that this was a ritual burial."

"So does that mark the end of your quest?"

"Yes, I believe it does."

"Then I shall, I think, be deserting you as of tomorrow. There is little more that I can do now, Charles. I have my suspicions of course, but only circumstantial data. However, I have much enjoyed my stay."

"You've been most welcome," Whitaker replied.

After Holmes had left the breakfast room, Whitaker scanned his post. Two bills, an enquiry about parish registers and a long cream envelope embossed with the initials "R. H." Whitaker, who recognised the monogram instantly, opened the envelope to reveal two sheets of cream foolscap writing paper, written in an untidy hand. It was from his old friend, Robert Houghton of Morwenstow.

"Dear Charles," the letter ran, "I was most pleased to hear from you again. I had imagined you were enjoying something akin to full retirement but from what you have told me, you have chosen to surround yourself with murder and mayhem. How ignobly sensational of you! Life here in Morwenstow is, at present, unutterably dull and I have nothing murderous to report, apart, of course, from my pursuit of the fox. Quite frankly, I miss the intrigues and skull duggery of Welcombe. Life in Morwenstow is, by comparison, a catalogue of monotony. I do very little these days, apart from sitting on the parish council, working on my histories of the Cornish saints and acting as secretary for the

Bristol Missionary Society. But to come to the point. You ask me about this fellow MacBride. He was indeed personally known to me during my time as the vicar of Welcombe. He was Romany by birth. In fact, his father was an immigrant who came to Cornwall by way of Ireland. During his time with us he made a reputation for himself as a self - styled "wizard" or cunning man. People came from far and wide for their charms to be renewed. This would happen once a year, usually in the spring. He was, however, a notorious swindler and confidence trickster and gambled away much of his ill - gotten gains on horse racing. You mention something called "The Horseman's Word". I fear I have no knowledge of this organisation, but I do know he had considerable influence over horses. I have personally witnessed his ability to stop a horse in its tracks by speaking to it in a certain way - a technique called "horse whispering".

"He had a book of astrological calculations and spells which he kept locked in a trunk in his cottage. It was an impressive looking volume, but I cannot vouchsafe as to its contents. He was, at one stage, a rival of mine, often conducting so - called "hand fasting" ceremonies. I complained to him, of course, but he simply took no notice. He had a voracious sexual appetite and I suspect that quite a few of his female clients fell for his charm. Among them he numbered at least two women of wealth and position. There was something very dashing and Byronic about him which women found irresistible.

"At one stage he had an accomplice - a young woman also of Romany extraction who came to the village with her parents for the annual horse trading. She soon set up shop with him and was equally proficient at the business of dispensing spells, aphrodisiacs and charms, especially to young women. At one stage she acted as a midwife in the village and was reckoned to have remarkable healing powers. Eventually, however, they fell out and she moved elsewhere. She gave birth to a child, which was MacBride's, and I do not know exactly what became of her. Maybe she rejoined her parents. I don't really know. She called herself Tamson Bright but I know that was not her real name, since I conducted the baptism for her. Her real name was Tamson Rachel Annis. She was a striking woman, large framed, with dark eyes and soft olive skin. There was something of the Spaniard about her."

As Holmes entered the room, Whitaker stood and greeted him. Down the corridor they could hear Mrs Annis talking to Augusta Bloxham in her usual full - bodied tones. Whitaker passed the letter to Holmes and the two men made their way into the study where a large fire was blazing cheerfully. They settled down in the leather armchairs by the fireside, awaiting the arrival of Lady Bloxham.

The door opened to reveal Augusta Bloxham. She was dressed in a long, black boucle dress, tapered at the waist, knee high boots and a short, green padded jacket. Her face seemed sad and wistful, and she seemed hesitant.

"Thank you, Mrs Annis."

Whitaker put the half - read letter down and ushered his tall, elegant, gaunt - faced visitor to a chair, where she sat, straight - backed, her hands folded in her lap.

"I felt I must see you both as a matter of urgency," she began. "There is something you should know. I have kept it to myself for so long now and frankly, I cannot bear it anymore."

Whitaker smiled reassuringly and extended his hand in support.

"Go on," he said.

"I thought I should tell you both the truth about my husband and William MacBride but you must understand that what I have to say now is strictly confidential. It may be that the police will have to be involved in this matter at some stage, but I do not wish it to become common knowledge in the village."

"I quite understand, Lady Bloxham. I can assure you your wishes will be respected," said Holmes, lighting his briar.

She released her hands and relaxed a little.

"May I offer you some tea?" asked Whitaker.

"No thank you."

"Then please continue."

"You must understand gentlemen, that William MacBride was a truly remarkable man. Our association with him began when he was employed as a part - time groom for my husband. William was quite unlike other men. He was gifted."

"So I believe," said Holmes.

"I know that he had something of a reputation for dishonesty, but he was a psychic of great power. My husband and I are – were, as you know - both spiritualists. We had been converted to the cause long before he came into our lives. In fact, we met him at a seance in Norwich. When our son died, he offered to help us contact him beyond the veil. We said we would pay him for his services, but he refused. He had great success and we were much comforted by the help he provided."

"MacBride and your husband were both members of a society known as The Horseman's Word?" asked Holmes.

"My husband had a great love of horses. He was initiated into the order many years ago when he was a member of the Norwich freemasons. When he came to Thorsford he was eager to establish a local chapter. He believed that MacBride would be an invaluable member because of his psychic powers."

"And was he?"

She nodded.

"He had the ability alright. He would talk to the horses in such a manner that Ronald would rely on him before a race to ginger the animal up. It worked every time - every time he was sober, that is."

"He had a drink problem?"

"He was very unreliable, especially when he'd been at the drink. In the end he crossed the line. Ronald could not forgive him for what he did."

"And what exactly did he do?"

"He spoke the Horseman's Word within the earshot of others."

"The Horseman's Word?"

"The secret word that no one must reveal outside the chapter. And this happened more than once."

"And what did your husband do about it?"

"He asked him to leave the order, but he refused. But there was something else."

She bent her head, revealing her long, slender neck. There was a silence. Then she spoke again, very softly, her head lowered.

"William and I - we were lovers."

"I see. Did Sir Ronald know of this?" asked Holmes.

"Not at first. After the seances held at Munnington Hall, I went to William's cottage in secret. I needed his support, but I knew that Ronald would never forgive me. It was an innocent liaison at first. I would take him things that belonged to our precious boy - his hairbrush, one of his cufflinks, an old diary he had kept before he had enlisted. He would practise psychometry with them. He even spoke with his voice. I found it deeply moving. I was certain it was him, speaking to me from the Summerlands. I felt a great sense of reassurance you see, of Christian love even, in his presence. I know it may seem odd saying this to you now, but it was true. William possessed great spiritual strength and I found that very comforting."

"And so you grew to love him?"

Augusta nodded.

"It was not a physical relationship – well, not at first. We would sit in that cottage and talk about all sorts of things. I learned about the beliefs of the Roma people, their customs and way of life. William was a mine of information. He had had no formal education, yet he was wise in the ways of the world. And he had lived a full life. He had loved women with all of his soul. I had never known a man with such a great and compassionate heart. It was on one of these visits that I told him I loved him. I don't know what I expected. Maybe I thought he would reject me. But he didn't. He spoke to me in a way that Ronald never could - from his heart."

"And after that?"

"After that we kept meeting at the cottage. We made love constantly. I suppose I thought that it would never end. That was folly, of course. I was deluding myself. One afternoon Ronald must have been riding in the area. He saw me leaving. After I had gone, he called on William and interrogated him. He admitted everything and they had words. When he got home that afternoon Ronald accused me of terrible things: of being a whore and an adultress, of bringing his reputation into disrepute - I told him I would leave Munnington Hall the following day but he said he would not allow it, that it would sully his reputation. So, in the end I stayed."

"And did Sir Ronald find it in his heart to forgive you?"

She shook her head.

"From that moment onwards, he turned his heart against me, and I knew that he was intent on revenge."

"Revenge - for whom? You or William?"

"For William. The night William was murdered - I must tell you about that. William had been drinking again. He had been at the Green Man all afternoon, drowning his sorrows. Ronald had left the hall in the afternoon and I did not see him again until the early evening. When he did return, I noticed his clothes were dusty and he looked strange - preoccupied. I asked him where he had been, but he refused to answer. The following day I heard that William had been bludgeoned to death. It is my certain belief that my husband killed him."

"But how can you be so certain?" asked Holmes.

"By his demeanour. A woman's instincts are rarely wrong."

"Then I will take your word for it, Lady Bloxham."

"I also found this among his belongings. It has bloodstains on it."

Reaching into her bag, she drew out a battered horseshoe and laid it on the study table.

Holmes peered at the item, turning it this way and that. Then he said at last:

"And did you not think of speaking to Inspector Gould about your suspicions?"

"I did not."

"Even though you knew your husband may have committed murder?"

"My husband may have ceased to love me, Mr Holmes but I consider the loyalty that exists between husband and wife to be a quality worth preserving."

Holmes gazed at her intently. Her own sense of loyalty had not been quite so robust when she had embarked upon her affair.

"Noble sentiments indeed, Lady Bloxham. However, I must tell you that I cannot just conceal this evidence from the police."

Lady Bloxham bowed her head.

"I understand."

She rose to leave.

"Mrs Annis will see you out. You may be required to give a statement to Inspector Gould, although I doubt you will have to appear in court."

"I shall do what is necessary, of course. Thank you for your time."

Holmes stood at the study window, watching her carriage leave. Flurries of snow were falling, whitening the driveway and the bare branches of the trees. He thought about the evidence she had provided. If Bloxham had truly murdered MacBride in a fit of jealousy, then it must have been he who had wrecked the inside of the cottage and smashed the window. Had he left the items on the table to suggest that MacBride had been the victim of some sort of ritual murder? And if so, who had murdered Ronald Bloxham? Clearly someone who had a knowledge of the Hall. Could that person have been Lady Bloxham herself? And did she have an accomplice?

As soon as Lady Bloxham had left, Holmes picked up the telephone and dialled.

"I'd like to speak to Inspector Gould. Oh, I see. When will he be back, then? My name is Sherlock Holmes. Yes, it's a matter of great urgency. Could you ask him to telephone me as soon as he returns? Thanks. My number is Thorsford 375."

Inside the "Archive Room", there was a smell of age. On one side, a series of dilapidated bookcases were stuffed to the brim with old papers, box files and cardboard boxes, marked in copperplate handwriting - Oakenfull's by the look of it. On the other side lay a jumble of dusty furniture, old, moth-eaten vestments, a broken rocking horse, three oak chairs with holed seats and a faded chintz sofa, spewing forth its horse hair. Holmes went to the window where he found a collection of small black candle holders and cleared them to one side to gain access to the window frame. He tried to open it but found that it was stuck fast, having been painted in on the outside.

He began to rummage through the cardboard boxes. A collection of damaged Common Prayer books, a large family Bible with a brass chain attached; a set of English Hymnals with faded gilt lettering were first. These he quickly discarded and scanned the ends of the boxes in search of the All Saints Day order of service. At last he spotted what he was looking for, filed in the S section. He took the box to the window ledge and opened it. "Notes on All Saints Day and Order of Service." Just what he was looking for. He skimmed through the document.

"All Saints Day is a celebration of the redeemed when we remember the souls of the departed and pledge our belief in the Holy Spirit. In 1725 Henry Bowne wrote: "When we leave this world, we lie down in our graves and rest from our labours. Sleep and darkness lay hold upon us, and there we abide to the last day, when the voice of the archangel shall awaken us that we may meet the Lord of Light and Day."

The popular notion that the dead are but 'sleeping' appears often on graves but we must remember that this is a pagan belief and originates from pre-Reformation times. Whatever we would like to imagine, the dead are the dead and all attempts to communicate with the spirits of the deceased are pure folly. So, on All Saints Day, we celebrate all those who have brought us close to the spirit of Christ..."

There was more of the same which Holmes did not bother to read through. It was turgid stuff, he thought, and less useful than he had hoped it would be. He put the papers to one side and began to rummage through the rest of the contents of the box. An obsolete funeral service pamphlet, a guide for missionaries, several letters from the Bishop, and what was this? A sealed foolscap envelope with an address label marked with the letters "MM". He hesitated for a moment, then ripped it open. Out fluttered a collection of grainy black and white photographs and a small paper bag. He opened the latter and found inside a long lock of dark hair, tied by a pink ribbon. He picked it up and placed it under his nose. A rich, heady perfume, sweet and rose drenched, drifted up to meet him.

He picked up one of the photographs. A young woman lay on a chaise longue, her legs spread eagled, her head thrown back. She was smiling, her eyes half closed as if she were half asleep. Her right hand dangled to the floor and her left clutched a glass. It was like looking at an Old Master for the porcelain flesh was etched against the darkness of the room. Above her, bending over her, stood a tall man with greying hair. He was dressed in a long dressing gown which fell open, revealing his bare chest. He was smiling, as if he and the young woman were sharing some joke. The depth of the photograph suggested it had been a slow exposure, for there was a slight blurring to the girl's hand where she had shifted slightly. There was something decadent about the picture as if the participants had thought up the notion of the photograph in some drunken, post-coital reverie. Across the bottom of the photograph Oakenfull had scrawled the words: "MM and me, rectory, summer, 1918."

Holmes lay the photo aside and leafed through the other pieces. There was a photo showing Mary Martin, the blacksmith's daughter, dressed as some sort of fairy. She wore wings and was dressed in a long, semi-transparent cloak. She was leaning against a tree, her long hair covering her breasts, laughing. The photo appeared to have been taken in a wooded area, possibly part of Wayland's Wood. There were other pictures, much more explicit. These he did not dwell on but returned them to the packet.

There was something strangely innocent yet obsessive about the images. He felt disturbed by them, yet part of him understood the terrible compulsion which must have consumed Charles' predecessor. He was about to thrust them into his jacket pocket when a piece of foolscap paper fluttered from the box onto the ground. He picked it up and examined it. Written in Oakenfull's hand, it consisted of three paragraphs and was entitled "The Goddess Andraste."

Who is this Great Goddess ? (Oakenfull had written.) Boadicea, Queen of the Iceni, invokes her prior to her great battle, supplicating her and praying for victory, yet she is mentioned but the once. Is this in fact the goddess called Andasta, worshipped by the fierce Vocontii of Gaul, a variant of Anu? Is she part of that great panoply of goddesses worshipped by the Celts, among them Dana, the Mother Goddess of the Tuatha de Danaan, associated with the hills of Kerry in Ireland, or in Scottish folklore the hideous hag Black Anu? Is this the same as the fearsome Morrigan, the death goddess, who wheeled as a raven over the bodies of slain warriors?

She is also Medb, the warrior queen of Connaught, of whom it was said that no king could rule unless married to her. Her armies invaded Ulster and killed its hero, Cuchulainn, and she was possessed of a voracious sexual appetite. In my own way, have I not succumbed to her power in insatiable desire for this young woman? She inspires my every waking moment and I live only for the feel of her warm flesh and the consummation of my desire for her. I am nothing without the power that emanates from her body. I worship the temple of her mons veneris. What am I saying? Sometimes I think I have gone down into the dark and will never return to the light of the Lord Jesus. Heaven help me, surely, I am lost.

Holmes looked up. He had been distracted by a sound from below. A spider was making its way slowly along a thin thread towards its cocooned prey which lay at the centre of the web. He watched in fascination as the spider squatted over its helpless victim and began to suck from its inert body. A terrible feeling of suffocation began to overcome him, and he left the room rapidly.

The phone had stopped ringing. Whitaker waited but it did not ring again. He stood in the hallway, listening. The silence was broken only by the ticking of the grandfather clock and the sound of his own rapid breathing. What day was it? Tuesday. Tuesday morning. It was the day Mrs Annis took the table linen to the village store ready for the laundry collection. He walked slowly to the scullery and peered through the crack in the door. Empty. So, then, she had not returned yet. He returned to the study and peered through the window. The path was deserted. Where was Holmes? Probably gone by now. He scanned the hill but could see no sign of his friend. He was alone in the house.

He returned to the telephone and waited for a good twenty minutes, but the silence closed about him like a glove. He decided there and then that he must act. He would send a wire to Gould from the village post office, then climb the hill, find Holmes and discuss the matter.

He had climbed the stairs and was about to turn down the corridor in search of his boots when a door opened immediately behind him. Before he could turn, there was a sharp blow to the back of his head and he fell to his knees, his sight fading to blackness.

The voices came and went, faint echoes as if heard in a dream. He was fading, slipping into sleep. He was cold, cold as ice. Cold as Death itself.

There was a voice now, somewhere outside the room, a voice that was familiar to him. He wanted to turn around, but he did not have the strength. As if in a dream, he saw the face of Mrs Annis.

Whitaker stirred in the wheelchair. His head ached and his

vision was blurred. He tried to move his hands but found they had been tied to the arms of the chair with thick rope. He realised now that he was in the locked room in the east wing, the place that had been concealed from him all along. And now he was here, he was beginning to understand why. Five women stood behind him, their eyes fixed on the altar. Around the room were several figurines, ancient representations of the Great Goddess whom Hebrews and Christians had abjured for so many centuries. And at the centre of the statues stood the figure of the ancient white horse. Here in this room, her acolytes had gathered to witness some arcane and ancient ritual. He could see clearly now as Sophia Annis stepped forward and lit the two beeswax candles on the altar. Then the five held hands and began to chant:

"Mighty Horse Goddess, Andraste.

She who is three parts in one,

She who is the three phases of the Moon,

She who waxes and wanes,

She of the Three Mothers,

She who is the Holy Trinity,

Mother and Grandmother,

Creator of all living things,

She whose bright cloth is embroidered with threads of gold,

We praise you.

Loud is your war cry, sharp are your spears and arrows,

You who flew across the battlefields, black as the blackest raven

Your bird cry filling the hearts of the living with dread,

We celebrate your power."

Whitaker shifted uneasily in the bed, then slowly opened his eyes.

He tried to sit up but found that weakness prevented him. From the side of the bed Sherlock Holmes smiled.

"Feeling a little better?"

"Where am I?"

"At home, at the Rectory. It's alright. Everything's under control. You have a visitor. Inspector Gould. Do you feel up to it?"

Whitaker nodded. Holmes helped his friend sit up in the bed and adjusted his pillows.

"What happened exactly?"

On the other side of the bed the comfortable, stocky form of Inspector Gould looked at the bedraggled, pale - faced clergyman.

"You had a narrow escape, sir. A very close shave it was. Had it not been for this gentleman arriving when he did, we might have lost you altogether."

The memory of the locked room and the women flashed through his mind. He reached for a glass of water and took a sip to assuage his thirst.

"I happened to return from the Archive Room earlier than I had expected," said Holmes. "I'd forgotten my pipe. When I came into the hall, I found your dog at the top of the stairs growling - kicking up a terrible fuss. I followed him and he led me to the east wing. Of course, when I saw you there in the chair, I realised something was horribly wrong. You were still semi - conscious, of course, but doubled up with stomach cramps. I saw what they'd given you to eat. Some sort of deadly mushroom. *Amanida phalloides* - death cap, as it turns out. It took me a while to get you out of there. Your housekeeper is a strong woman. She put up quite a fight, by the way. The others didn't seem to have much of an appetite for it and fled. Sophia Annis was the moving force behind it all. It seems that they were all part of some goddess worshipping group who regarded men as inferior. It was almost as if she and her friends had no self - will left, as if they were mesmerised. Sophia was totally in control. I realised then that I had to do something about your condition pretty quickly, so I got a bottle of vinegar from the scullery and made you down it.

Drastic treatment, I'm afraid, but it had to be done. Once you'd vomited up the ghastly stuff, I knew you had a fighting chance of survival. They'd also given you a sleeping draught - a mixture of valerian and vervain I subsequently discovered - a knockout drink. That explains why you were so comatose when I found you.

"Plus the bang on the head," intervened Gould.

Whitaker looked apprehensively about the room.

"Don't concern yourself," said Gould. "The women are all now in custody."

"The Inspector here has already interviewed Sophia Annis and her friends. They have made full confessions regarding the murder of Ronald Bloxham. After some persuasion, I might add!" said Holmes.

"But what on earth was their motive?" asked Whitaker.

"Revenge, in a word. Well, at least on Sophia Annis's part. And, of course, you, Charles, would provide a suitable subject for a sacrifice."

Holmes leaned forward.

"You will recall the letter send to you by the vicar of Morwenstow? Houghton had not given any dates in his letter, so it was difficult to work out the timescale. But he was in his seventies, so this would have been thirty or so years ago. "Dark eyes and olive skin". Surely, I reasoned, it could not be mere coincidence - *Tamson Annis was the mother of Sophia Annis.*"

Whitaker gasped in astonishment.

"I confess I read it but did not see the connection."

"Sophia Annis was the illegitimate daughter of William MacBride, Charles. The information about her from Robert Houghton of Morwenstow clinched the case. That was what I had hoped to tell you, Inspector."

"I'm only sorry we didn't get to you sooner!" said Gould. "It appears that the day MacBride was murdered, Annis had gone over to his cottage by way of Wayland's Wood. When she was halfway down the hill, she saw Bloxham and MacBride going into the cottage. It was obvious to her that MacBride was the worse for drink. She thought she would wait until he'd got rid of his visitor but when Bloxham left, she entered and found him much as you had discovered the body much later. It was obvious to her that there had been a violent struggle. Before he left, Bloxham had added a few touches of his own, to give the impression that he had died of unnatural causes."

"Augusta Bloxham believed as much," added Holmes. "She told me us she had had an affair with MacBride. She suspected that Sir Ronald had discovered their liaison and had confronted him with it. It appears that Sophia Annis was brought here when she was a young girl by her mother, Tamson, Her mother had followed MacBride from Cornwall where both had set up practice as cunning folk. When the mother died, Sophia and her sisters were fostered by an elderly couple in the village. Then, when she was fourteen, she was put into service."

"And she remained friendly with her father?" asked Whitaker.

"She adored him, apparently. She became very concerned about his drinking bouts and often got him out of scrapes. But she kept their relationship a secret all those years."

Whitaker coughed suddenly, his bruised ribs aching. When he had regained his composure, Holmes continued.

"Mrs Annis was in the habit of collecting wild mushrooms for Oakenfull. They were a delicacy of his. It's my belief that she gave him a portion of death cap. She won't admit it of course, but I'm certain of it."

"The same treatment she intended to mete out to you, Charles," observed Holmes.

"Only you were luckier," said Gould.

"I owe you a great debt, gentlemen," said Whitaker. "It seems you arrived in the nick of time."

"If I hadn't, by now you would be the other side of Hades, or whatever version of the underworld these ladies had prepared for you. You were most certainly chosen as some sort of sacrifice," said Holmes. "Remember, Charles, that Mrs Annis had killed before. The means of your intended death is horribly reminiscent of the first phase of what the Celts once called "The triple death" - a ritual sacrifice to the gods of the Celtic pantheon. When I intervened, Mrs Annis and her friends were chanting the name of the Morrigan - the warrior goddess of death and destruction."

Inspector Gould shook his head in disbelief.

"I can hardly believe that in the twentieth century we should even consider such events to be possible, Mr Holmes," he said.

"Well, believe it or not, we have to accept it as fact," Holmes replied. "There is nothing more dangerous than religious zealotry, wouldn't you agree, Charles?"

But Charles Whitaker was staring out of the window at the hills beyond. The outline of the old figure was stark and clear, its chalk contours picked out by the cold November sun. On one side stood the dark margin of Wayland Wood, on the other the hill swept down to a broad, open swathe of flat fields. Here, centuries before, the tribe of the Iceni had cultivated the land, grazed their animals and performed their sacrifices to ancient gods. In the time that had passed since then, had humanity really changed or progressed? He did not think so. He thought of the mass slaughter of the Boer War and The Great War, and it struck him that in many ways his own age was more barbarous than any which had gone before. For a few moments his eyes filled with tears and he was lost in reverie.

About the Author

Kelvin I. Jones has been a prolific writer for a quarter of a century. Born in Kent in 1948, he has published many books about Sherlock Holmes, a trilogy about the sleuth, entitled 'The Peculiar Persecution of Sherlock Holmes, and the first ever study on Conan Doyle's interest in spiritualism, as well as numerous short story pastiches and articles about the Victorian detective (see R De Waal's 'Universal Sherlock Holmes,' online edition, 2000). He recently published Holmes' comprehensive work on Victorian criminology, 'The Art of Detection' as well as an edition of Holmes' much sought after monographs, 'Upon The Chaldean

Roots of the Ancient Cornish Language' and 'Upon the Tracing of Footprints'. Because of his wide - ranging knowledge of Victorian crime, and his exhaustive research into the work of Conan Doyle, he has been described recently by an American Holmesian as 'A Master Sherlockian.' Ed Hoch, the renowned American crime writer, has said of his Sherlockian work: "Kelvin I Jones reveals a sensibility and knowledge of 19th Century literature that extends far beyond the world of Sherlock Holmes." (Introduction to 'Sherlock and Porlock,' Magico, 1984). He is also the author of many supernatural stories, among them Carter's Occult Casebook, about a psychic Edwardian detective. Of his gothic tales, Francis King, the novelist and critic, has written, "(Kelvin's work) piquantly suggest the work of a modern M.R. James." (Introduction to 'Twenty Stories.') His work is also cited in Ramsey Campbell's 'Meddling With Ghosts' (2002), where he is described as one of the 'James gang.' He has recently published a biographical edition of the work of the lyrical Victorian poet and 'decadent', Ernest Dowson, and has edited an annotated six volume edition of the anonymous Victorian erotic memoirs of 'Walter', entitled 'Satyriasis.' He has published a two - volume edition of Krafft Ebing's ground breaking work on Victorian deviant sexuality, 'Psychopathia Sexualis.' His definitive 1984 study of the literary influences in the Holmes stories, 'Sherlock And Porlock,' was reissued in 2019 in a greatly enlarged edition.

A BRIEF SOCIAL HISTORY OF TOBACCO USE IN SHERLOCKIAN ENGLAND

By Wendy Heyman - Marsaw

Historical Overview

"I have been guilty of several monographs. They are all upon technical subjects. Here, for example is one 'Upon the Distinction Between the Ashes of Various Tobaccos'. In it I enumerate a hundred and forty forms of cigar-, cigarette- and pipe tobacco, with coloured plates illustrating the difference in the ash."

~ Sherlock Holmes, The Sign of Four

27 July, 1586 is the commonly accepted date when Sir Walter Raleigh formally introduced tobacco to the English court from the colony of Virginia.

But it was actually in 1573 that Sir Francis Drake brought tobacco in large quantities to England from "The Americas". Prior to that time, around 1565, English sailors obtained chewing or smoking tobacco from their fellow Spanish or Portuguese counterparts. Drake discovered a method of curing the tobacco so it could be stored and transported economically. The East India Company viewed tobacco (and many other exotic items) as a source of potentially great income. Soon the exchequer was enjoying considerable revenues from the huge increase in the popularity of smoking. The relatively high cost of tobacco meant that the dried leaves were largely smoked in small, clay pipes. Broken remnants of these are still regularly found along the banks of the Thames.

In 1586, the sight of the colonists puffing away on their pipes started a craze at Court. (Legend says that in1600 Sir Walter Raleigh tempted Queen Elizabeth 1st to try smoking but to no avail.) The court behaviour was copied by the population as a whole and by the early 1600s the smoking habit was commonplace and had become a cause of concern. King Philip I of Spain denounced it. King James I wrote "A Counterblast to Tobacco" in 1604 which dismissed smoking as "loathsome to the eye, hateful to the nose, harmful to the brain [and] dangerous to the lungs". Regardless of these warnings, the number of tobacconist shops grew to over 7,000 by 1614.

In 1619, in an effort to maintain tight control over the excise, King James I ordered that all tobacco must enter the country via London. Pipes were to be made only by a group of manufacturers in Westminster, to whom he granted a Royal Charter. This first group of pipe makers was reincorporated by Charles I in1634 under the name of "The Tobacco-pipe Makers of London and Westminster and England and Wales", which today is "The Worshipful Company of Tobacco Pipe Makers and Tobacco Blenders".

In 1638 around 3,000,000 pounds of Virginian tobacco was sent to England for sale and by the 1680s Jamestown was producing over 25,000,000 pounds of tobacco per year for export to Europe.

The demand for tobacco continued in England. Its supposed medical properties were extolled during the "Great Plague" of 1665-66. The pungent smoke was thought to protect against disease miasmas. At the height of the plague, smoking was made compulsory at Eton public school.

During the 17th and 18th centuries, coffee was king rather than tea in England. Over 2,000 coffee houses sprang up in London and catered to a wide variety of patrons, many of whom had adopted the penchant for smoking. Merchants, writers and politicians were amongst the many who filled these coffee houses. Runners went from coffee house to coffee house to relay the events of the day. On December 23, 1675, King Charles II made a proclamation to suppress coffee houses. Widespread citizen protests caused the rule to be revoked on January 8, 1676.

Snuff

"He held out his snuffbox of old gold, with a great amethyst in the centre of the lid. Its splendour was in such contrast to his homely ways and simple life that I could not help commenting upon it."

~Dr. John H. Watson in "A Case of Identity"

Snuff, a finely ground tobacco with or without flavorings, originated with the Spanish in the 16th century. Snuff use gained popularity in England at the time of the "Great Plague" due to its perceived medicinal properties. But it also had serious detractors, among them Pope Urban the 8th who threatened to excommunicate snuff-takers.

By the 18th century in England, however, snuff became all the rage amongst aristocrats. Its use became most popular during the reign of Queen Anne (1702-1714). Snuff was extremely popular among the George Bryan "Beau" Brummel-type Regency dandies. England began manufacturing snuff and some of the lower classes prepared it at home.

Snuff was taken from exquisitely crafted and ornate snuff boxes by the élite. Snuff boxes were made in two sizes – one for personal use and one for the table. It was taken generally between the thumb and index fingers and sniffed through the nose. Notables who used snuff included Lord Nelson, the Duke of Wellington, (who forbade the use of other forms of tobacco amongst his officers), Samuel Johnson and Benjamin Disraeli..

Nineteenth century England saw some scurrilous claims on the health and curative benefits of snuff including the ability to read without spectacles. Victorian England, however, generally became less tolerant of the habit and snuff started to be frowned upon. Snuff remained popular with the professions where it wasn't socially permissible possible to smoke or to be seen to smoke such as doctors, lawyers, judges, clergymen and miners. (Sir Arthur Conan Doyle obviously did not share the belief that smoking should be banned for physicians. He, himself, smoked, as did Dr. Watson.) Mycroft Holmes used snuff ("The Greek Interpreter"). Dr. Watson humorously compared snuff to "the devil's foot-powder" ("The Devil's Root").

The beginning of the end for snuff-taking was the invention of the automatic cigarette rolling machine in 1881 (which shall be examined later in greater detail.) Up to that point, manufacturers rolled cigarettes by hand at considerable expense. The First World War saw the virtual death knell for snuff, as cigarette companies literally flooded the trenches with free cigarettes.

Pipes

"It is quite a three - pipe problem and I beg you won't speak to me for fifty minutes'"

~Sherlock Holmes in "The Red Headed League"

Pipe smoking was the oldest form of tobacco use in England and endures to the present day. Historically clay pipes at first were used universally amongst pipe smokers. Clay was an excellent smoke, as the pipe feels nice in the hand, burns cool and imparts no flavour to the tobacco used in it. It was easy to come by and was available in an assortment of sizes. Although pipe smoking was believed to be a male-dominated experience (more on that later) lower class women would use it as well. (Catherine Eddowes, one of Jack the Ripper's victims, had two clay pipes in her possession when her body was discovered.) The smoldering pipe tobacco was generally taken into the mouth but was infrequently inhaled into the lungs as well.

In the 19th century, pipes began to be fashioned from an assortment of materials including briar, clay ceramic, corncob and glass. meerschaum (a soft white clay mineral) or beech wood and bog oak (an ideal material which is especially resistant to burning and provides a neutral taste during tobacco smoking). The classic English calabash pipe, although linked to Sherlock Holmes's imagery, was not described in the Canon and was first used by stage and screen actor William Gillette. It permitted actors to speak whilst smoking the pipe, as the leverage was better; a straight stemmed pipe would put more strain on the teeth making clear speech almost impossible. It also allowed the actor to put his hands on the pipe without distracting attention to his face. However, for Holmes, it would have been an impractical and unwieldy pipe.

Holmes kept his pipes and tobacco pouches scattered on the mantelpiece in his bedroom ("The Dying Detective") and was not particularly careful with them. He favoured just 3 types of pipes:

- a blackened (or dirty) and oily clay pipe. It is likely that this was at first a white clay or meerschaum pipe that became blackened by heavy use. His use of a coal from the fireplace to light his pipe would also tend to blacken a white clay pipe. He uses this pipe in several stories including "The Creeping Man", "A Case of Identity" and "The Solitary Cyclist". It is not taken with him on his adventures – its use was generally for "contemplative" purposes and was restricted to 221B.

- a cherrywood, often referred to as a "churchwarden" has a stem that is three or more times longer than an average pipe. It is associated with Holmes when he was in an "argumentative" mood. It imparts a cooler smoke since you are not pulling hot fumes right from the bowl.

- a briar pipe, somewhat older, used in *The Sign of Four*. Often such pipes were handed down from father to son and easily reconditioned.

Holmes generally held that pipes had more "individuality," with the exception of watches and bootlaces.

Briar pipes were the primary choice of 19th- century gentlemen. Briar is a particularly well suited wood for pipe making for two main reasons. The first and most important characteristic is its natural resistance to fire. The second is its inherent ability to absorb the moisture that is a byproduct of the combustion of tobacco. Briar is the burlwood of the white heath tree which grows in the region surrounding the Mediterranean Sea. The burl grows underground between the root and the trunk of the tree and can be harvested without destroying the arbour. The bulk of fine briar pipes are made in Italy. The burl can be crafted into beautiful shapes. Briar burls are cut into two types of blocks: ebauchon and plateaux. The former is taken from the heart of the burl while the latter was taken from the outer part of the burl. While both types of blocks can produce pipes of the highest quality, most artisan pipe makers prefer to use plateaux because of its superior graining. Briar bowl finish types include brushed, carved, rustic, sandblast and smooth.

Pipe were available in over 12 basic shapes with a multitude of variations within each shape (for example, bowl size and bend). The pipe stem also permitted the customer further options to customize their pipes.

Inderwicks and Company, founded in 1797, is reputed to be England's oldest pipe maker. It could originally be found at 45 Carnaby Street. In more recent years, however, Inderwicks had a shop on Bear Street which in the 1990s became part of the Bear and Staff pub.

Loose Tobacco & Tobacconists

"I give you that for three days I have tasted neither food nor drink until you were good enough to pour out that glass of water. But it is the tobacco which I find most irksome."

~Sherlock Holmes in "The Dying Detective"

The tobacco store of Robert Lewis first opened its doors in St James's Street in 1787. It claims many famous customers, including Sir Winston Churchill (whose ledger and chair are still to be seen in the store), Oscar Wilde and many members of royal families from the UK and further afield. In September 1992 the business was acquired by the Dublin-based tobacconist James J Fox and the store has now traded in all forms of tobacco for over 230 years. The tobacconist shop frequented by Holmes and Watson was Bradley's (*The Hound of the Baskervilles*).

Sherlock Holmes's pipe tobacco was common black shag. Black shag in the Victorian period was much more coarsely cut than what we think of as shag today and it would have been a strong tobacco of fair to poor quality. Generally, shag tobacco dries out very easily and should be kept in an airtight container. Given the amounts Holmes consumed, however, it was unlikely to go stale in the Persian slipper he used as his main tobacco pouch at home ("The Empty House", "The Illustrious Client", "The Musgrave Ritual" and "The Naval Treaty"). He also kept the dottles of his day's smoking on the mantel piece to be consumed the next morning.

The use of tobacco in Victorian England was considered to be healthy since it was believed to ward off diseases like tuberculosis and pneumonia. Sherlock Holmes never seemed to have met a form of tobacco he didn't like. Nor was the term "moderation" one that could be applied to his smoking. Dr. Watson commented on how dense and foul the clouds of bluish smoke would have been when he returned home whilst Holmes was concentrating on a case. Watson once described Holmes as putting away a pound of tobacco in the space of a few hours ("The Man with the Twisted Lip"), an almost inhuman feat, since the average pipe smoker would go through an ounce or two in a week. Little wonder then that Dr. Watson describes Holmes as a "self-poisoner by cocaine and tobacco" ("The Five Orange Pips").

Dr. Watson's initial preference was a ship's tobacco ("*A Study in Scarlet*"). Tobacco made in this form is tied round tightly together with rope, and has been often prepared in this way by sailors on board British gunboats visiting Tamsui (off the northern tip of

Taiwan). It is said to have been much appreciated by everyone fond of a pipe. It may also have been flavoured with rum. He later switched to an Acadian mixture. This is a shag-cut blend of light and medium brown Virginias with a high percentage of fruity black Perique, a type of tobacco from Saint James Parish, Louisiana, known for its strong, powerful, and fruity aroma. The Tobacco Institute of the United States (founded in 1958) states that Perique has been shipped out of New Orleans for more than 250 years. The Acadian blend had a mild, naturally sweet, pure tobacco flavor.

Most men of the period preferred tobacco blends and would often have a custom blend mixed at their tobacconist. Up until 1986, additives were not permitted in tobaccos made in England. For this reason, these tobaccos were referred to as English blends even though aromatic tobaccos were manufactured all over the world. A true English blend is considered to be any blend consisting of Oriental tobaccos, and most notably Latakia. This tobacco is a specially prepared and originally produced in Syria and named after the port city of Latakia. It has an intense smoky-peppery taste and smell. Too strong for most people's tastes to smoke alone, it is used as a "condiment" or "blender" (a basic tobacco mixed with other tobaccos to create a blend), especially in English classic blends. The most common English blend consists of Latakia, Virginia and Perique. Depending on how much Latakia is mixed into the blend ultimately determines the overall strength of the mixture, described as a mild, medium or full-bodied English blend.

Cigars and Cigar Divans

"You don't mind the smell of strong tobacco I hope?"

~Sherlock Holmes in A Study in Scarlet

Unlike his pipe tobacco, Holmes's taste in cigars was definitely more discerning, with his preference being Cubans. But rather than keep these fine, expensive cigars in a humidor, he preferred to keep them in a coal scuttle near the fireplace.

The word cigar originated from "sikar", the Mayan-Indian word for smoking. This became "cigarro" in Spanish, although the word itself and variations did not enter common usage until the mid-18th century.

Cigars, more or less in the form that we recognize today, were first made in Spain in the early 18th century, using Cuban tobacco. At that time, no pre-made cigars were imported from Cuba. By 1790, cigar manufacture spread north of the Pyrenees, with small factories being set up in France and Germany.

The Dutch began making cigars, using the tobacco from their Far Eastern colonies. East Indian Cigars were also available and were very strong in flavour. ("The Speckled Band").

Entering a tobacco house during the time of James I, each customer would be greeted by a statue of an elaborately plumed aboriginal North American Indian with a giant pipe – as can still be seen today inside the window of James J. Fox at 19 St. James Street, one of the oldest cigar merchants in the world.

The roots of the United Kingdom cigar scene can be traced back to 1814, when officers returned from the Peninsular War with cigars gifted by their fellow Spanish officers. The officers' messes and gentlemen's clubs of London started to seek out fine examples of the smoke, made with tobacco from Cuba.

The production of "segars" began in Britain in 1820, and in 1821 an Act of Parliament was needed to set out regulations governing their production. Because of an import tax, foreign cigars in the UK were already regarded as a luxury item.

The coffee houses of the 17th and 18th centuries evolved into "Cigar divans", which specifically catered to tobacco smokers. These venues featured musicians and poets. The cigar divans became highly successful and were very fashionable establishments for men. The original divan was thought to be Mr. Giddon's Cigar Divan, opening at 42 King Street on 8 February, 1825, by Anne Giddon. The idea had come from Giddon's brother who travelled extensively in the East. The salon, it was said, was hung "like an eastern tent, the drapery festooned around you...."

What is now Simpson's in the Strand first opened in 1828 as a chess club and coffee house and then became known as "The Grand Cigar Divan". It soon became known as the home of chess, attracting such luminaries as Howard Staunton, the first English world chess champion, through its doors. Today the main restaurant is still called "The Grand Divan".

By 1845 tobacco replaced coffee as Cuba's chief export and cigars became a symbol of wealth for Europeans. Soon cigar smoking was all the rage in Spain and finally the rest of the Western World. There was a growing demand for higher quality cigars in Europe. Spanish cigars were superseded by those made in Cuba, which was then a Spanish colony. Cigar production in Cuba began in the mid-18th century. Pre-made cigars, European smokers discovered, travelled better than tobacco. One of the oldest cigar brands still in production, H. Upmann cigars, was founded in 1844.

The cigar band became an industry standard and many still exist, including Punch and Partegas which remain virtually unchanged today. By 1873 France owned the Havana cigar trade and was selling over one billion cigars a year. England was the chief importer at this time and began to influence a wider variety of shapes and sizes.

Cigar and tobacco use in general in Great Britain was affected by the active disapproval and disgust of Queen Victoria. Although her beloved Prince Albert was known to have enjoyed cigars since the 1840s, he was never permitted to smoke in her presence or in any room she occupied. It was only after the 1901 accession of King Edward VII - (an avid cigar enthusiast), made his first after-dinner pronouncement, "Gentlemen, you may smoke." that cigar smoking became *de rigueur* amongst society men. He also inspired a brand of cigar that exists today. It was also around this time that more new shapes evolved, which were inspired to some degree by the request of London financier Leopold de Rothschild and the Earl of Lonsdale.

During the Edwardian period, cigar smoking had become so popular amongst gentlemen in England and France that European trains introduced smoking cars to accommodate them.

Hotels and clubs boasted of smoking rooms. The after- dinner cigar, accompanied by glasses of port or brandy, also became a tradition if not a ritual.

Cigarettes

"I exchanged some remarks with him, therefore, and obtained his courteous permission to write the short note which you afterwards received. I left it with my cigarette-box and my stick, and I walked along the pathway, Moriarty still at my heels."

~Sherlock Holmes in "The Empty House"

Only after the Crimean war (1853-56) did cigarette smoking gain some popularity. By the middle of the 1860s cigarette shops began to appear in London. Up until 1881 cigarettes were handmade, expensive and accounted for a tiny fraction of tobacco sales. The advent of automatic cigarette-making machines by W.D. and H.O. Wills meant the cigarette had come to Great Britain to stay. The machinery employed by the company could produce 200 cigarettes per minute. This heralded a complete transformation of the tobacco market. By drastically reducing production costs, these machines provided mass production for new mass markets. In the early 1880s "Wild Woodbine" had become one of the most popular brands in the country and the price of cigarettes dropped as low as a penny. Year on year cigarette sales grew dramatically and consumption steadily increased by 5% per year.

Because cigarettes were sold in paper packets, it was common practice to insert a piece of cardboard in order to keep the cigarettes from being crushed. This led to the practice of putting pictures on cards in the packages. Sets of cards were produced with one card inserted per pack. This marketing scheme would encourage consumer loyalty to achieve a complete set. It worked extremely well.

Cigarettes did not always have an appeal to the upper classes. This culture worshipped their cigars and pipes at the expense of the cigarette and felt that the latter was commonly associated with the effete and those from the East. The cigarette was perceived as a miserable apology for the manly pleasure of a cigar or a pipe. The cigarette smoker was a passive consumer, whilst the pipe or cigar aficionado was knowing and discriminating. But the cigarette became elegant and fashionable among society men as the Victorian era gave way to the Edwardian. The Pall Mall brand was introduced in 1899 by the Black Butler Company (UK) in an attempt to cater to the upper class with the first "premium" cigarette. Increasingly, jewellers were tasked with the creation of both personalized and ornate jewelled cigarette cases in silver and gold.

Cigarettes suited Sherlock Holmes and Dr. Watson very well. They were more portable than a pipe and tobacco and required less active attention. They were certainly more affordable than expensive Cuban cigars and could be used or discarded at a moment's notice with minimal waste.

The Social Impact of Smoking in Victorian and Edwardian England

"'This is Mrs. Merrilow, of South Brixton,' said my friend with a wave of the hand. 'Mrs. Merrilow does not object to tobacco, Watson, if you wish to indulge your filthy habits.'"

~Sherlock Holmes in "The Veiled Lodger"

For the middle to upper class societies, smoking was the purview of men whilst the social proprieties were governed by deference to women. A litany of rules of etiquette regarding smoking began in the 1850s and continued until the "Roaring Twenties". The 1860s ushered in a time when men who took pleasure in the "divine weed" developed a culture of connoisseurship. They wrote odes and even novels about tobacco.

A woman of means could not be seen to be smoking as it carried obscene perceptions of a "fallen woman" or an outright prostitute. Indeed, women who posed whilst smoking were common in Victorian erotic photographs. Only rebellious intellectuals and artists such as George Sand dared to challenge the strict censure of female smoking.

The rules for men evolved as smoking became a more popular occurrence. At first, there was more emphasis on the negatives of smoking in a general sense. In 1860s, "Habits of a Good Society" noted that "All songs you may see written in praise of smoking in magazines or newspapers, or hear sung upon the stage, are puffs, paid for by the proprietors of cigar divans and tobacco shops, to make their trade popular – therefore never believe nor be deluded by them."

"One must never smoke, again, in the streets; that is in broad daylight. The deadly crime may be committed, like burglary, after dark but not before."

> - Cecil B. Hartley, 1873 in - *The Gentlemen's Book of Etiquette and Manual of Politeness / Being a Complete Guide for a Gentleman's Conduct in all / his Relations Towards Society*

By the 1870s, as smoking continued to grow in popularity, social rules became more specific and restrictive and for the first time acknowledged the need for protection of the "fairer sex". In his afore mentioned book, Cecil B. Hartley wrote a litany of rules:

- One must never smoke, nor even ask to smoke, in the company of the fair. If they know that in a few minutes you will be running off to your cigar, the fair will do well – say it is in a garden, or so – to allow you to bring it out and smoke it there.

- One must never smoke in a room inhabited at times by ladies; thus, a well-bred man who has a wife or sisters, will not offer to smoke in the dining-room after dinner.

- One may smoke in a railway-carriage in spite of by-laws, if one has first obtained the consent of everyone present; but if a lady there, though she gives her consent, smoke not. In nine cases out of ten, she will give it from good nature.

- One must never smoke in a closed carriage; one may ask and obtain leave to smoke when returning from a pic-nic [sic] or expedition in an open carriage.

- One must never smoke in a theatre, on a race course, nor in church. This last is not, perhaps a needless caution.

- One must never smoke a pipe in the streets; one must never smoke at all in the coffee room of a hotel.

- One must never smoke, without consent in the presence of a clergyman; and one must never offer a cigar to any ecclesiastic.

- You should never smoke in another person's house without leave, and you should not ask leave to do so if there are ladies in the house. When you are going to smoke a cigar, you should offer one at the same time to anyone present, if not a clergyman or a very old man. You should always smoke a cigar given to you, whether good or bad, and never make remarks on its quality.

Victorian mores gained increasing traction and rigidity. Men retired to separate smoking rooms, often billiards rooms, studies or libraries, to smoke and drink whilst the ladies went to the parlour. Here men also had the type of conversations where women were excluded. It was a masculine retreat equivalent to the female domains of the morning room or boudoir.

In country homes it was easier to accommodate this segregation due to the prevalence of more social spaces. But even in town, middle to upper class folk actually looked to purchase real estate that had specific "private" areas with separate spaces for men to smoke. Thus, gender segregation became even more entrenched. It was said, by etiquette writer Jessica Sewell that the "pipe was the worst rival a woman can have...because it was never nagging or needy and offered calm pleasures. Indeed, it can be said that smoking and masculinity were conceptualized as a most private relationship. Tobacco was placed alongside a number of commodities, such as fine wine, tailored clothing and mechanical gadgets that could only be appreciated by tasteful and rational, bourgeois male consumers.

Smoking influenced men's attire and grooming as well. The previously mentioned 1870s Cecil Hartley's etiquette book stated, "...if you smoke or if you are in the company of smokers, and are to wear your clothes in the presence of ladies afterwards, you must change them to smoke in. A host who asks you to smoke will generally offer you an old coat for the purpose. You must also, after smoking, rinse the mouth out well, and if possible, brush the teeth." Lady Constance Howard in Etiquette: *What to Do and How to Do it* published in 1885, wrote that "In country houses in the evening gentlemen usually don a smoking suit, which suits are composed of velvet, satin, Indian silk, cloth braided, etc. according to the wearers' taste and finances. Slippers are worn instead of boots, but on no account what is called a 'smoking cap' – that is an article of male attire happily consigned to oblivion."

We know that Sherlock Holmes had at least three dressing gowns. One was an unfortunate "mouse coloured" one ("The Bruce Partington Plans" and "The Empty House") that he wore most often between cases as it suited his rather morose mood at those times. Holmes had two more presentable ones: blue ("The Man with the Twisted Lip") and purple ("The Blue Carbuncle"). It appears, from a review of Sidney Paget's illustrations, that he wore these as casual at home smoking attire. It is difficult to discern from the images whether he or Dr. Watson wore actual smoking suits, or more specifically smoking jackets. No illustrations of either Sherlock Holmes or Dr. Watson smoking in the presence of women could be found.

This "ritualistic" approach to smoking behavior continued into the 1890s when Lady Gertrude Elizabeth Campbell wrote in *Etiquette of Good Society* that "A gentleman...will never smoke in the presence of a lady without first obtaining her permission, and if, when smoking out of doors, he meets any lady, be she friend or foe, he will take his cigar out of his mouth while passing her".

Among the impoverished lower classes, there were no social stigmas or rules of etiquette to be followed with regard to smoking. Both men and women enjoyed a clay pipe of tobacco or a cigarette when finances permitted. The rules and rites governing the upper class had no influence. The mere notion of a separate smoking area was outlandish.

The vast slums of London, however, steadily evolved into more decent neighbourhoods, because of the Industrial Revolution. A new working class began to emerge. Working class males began to adopt some of the upper-class smoking traditions and trappings. They became aware of and tried to aspire to smoking as an important component in self-fashioning as did their bourgeois contemporaries.

The advent of inexpensive cigarettes in 1881 and King Edward's ascension to the throne in 1901 coincided with the increasing strength of the women's suffrage movement. February 1907 marked the largest open air demonstration ever held (at that point) – over 3000 women took part. In this year, women were admitted to the register to vote in and stand for election to principal local authorities. Smoking became an accepted habit amongst the more radical factions within this women's movement.

World War I proved to be a watershed in both the emancipation of women and the spread of smoking among women. During the war women took on traditionally male occupations. They also began to wear trousers, play sports, cut their hair and smoke. Attitudes towards female smokers began to change. The cigarette became a weapon to challenge traditional ideas about women.

Nevertheless, there still existed some resistance to these sociological changes. In Emily Post's 1922 book *Etiquette,* this is clearly evident: "In the country, a gentleman may walk with a lady and smoke at the same time – especially a pipe or a cigarette. Why a cigar is less admissible is hard to determine, unless a pipe somehow belongs in the country. A gentleman in golf or country clothes with a pipe in his mouth and a dog at his heels suggests a picture fitting to the scene; while a cigar seems as out of place as a cutaway coat. A pipe on the street in a city, on the other hand, is less appropriate than a cigar in the country, In any event he will, of course, ask his companion's permission to smoke." No reference to women's smoking is mentioned.

In the 1920s the Flapper movement consisting of young women who sought to flaunt society's social, political and economic constraints became an important group in the emancipation of women, They included cigarette smoking along with bobbed hair-dos, short skirts and very long and ornate cigarette holders. The cigarette became synonymous with women's emancipation – a kind of "Torch of Freedom".

A final anecdote involves Princess Louise, the sixth child and fourth daughter of Queen Victoria and Prince Albert. The Princess, who was known for her unconventional lifestyle, was a secret cigarette smoker. She somehow managed, perhaps with assistance from her brother Bertie (later King Edward VII), to find hideaways in Buckingham Palace where she could smoke. It was not until 1901, when her brother became king, that Princess Louise could openly enjoy a cigarette in the smoking rooms of the royal palaces. She died in 1939 at the age of 91 with an unpaid bill to cigarette shop R. Lewis Limited, located near the palace.

Rudyard Kipling and Arthur Conan Doyle were friends for many years. It may then be judged fitting to end this monograph with a poem about cigars written by Kipling that was first published in book form in *Departmental Ditties* written in 1886. It was inspired by a "Breach of Promise" case that occurred in 1885.

The Betrothed

Open the old cigar-box, get me a Cuban Stout,

For things are running crossways, and Maggie and I are out.

We quarrelled about Havanas – we fought o're a good cheroot,
And I know she is exacting and she says that I'm a brute.'

Open the old cigar box – let me consider a space;
In the soft blue veil of the vapour musing on Maggie's face.

Maggie is pretty to look at – Maggie's a loving lass,
But the prettiest cheeks must wrinkle, the truest of loves must
pass.

There's peace in a Lananga, there's calm in a Henry Clay;
But the best cigar in an hour is finished and thrown away –

Thrown away for another as perfect and ripe and brown –
But I could not throw away Maggie for fear o' the talk o' the town!

Maggie, my wife at fifty – grey and dour and old –
With never another Maggie to purchase for love or gold!

And the Light of Days that have Been the dark of the Days that
Are,
And Love's torch stinking and stale, like the butt of a dead cigar –

The butt of a dead cigar you are bound to keep in your pocket-
With never a new one to light tho' it's charred and black to the
socket!

Open the old cigar box – let me consider a while.
Here is a mild Manilla – there is a wifely smile.

Which is the better portion – bondage bought with a ring,
Or a harem of dusky beauties fifty tied in a string?

Counsellors cunning and silent – comforters true and tried,
And never a one of the fifty to sneer at a rival bride?

Though in the early morning, solace in time of woes,
Peace in the hush of the twilight, balm ere my eyelids close.

This will the fifty give me, asking naught in return,
With only a *Suttee's* passion – to do their duty and burn.

This will the fifty give me. When they are spent and dead,
Five times other fifties shall be my servants instead.
The furrows of far-off Java, the isles of the Spanish Main,

When they hear that my harem is empty will send me my brides again.

I will take no heed to their raiment, nor food for their mouths withal,
So long as the gulls are nesting, so long as the showers fall.

I will scent 'em with best vanilla, with tea will I temper their hides,
And the Moor and the Mormon shall envy who read of the tale of my brides.

For Maggie has written a letter to give me a choice between
The wee little whimpering Love and the great god Nick o' Teen.

And I have been a servant of love for barely a twelvemonth clear,
But I have been Priest of Cabanas a matter of seven year.

And the gloom of my bachelor days is flecked with the cheery light
Of stumps that I burned to Friendship and Pleasure and Work and Fight.

And I turn my eyes to the future that Maggie and I must prove,
But the only light on the marshes is the Will-o'-the – Wisp of Love.

Will it see me safe through my journey or leave me bagged in mire?
Since a puff of tobacco can cloud it, shall I follow the fitful fire?

Open the old cigar box – let me consider anew –
Old friends, and who is Maggie that I should abandon *you?*

A million surplus Maggies are willing to bear the yoke;
And a woman is only a woman, but a good Cigar is a Smoke.

Light me another Cuban – I hold to my first-sworn vows.
If Maggie will have no rival, I'll have no Maggie for Spouse!

Recipe: Smoker's Coffee

Serves 2

Ingredients: ¼ cup green crème de menthe, ¼ cup Tia Maria or Kahlua, 1 ½ cups hot, strong coffee, ½ cup heavy cream, whipped. Garnish: 2 "After 8" square or long chocolates

Mode: Divide the 2 liquors equally into 2 tall glasses – preferably with handles. Fill each glass equally with coffee. Top with whipped cream. Garnish with "After 8" chocolates.

About the Author

Wendy Heyman-Marsaw was born in New York City and moved to Canada in 1979. Her interest in the world of Sherlock Holmes was kindled by her father, a devoted deerstalker-wearing and pipe smoking Sherlockian. She began reading the Canon at the age of 8. Her father gave her a grey suede Lady Dunhill pipe whilst she was in University. Wendy frequented Dunhill's in New York City for her specially blended tobacco. She worked in advertising for over 35 years on numerous multi-national clients including Rothman's – Benson and Hedges. She is a close friend of the #2 cigar sommelier in the world. She has attended seminars on cigar history, manufacturing, current trends, and beverage pairings.
Wendy is a long-time member of three Sherlockian societies: The Sherlock Holmes Society of London, The Bootmakers of Toronto (where she is a Master Bootmaker), and The Spence Munros of Halifax.

She is the author of "Memoirs from Mrs. Hudson's Kitchen" (edited by Mark and JoAnn Alberstat, MX Publishing, 2017). Her articles appear in "Sherlock Holmes is Like – Sixty Comparisons for an Incomparable Character" (edited by Christopher Redmond, published by Wildside Press, 2018) and "Saratoga at the Finish Line From 'Silver Blaze' to 'The Crooked Man'" (edited by Donny Zaldin and Barbara Rausch, published by The Baker Street Irregulars, 2019). Wendy also has a website and blog that can be accessed at *www.mrshudsonskitchen.com*. Wendy and her husband reside in Dartmouth, Nova Scotia, Canada with their Miniature Schnauzer, Wolfie Watson.

HONEYDEW FOR THE NEWSPAPERS

By James C. O'Leary

In July 2013, the late Don Libey[1] posed this question on an online forum: "Dr[2] Watson uses the word 'honeydew.' Full particulars please; not just the Google gloss.[3]" I was intrigued and had some questions that I wanted to answer; how did honeydew tobacco get its name, what was it origins, what brand could the cardboard box received by Sarah Cushing have been? One does start by googling, but the paucity of information does force the researcher to delve deeper.

The first thing that turns up in a Google search of "honeydew tobacco" is the sweet secretions left like drops of dew by aphids or naturally secreted by the plants themselves. In *History and Status of the Green Peach Aphid as a Pest of Tobacco in the United States* by Frank Shirley Chamberlin (USDA, 1958) there is this quote: "Heavy infestations of aphids can severely stunt the growth of young tobacco plants in the field. As the initial distribution of aphids in a field is likely to be irregular, an uneven crop can result from early attacks. Stunting of older plants and withering of leaves may be caused by large populations of aphids. Their feeding on the foliage produces tobacco leaves of an inferior or worthless quality, this condition being accentuated in the relatively thin cigar-wrapper types. On such types of tobacco, which are harvested by cutting the whole plant, the yield and qualjty may be reduced by premature ripening of the lower leaves. Feinstein and Hannon have shown that aphid-damaged tobacco

---

[1] https://multichannelmerchant.com/news/remembering-don-libey/
[2] Don used the British abbreviation without period.
[3] This was a very nice pun on Google Glass. For those who don't remember that Edsel of the 2013 tech world, google it.

contains less nicotine than comparable undamaged tobacco. Injury is believed to be due mainly to the removal of plant juices but may be caused in part by injected salivary secretions absorbed and translocated by the plant. This deposition prevents normal curing and causes disfiguration due to the presents of adhering cast skins and sooty moulds."[4] Does this have anything to do with honeydew being a "kind of tobacco moistened with molasses?" There is no evidence that growers took the damaged tobacco and sweetened it to hide a substandard product. There is, in fact, evidence that growers took pride in producing a superior product. Early use of quotation marks around the term "honey-dew" would indicate it was perhaps named by analogy.

ORIGINS

According to *History of American Manufactures From 1608 To 1860, Volume 3* by J. Leander Bishop (Edward Young and Co., Philadelphia, 1868, third printing)[5], James Thomas, Jr., a manufacturer of plug tobacco, specialized in lighter, "bright" tobaccos that made him well-known in the US and Europe.

Plug or cut tobacco are cured leaves pressed together into a cake or "plug" and wrapped in a tobacco leaf, twisted and/or pressed, usually for chewing but can also be smoked in a pipe. It was sweetened with molasses, liquorice, or rarely, honey.

"The art of sweetening tobacco with mass liquorice was discovered about this time ["sixty years ago"] by Mr. Jesse Hare, also of Richmond, and this discovery may be said to be the first step taken towards elevating the business to one of national importance. "Honey Dew" tobacco, as several of the varieties containing this ingredient were afterwards called, yielded its supremacy at length to the bright-assortments subsequently

---

[4] http://ageconsearch.umn.edu/bitstream/157227/2/tb1175.pdf
[5]http://books.google.com/books?id=EtQrAAAAYAAJ&pg=PA527&dq=History+Of+American+Manufacturers+From+1608+To+1860,+honey+dew+tobacco&hl=en&sa=X&ei=DY8nUobMG-r94AOtkoDgBw&ved=0CDUQ6AEwAQ#v=onepage&q=History%20Of%20American%20Manufacturers%20From%201608%20To%201860%2C%20honey%20dew%20tobacco&f=false

introduced, and of which James Thomas, Jr., may be considered the pioneer and founder." (p. 527)

Another well-known name associated with honeydew tobacco is that of the Gravely family of Henry county, Virginia. According to Steve Rucker in "The Tobacco Industry in the City of Martinsville and Henry County,"[6] in 1792 "In1792, B. F. Gravely and Sons built a factory in Leatherwood. Benjamin is credited with adding the essence of liquorice to improve the flavour of plug tobacco. Around 1800, Gravely became world famous as a processor of plug tobacco." Their flue-cured bright tobacco was sold as the popular brands, "Payton Gravely," "J.G. Gravely Fine pounds," "Honey Dew," "Kate Gravely Fine 9 inch." John Redd Smith's article "Early Settlers of the Territory Now Occupied by Patrick and Henry Counties in Virginia"[7] notes:

> When I (the writer) was an undergraduate medical student in New York City, something over a half century ago, I walked into a fashionable tobacco store on Broadway and requested the proprietor to show me a plug of the very finest chewing tobacco. Without the slightest hesitation he reached up to a shelf and took down a plug of B. F. Gravely's "Superior," and laid it on the counter with an air of finality, as if there could be no room for discussion....Many years ago, when the great explorer, Henry M. Stanley, forced an expedition through six hundred miles of seemingly impenetrable forests to the rescue of Emin Bey [Mehmed Emin Pasha b. March 28, 1840 d. October 23, 1892], and when he and Emin met formally on the shore of the lake [Lake Albert, 1888], it seemed the proper thing for them to exchange diplomatic presents. Emil [sic] Bey's gift to Stanly included a pound of Peyton Gravely's "Honey Dew" tobacco.

---

[6] http://www.mhchistoricalsociety.org/2018/05/15/the-tobacco-industry-in-the-city-of-martinsville-and-henry-county/
[7] Pedigo, Virginia G. and Lewis G., *History of Patrick and Henry Counties*, Reginal Publishing Co., Baltimore, 1977. Originally published Roanoke, Virginaia, 1933.

Honeydew was a popular chewing tobacco enjoyed as "chaw" or in a pipe by both men and women in the US. Chaw was also very popular with sailors, from many nations, especially because of the fire hazard of smoking on wooden ships.

Honeydew spread throughout Europe and the world. "Honey-dew tobacco was advertised for sale in *The New Zealander* in Auckland at 4 shillings a pound in 1852 and described as 'The best in town.' "[8]

THE CARDBOARD BOX

How did Jim Browner use tobacco? There is actually no evidence within the story to form an opinion. No pipe or sealskin tobacco pouch in evidence; no quid in his mouth. No cigarettes or cigars. In fact, the cardboard box might even have been someone else's discard picked up from the trash. While English sailors were more likely than the average Briton to chew tobacco, any conclusion one could make would be mere guesswork.

While one can find many vintage honeydew tobacco tins, especially W.D. & H.O. Wills Gold Flake Honey-Dew cigarettes, cardboard would appear far more ephemeral. A clue, though, can be gleaned from W.R. Loftus' *"The Tobacconist"* A Practical Guide to the Retail Tobacco Trade in all its Branches.[9]

Cut Honeydew. ---Honeydew is a general name given at the present day to leaf-tobacco of a light colour that has been pressed after a slight damping into frames of moulds, and then sold either in a cut or an uncut state. Not having undergone fermentation to any extent like shag or Birdseye, honeydew is of necessity strong-smoking. It is, in fact, Cavendish without the dark colour which the great bulk of Cavendish possesses, unless sold in stamped custom wrappers, without the molasses or liquorice used in the preparation of sweet Cavendish. As very little water is added to the leaves employed in the making of honeydew, it is requisite to

---

[8] http://www.tinderbox.co.nz/clay_pipes.html
[9]Simpkin, Marshall & Co., London, 1881.

charge a higher price for it that for shag or birdseye in order to compensate for the loss of the profit realised by selling these tobaccos in a damp condition. The Hence honeydew is consumed chiefly by the well-to-do classes, and by those only amongst them who can tolerate or enjoy a strong smoke. *It is rarely sold loose. The different makers send it out almost entirely done up in fancy packets of various sizes.* [Emphasis added.]
Loftus expands on this in the section *Packet Tobacco*:

> The increasing sale of almost every kind of tobacco in packets of definite weight, ready made up and labelled, has greatly changed the character of the retail trade throughout the country. All difficulty as to loss of weight by drying up in stock is thus removed; for, apart from the cases in which the tobacco is enclosed by the manufacturer in lead foil, which practically prevents evaporation of the moisture, each package is sold to the customer as of the weight invoiced by the manufacturer, no allowance being made or expected for any difference of weight caused by keeping, so long as the tobacco remains enclosed in the original package, and has evidently not been tampered with since it came into the hands of the retailer.

Under the subhead **Cake and Roll Tobacco**, Loftus says both cavendish and honeydew come in two types, sweetened and unsweetened and "sweetened tobacco must, by law, be enclosed in stamped Government wrappers before it can go into home-consumption. A heavy fine is imposed for any violation of this rule."

So, apparently, honeydew and other tobaccos were sold to local tobacconists directly imported from the tobacco manufactures in pre - weighed packets, with the sweetened type of cake tobacco further enclosed in official wrappers.

In my online search I came across a photo of a yellow(ing) cardboard box of honeydew tobacco. In 2012, renovations of the Inverness Steeple, in Inverness, Scotland, uncovered papers wrapped in wax paper tied in sisal string. Those papers along with other modern day items, including a Nokia cell phone were placed in a time capsule that November, to be opened in 100 years' time, in 2112. Then in May 2013, there was another find: "Joiners working at Inverness town steeple on the corner of Bridge Street and Church Street have uncovered another time capsule during the historic building's renovation works. This earlier find is believed to date from 1878 and is the second discovery within the past 8 months. It predates, by 45 years, another package dating from 1923 which was discovered during October 2012 in the steeple. Tony Russell and Jordan Fraser of D.Y. Fraser Joiners, Inverness were carrying out works on the interior of the steeple building for The Highland Council when Tony revealed the find on Thursday 9 May 2013."[10] In a recess that was later covered over by a staircase Russell and Fraser found a Havana cigar box which contained:

- A booklet published by the American Sabbath Tract society itemising "The brief grounds serving to prove that the Ten Commandments are in full force and shall remain so..."

- A Savings' Book of Inverness Bank dated 1878;

- A notebook with the signature of Angus McNeill;

- A small envelope with a Penny Brown Stamp posted in Manchester on Jan 1878 and addressed to – Mr D.C.Taylor, Tobacconist, 1 Church Street, Inverness;

- Inside the envelope were receipts dated 1877 from Sutton Company Parcel Express and their agents Robert Paton of Glasgow; and a Happy New Year message on a memo from Alexander Taylor, Pawnbroker, Manchester to Mr Taylor in Inverness.

- Headed notepaper of the Prudential Assurance Company, 62 Ludgate Hill, London;

---

[10]

https://www.highland.gov.uk/news/article/7051/inverness_town_steeple_reveals_more_secrets_from_the_past

- 3 Promotional cards itemising "Free Fishing Days on the River Ness" published by the Inverness Advertiser in February 1878, and

- A small 'Honey Dew' tobacco box containing coins including old pennies and shillings with dates ranging between 1851 and 1877.

Based on the coins inside the box, Greg Ruby, in a private conversation, surmised the box was about three inches square (the average human ear is about 2.6 inches square). The cover has a printed red ribbon reading "Bright Flaked Honey Dew" but no other markings as to size or brand. Holmes says of the box sent to Miss Cushing, "The box is a yellow, half-pound honeydew box, with nothing distinctive save two thumb marks at the left bottom corner." This description would fit the box shown; nothing distinctive, just the type of tobacco, not even the weight of the contents, although Holmes and most other tobacco users would probably be able to tell the amount. Now we have an example of a honeydew cardboard box.

About The Author

James C. O'Leary is a long-time Canoncentric Sherlockian with an interest in Higher Criticism and Chronology. He irregularly posts on the 'I Hear of Sherlock Everywhere' blog and in various scion publications. His own blog is: Others Perhaps Less Excusable – The wide, wide world of Sherlock Holmes. Member of the Speckled Band of Boston, Sons of the Copper Beeches and diverse other scions.

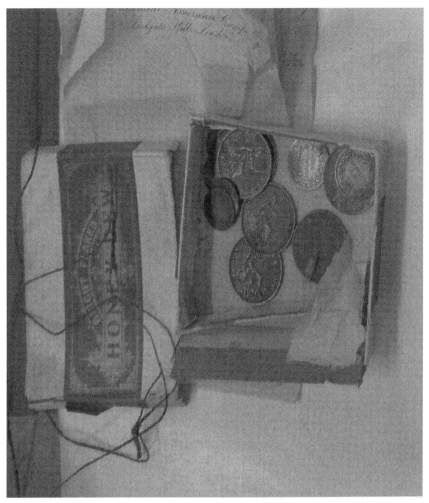

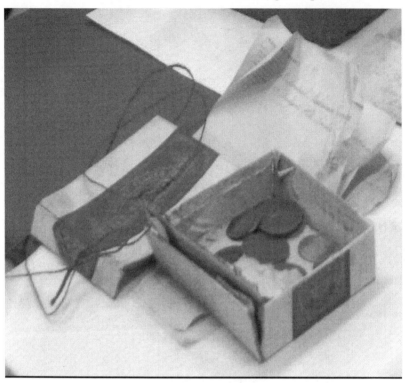

NO FIRE WITHOUT SOME SMOKE

By John L. Hicks

'The pipe draws wisdom from the lips of a philosopher and shuts up the mouths of the foolish; it generates a style of conversation, contemplative, thoughtful, benevolent, and unaffected; in fact, dear Bob – I must out with it – I am an old smoker. I have done it up the chimney rather than not do it...'

~William Makepeace Thackeray

"GENIUS," says William James, Sherlock Holmes's great contemporary, "in truth, means little more than the faculty of perceiving in an unhabitual way." 1 The Great Detective of course had that faculty in a higher degree than any other man of his time. Another philosopher, Thomas Carlyle, who was also living during the period of Holmes's early cases, speaks of genius as the "transcendent capacity for taking trouble first of all," 2 and Holmes, again, undoubtedly qualified. In *A Study in Scarlet* he remarks, "To a great mind, nothing is little."

But where and how, one may ask, did he acquire the "faculty" of observation and the "capacity" for taking pains? His musical talent, his aptitude for scholarship, his scientific ability - these were doubtless all inherited from ancestors that produced the French artist Vernet and the American scholar and scientist Oliver Wendell Holmes. The Master himself says, in *The Adventure of the Empty House*: "I have a theory that the individual represents in his development the whole procession of his ancestors .... ` He would not have evolved such a theory if his own qualities had not offered evidence supporting it. "To some extent," also, as he declares in *The Greek Interpreter*, "systematic training" increased his facility. His power of observation and his faculty of patiently attending to details, however, cannot be wholly explained in this manner. Moreover, his ability to use the data he gathered by observing carefully and not neglecting details-his great power of deduction - could not have been due entirely to heredity and training. It is true that in *The Greek Interpreter* he attributes his artistry in reasoning partly to his ancestors and offers as proof the superior abilities of Mycroft, but this is only a partial explanation.

A close study of the Sacred Writings reveals that Sherlock Holmes's great powers of concentration were due largely to his pipe-and primarily to his briar pipe. Mycroft, of the keen mind and capacious memory, was exceedingly lazy; indeed, he could be greatly moved only when, as *in The Bruce-Partington Plans*, the welfare of his country was threatened. He received inspiration from tobacco, but the tobacco was in the form of snuff.

Sherlock was not only a thinker but also a man of action, and he, significantly, smoked a pipe. The difference in the forms in which the two brothers used tobacco explains their dissimilarity in temperament.

No one can seriously question that the Master preferred a pipe to cigars and cigarettes. He smokes a pipe in thirty-five of the sixty cases in the Canon, probably does in three others, and in still another, talks about his pipe without, as far as the reader knows, actually lighting it. 3 He smokes nothing but a pipe in twenty-nine or, if one includes the doubtful instances, thirty-two instances. He definitely indulges in cigars in eight tales and probably in one other, and in cigarettes definitely in nine and probably in one other. In only ten cases does he smoke cigars and/or cigarettes but not a pipe. In eleven tales there is no mention of smoking by Holmes, but there is no reason to believe that the great man stopped the habit at any time, especially since these cases are scattered throughout his career. Holmes very likely smoked a pipe during the adventures recorded in the eleven tales in which there is no reference to smoking, as well as during those of the ten in which Watson names only cigars and cigarettes.

The great man's liking for a pipe began early in life and lasted long; in fact, one cannot doubt that he still smokes one as he contemplates the industrious bee. The earliest mention of Holmes's lighting a pipe is in *A Study in Scarlet,* which records an adventure of 1882. 4 The pipe that he enjoys in *"The Gloria Scott"* is, of course, on "one winter's night" when he tells Watson of his first case. The last reference to a pipe is in *The Creeping Man,* whose date of occurrence is 1903, the year of his retirement.

Most admirers of Sherlock Holmes have believed that his favourite pipe was made of clay. "Let us consider our data." In six tales Watson specifically mentions a clay pipe and since in three of these accounts it is a "black clay pipe," 5 perhaps the "old black pipe" of *The Creeping Man* is also clay. Watson tells us in *A Case of Identity* that the "old and oily clay pipe" was to Holmes "as a counsellor" and in *The Copper Beeches* that a cherry-wood pipe "was wont to replace his clay when he was in a disputatious rather than a meditative mood." The latter statement might at first seem to indicate that the clay was the favourite among Holmes's pipes, and it is undeniable that the Master was fond of his clay. But since *The Copper Beeches* is concerned with a case of the year 1890 and was published only two years later, the pronouncement can apply only to the first fifteen years of Holmes's professional career and may apply only to the time of the Adventures.

Concerning the "old black pipe" of *The Creeping Man,* Watson says, "As an institution I was like the violin, the shag tobacco, the old black pipe, the index books, and others perhaps less excusable." This remark occurs in an adventure of 1903, and the pipe referred to would seem to have been an "institution" during nearly all of Holmes's professional career. *The Creeping Man,* however, was not published until 1923, and it is hardly necessary to add that the doctor's memory was not always reliable, even for periods of much less than twenty years. As Mr. Anthony Boucher has pointed out, 6 another "institution" in this list, the violin, was not, according to the available evidence, played by Holmes after 1891. It may be that the "old black pipe" is not a particular pipe, but all the pipes that Holmes smoked, confused and blended in the mind of the somewhat elderly Watson. Finally, the Master did not treat his clay pipe as a devoted pipe smoker would treat a favourite: in *Charles Augustus Milverton*, he even "lit it at a lamp."

Now let us consider the briar. In only two of the adventures -*The Sign of the Four* and *The Man with the Twisted Lip* - does Dr Watson say that Sherlock Holmes smoked a briar pipe. In the former tale it is an "old brier-root pipe" and in the latter and "old briar pipe." The adjective 'old' is significant. When these two cases occurred, Holmes was probably thirty-four and thirty-live years old. Since a devotee of pipes does not call a pipe old, unless it has been in use for at least nine or ten years, and since Watson as well as Holmes was a veteran pipe smoker, the latter very likely had cherished this pipe from the time of early manhood. His clay pipe, it is true, is once called old; but for Holmes, who was careless in his habits, a destructible clay pipe would have been old if he had kept it six months. In addition to the two above-mentioned adventures there are several in which, although the word briar is not used, the pipe is almost certainly used.

One can hardly doubt that when in *Shoscombe Old Place*, Holmes lit "the oldest and foulest of his pipe' he was lighting the "old briar pipe" of *The Man with the Twisted Lip* – a pipe mellowed by eight more years of devoted attention. In the events of *The Priory School*, the events which occurred twelve years after *The Man with the Twisted Lip*, Watson speaks of the 'reeking amber of Holmes's pipe. A briar pipe might have an amber stem but not a clay pipe. The old briar pipe Holmes smoked at The Cedars at the home of Neville St Clair in *The Man with the Twisted Lip* - and it was presumably the same pipe he smoked on the journey to The Cedars – A man who planned his course of action of action as carefully as did Holmes would carry a durable briar rather than a breakable clay when he went abroad.

For that reason, the pipe he smoked on the doorstep of Pondicherry Lodge in *The Sign of the Four*, was likely a briar as was the pipe he had with him at Poldhu Cottage.in the *Devil's Foot.*

In *Charles Augustus Milverton*, disguised as a "rakish young workman," he did descend to the street with a clay pipe in his mouth, but that pipe was part of his disguise. In *The Yellow Face,* speaking of the pipe that Mr. Grant Munro left behind in the sitting room at 221B, Holmes affectionately calls it a "nice old briar," and points out that it has been given careless treatment, for it is charred down one side as a result of being lighted at lamps and gas-jets.

In twenty-two tales Holmes smokes a pipe of which the material is neither identified nor implied. Who can deny that in each instance the pipe is every bit as likely to be a briar as it is to be a clay? The evidence supports the theory that Holmes liked a briar pipe better than any other kind, and that he lit his "old briar pipe" oftener than he did any other.

One might infer from many of the tales that Holmes had only one pipe at some periods; for example, in *The Illustrious Client* he says to Watson, "Put my pipe on the table." If there are several pipes from which to choose, how does Watson know which one to put on the table? Holmes had in mind, of course, his favourite-his well-loved briar. Briar, clay, and cherrywood pipes are, by the way, the only ones mentioned in the Sacred Writings. Neither Holmes nor Watson ever mentions a curved stem; it is possible, however, that the Master followed the fashion of his time and did have one or more pipes with curved stems.

Watson, divers times, speaks of the help that Holmes received from his pipe. He calls it "the companion of his deepest meditation"7 and his "meditative pipe." 8 When the Master attacked the mystery of the death of Sir Charles Baskerville, he prepared to spend several hours of "intense mental concentration" by asking Watson to leave and to have the tobacconist send up2 a pound of the strongest shag." When he was working on the problem of the disappearance of Neville St. Clair, he sat up all night with a briar pipe and an ounce of shag- and of course he solved the mystery.10 He smoked a pipe when he tackled the problem of the abduction of the only son of the Duke of Holdernesse,11 when he pondered the mystery of the disappearing bridegroom of Miss Mary Sutherland,12 and when he became "lost in the deepest thought" concerning the problem, brought to him by Lord Bellinger and the Right Honourable Trelawney Hope. 13 Frequently, when he had a particularly difficult matter to consider, he smoked two or more pipefuls in succession: for example, in *The Hound of the Baskervilles* and *The Man with the Twisted Lip* (these incidents are referred to above); in *The Red-Headed League*, which was a "three-pipe problem"; in *Thor Bridge*, in which he smoked two pipefuls in a row; in *The Crooked Man*, in which, having gathered some facts, he "smoked several pipes over them, trying to separate those which were crucial from others which were merely incidental"; and in *Silver Blaze*, in which he devoted a whole day to rambling "about the room with his chin upon his chest and his brows knitted, charging and recharging his pipe with the strongest black tobacco."

The evidence is so great that one might easily conclude that Holmes did not solve a single difficult case without the help of his pipe. It is true that in *The Norwood Builder* the Master spent a sleepless night smoking innumerable cigarettes; but it is also true that on the following morning he was nervous and pessimistic about the prospects of his client.

Colonel R. D. Sherbrook-Walker, in a recent article, states that Holmes was not a discriminating user of tobacco but was merely a slave of habit. 14 He cites the great man's choice of shag; his custom of smoking a before breakfast pipe, composed of all the plugs and dottles, left from his smokes of the day before all carefully dried and collected on the corner of the mantlepiece, 15 his puffing too rapidly (he allotted "fifty minutes to three pipefuls

16); his practice of keeping his tobacco in the toe of a Persian slipper, where it would dry out and be covered with dust. No real lover of pipes and good tobacco can help deploring the lack of refinement of the Master's palate17 and the carelessness of his habits. But it is unjust for one who likes the more subtle and expensive blends of tobacco to assert that a smoker who prefers a strong and coarse tobacco does not enjoy his pipe. Sherlock Holmes was faithful to shag because he liked it, His uneducated palate and eccentric habits, moreover, did not detract from the aid and sustenance he received from his pipe and his shag.

It is reported that on one occasion when Thackeray visited his friend Alfred Tennyson, they smoked shag tobacco while praising Miss Barret's poetry. 18 Great Victorians, both early and late, had a preference for shag as an aid to ratiocination.

NOTES

1. *Psychology*, ch. xx.

2. Frederick the Great, bk. IV, ch. 3.

3. l am indebted to the references in the concordance by Jay Finley Christ (*An Irregular Guide lo Sherlock Holmes*), but l have made the following emendations. Dr. Christ includes The Mazarin Stone among the tales in which Holmes smokes a pipe, but one cannot be sure he lights it. Holmes smokes a pipe in Shoscombe Old Place, which Dr. Christ does not list. And Dr. Christ includes "The Gloria Scot" among the tales in which Holmes smokes a cigar, but his instance seems to me to be doubtful.

4. I am using the chronology suggested by Edgar W. Smith in "Dr. Watson and the Great Censorship," BSJ (NS) 2 (1952), 138.

5. The Blue Carbuncle, Charles Augustus Milverton, The Copper Beeches, The Hound of the Baskervilles, A Case Identity, The Red Headed League.

6. "Was the Later Holmes an Impostor?" in *Profile by Gaslight.*

7. The Valley of Fear.

8. The Solitary Cyclist.

9. The Hound of the Baskervilles.

10. The Man with the Twisted Lip.

11. The Priory School.

12. A Case of Identity.

13. The Second Slain,

14. "Holmes, Watson, and Tobacco," *The Sherlock Holmes Journal,* 1 No. 2 (September 1952), 7-12.

15. The Engineer's Thumb.

16. The Red-Headed League.

17. A lack of refinement in regard to tobacco, but not to food. See Fletcher Pratt, "The Gastronomic Holmes," BSJ (Ns) 2 (1952), 94-99.

18. Lionel Stevenson, 'The Shantyman of Vanity Fair' (London, 1947), p. 105.

About the Author

(Editor's note: this article first appeared in the *Baker Street Journal,* in January 1955 and is reproduced here for the first time by permission of the present editor of the BSJ. Despite several lines of enquiry, alas, I have been unable to trace any of the descendants of Mr Hicks to gain their permission to reprint this fine piece.

THE DORSET SQUARE BUSINESS

By David Marcum

We had rambled west that night after our return to London, ranging to Paddington and beyond, perhaps going too far without considering the threat of rain. Our earlier arrival in Baker Street had been very late, as we'd no wish to remain in the Hampshire village of Ecchinswell, following the completion of our latest distasteful investigation. After paying the cabbie, we had stood outside our front door before spontaneously deciding to walk a little distance. Leaving our bags just inside, we ambled back the way we'd just travelled, eventually crossing Edgware Road, and then down Praed Street, and past the station, where we had only just arrived less than an hour before, on a very early train. We didn't speak, our minds turning over the events of the previous day.

We'd been summoned to one of the downs, three or so miles north of Litchfield, where a terribly mutilated corpse had been discovered near a rabbit warren. It was too beautiful a spot to have witnessed such a horrific crime, but the thought crossed my mind, while Holmes made his initial investigation, that there were likely stories at that site of similar viciousness from ages past, unknown to us and never to be told. At least justice might be found in this case for the young schoolteacher, cut down so tragically.

The details of the affair were straightforward, and yet so shocking that the full account can only be placed with those other records of a similar nature in my tin dispatch box, which is kept under lock and key. I will never forget the long vigil that we kept by the warren as the daytime beauties of Watership Down faded and were lost in the creeping darkness of night. It was only in those very late hours, when the human soul's tenuous link to its clay is at its weakest, that the villain revealed himself.

Inspector Dunleavy, who had joined us at the warren, had to be restrained from taking vengeance upon the mad slayer. We had not known until then just how close were his relations to the poor victim, for the inspector is a man who keeps his emotions tightly in check. It was of no concern to the murderer that we prevented the inspector from carrying out his own form of justice. Rather, it was to save him from becoming a killer – although he would never be the same, regardless of what happened that night. Moreover, I suspected that the murderer's final days in Broadmoor – for there was nowhere else that someone so insane might be placed – would end abruptly at the hands of another inmate.

At some point during our walk, Holmes and I each seemed to have found a way to move past the terrible events of what we had seen earlier that night. We had looped west, and then back again, returning to our door in Baker Street just as the sky was beginning to lighten.

We entered and retrieved our bags. Upstairs, we paused upon the first-floor landing and wished each other a good night, having left Mrs. Hudson a note, explaining that each of us intended to sleep late that day. Holmes entered his room, and I continued up another flight to my own. My chamber, on the west side of the house, looked out upon the poor little rear yard where our diminutive plane tree eked out its bleak existence. Beyond, on the back windows of the houses opposite, I could see a few reflected streaks of the sun, rising in the east.

I had pulled off my coat and was reaching to undo my necktie when an urgent pealing of the doorbell filled the pre-dawn silence, followed by a frantic pounding upon the door. This marked the start of our involvement in what Holmes would later discreetly call the Dorset Square Business. With a sigh, I turned, opened my bedroom door, and quickly descended, hoping to reach the street door before poor Mrs. Hudson was awakened – although that was unlikely.

As I passed by Holmes's room, he came out, a wry smile upon his face. He followed behind me, and then we were at the front door. I undid the locks and pulled it open revealing a constable, about to pound on the door again. He arrested the motion of his upraised fist.

"Doctor Watson!" he cried. He was a young fellow, not more than twenty-five, and his eyes were wide. "Hurry, Doctor! Get your bag! Hurry!"

I made to return upstairs, but Holmes said, "I'll get it," and dashed toward the steps, belying that he was a man now in his mid-forties.

"And get my coat!" I called. He tossed a hand in acknowledgement and then rounded out of sight at the top of the landing.

I put my hands on the young constable's shoulders, trying to infuse him with some sense of calm. "What has happened?" I asked, giving him a small shake for emphasis. It appeared to work, and he regained some focus in his eyes, seeing less of whatever it was that had unnerved him.

"It's Riley, Doctor. He . . . he was on fire, and then he jumped through the window! I was walking past on my rounds when I saw him come crashing through, and then he hit the pavement. He . . . I ran up and rolled him back and forth until the flames were out, but he's hurt terribly. I blew my whistle, and Ernest came running. He's with him now. I knew that you lived nearby, so I ran for you."

I could hear Holmes returning. I reached down and took the constable's wrists, holding them up so that I could examine them in the faint glow of the street's nearby gaslight. As I'd suspected, his palms were burned from where he had taken hold of his fellow constable, Riley – whom I knew – in order to put out the fire. He would need treatment as well, and I feared that he would have scars for the rest of his life, as a payment for his thoughtless act of selflessness.

Holmes stopped behind me. I turned and took my proffered coat, while he set down my bag and began donning his Inverness.

He held my overcoat, which I pulled on. Then he handed me my hat, placed his own fore-and-aft cap upon his head, and leaned down to pick up my bag. I led the young constable outside, and Holmes pulled our door shut, locking it, and then nodding.

The constable pivoted smartly and set off down the empty street. Soon he turned the corner, and we stayed with him. Within just a moment or two, he led us into Dorset Square, and around to one of the buildings standing along the north side. Even without his help, I would have known by then that this was the correct destination, for the house was lit up, neighbours watching from a distance on either side, or out of their windows. There were several constables grouped before the house, clustered around a figure crumpled upon the ground. High above him, one of the tall second-story windows was shattered, the broken woodwork extending outward, indicating the direction that Riley had taken when he had defenestrated. I could hear muffled voices coming from the high window, although no one was looking outside.

I pushed my way through the men surrounding the figure lying in the street, calling for them to move aside so that I had more light. Kneeling, I nearly retched as I smelled the odour of charred flesh. And there was something else which made itself obvious just seconds later – the reek of lamp oil. The man's clothes were soaked in it. If the flames hadn't been put out, he would have been dead immediately from the fire, regardless of the injuries sustained after his great fall. And yet, there were still signs of life in him.

I carried out my examination, vaguely aware of Holmes questioning the men standing nearby. I gathered that the young constable who had summoned us was named Carrick. He repeated what he had told me – he was making his usual rounds through the Square when suddenly he heard a crash. He only had time to look up before Riley was hurtling through the air, a flaming nightmare arcing from the second - floor window, screaming until his impact with the hard street silenced him. He continued to burn even as Carrick rushed forward, rolling him and trying to put out the flames. I didn't have the heart to negate the lad's bravery and quick thinking by pointing out that he could have smothered the flames just as easily by throwing his heavy coat over the man, sparing himself from his own injuries. Turning the injured man probably hadn't done that poor broken body any good, either.

Riley was in terrible shape. Most of the burns seemed to be located upon his chest, and his clothing there was gone, burned away, as was much of the flesh. His ribs and sternum were terribly exposed in places, while charred muscle showed elsewhere. The pain would have been excruciating, but he had also suffered several broken bones when he impacted with the pavement, including an apparent skull fracture that had left him unconscious. There was no need to dose him with morphine – the time for that would come soon enough when he awoke. If he awoke.

The sound of the ambulance arriving was nearly concurrent with my awareness when I heard Inspector Lestrade's voice, mingled with Holmes', in questioning Constable Carrick behind me. I surrendered my place at Riley's side to the attendants from the ambulance, giving a few quick comments to the doctor who had accompanied them. It was decided that the nearest and best facility was St. Mary's Hospital in Paddington. Riley was quickly loaded, and then I checked to see if Holmes and Lestrade had obtained all that they needed from Carrick before packing him into the ambulance as well, in order to obtain treatment for his hands. I could see that the shock of the event was passing, as was the adrenalin that had kept his pain at bay. The young man was in for a bad time of it.

I turned back to Holmes and Lestrade, who was explaining the significance of the house. "This is Donald Armilus's residence."

My eyes widened, and I could see that Holmes was suddenly more interested as well, for this particular building had been of some curiosity to the public for the past year.

In late 1897, about ten months earlier, Donald Armilus had unexpectedly bought the house and moved there from the United States. He was the grandson of a Bavarian who had emigrated to America long before, making his money in a variety of dubious enterprises, beginning with catering to the lowest base desires of men involved in the California Gold Rush. His own son Frederic had taken that small fortune and greatly expanded it through various questionable and seamy New York ventures. Frederic's son Donald had inherited the entire thing, and dark rumours had swirled for years that receipt of this legacy was rushed along by the curiously suspicious death of both Donald's older brother, and then Frederick, after a short illness in which Donald allowed only one amateur nurse – a woman of little medical experience who was employed at one of the family's more disreputable business enterprises – to be in attendance.

Donald Armilus had been married several times and had always tried to crack the upper tiers of American Society, but he was never welcomed. The old American nobility had recognized him for what he was: A tainted and corrupt boor of low-class antecedents who would never be accepted as one of their own. Finally, in disgust, and no doubt in connection with a growing myriad of accusations and likely criminal indictments mounting against him, he had unexpectedly and mysteriously relocated to London, taking an uncharacteristically small house in Dorset Square as his refuge. Not long after, mere days in fact, he was discovered in the middle of the night, sitting alone in his second-floor study, staring fixedly across the room at a blank wall, screaming unceasingly – deep within a madness from which he'd never recovered.

He had seemed to be broken and bitter after his flight from America, intending to burrow in and live the life of a recluse. His only servants, hired by his British agent who had bought the house for him, had been a housekeeper and a handyman, who served as something of a butler and caretaker. It was this man who had been awakened by the screaming. He burst into the study to find that Donald Armilus had lost his mind. There was no apparent reason for his breakdown, and nothing could be done to abate his terrible shrieks. By the time that the police had arrived, his cries had already permanently damaged his throat. Only sedation caused the screaming to stop, and when he awoke, it began again, although by this point his vocal chords were so shredded that he would never make actual sounds again. Reports indicated that he was still screaming, locked away in an expensive institution in a fine London neighbourhood, staring straight ahead and making all the urgent motions of a man howling in madness and pain – but never producing a sound beyond his laboured breathing.

Afterwards, the house had remained empty. But just the week before, Donald Armilus's eldest son, a sly and spoiled young man named Nicky had decided to visit London – his first time there, as neither he nor his younger brothers had bothered to make the journey the previous year when their father lost his mind, or at any time since, for that matter. Nicky's solitary sojourn to the British capital, *sans* the company of his siblings, was widely reported in the press, and I saw him once, as I was passing through Piccadilly Circus on an errand related to one of Holmes's investigations. He was a dark thin fellow, nothing like his obese and thoroughly unpleasant-looking father. He had shadows of a heavy beard on his face, and a dissipated and unhealthy aspect about his bruised-looking eyes. The rumour was that he was an addict to all sorts of detrimental sensations, and unlimited access to his father's funds had only served to ruin him that much faster.

He stayed initially at the Langham, but an incident with the staff resulted in his almost immediate move to his father's house in Dorset Square, which had been kept intact throughout the past year by the continued residence of the housekeeper and the caretaker, both remaining in the family's pay, as if no one had remembered to terminate their services as being unnecessary.

Young Nicky had moved in on a Tuesday morning, to great fanfare and under the scrutiny of the press. On Wednesday morning, he was found in the second floor sitting room, the same room where his father had gone mad, dead from blood loss. His unclothed body was covered in a multitude of shallow cuts, all apparently self-inflicted from his small penknife. He had used his own blood to draw various obscene sketches upon the walls, a task that seemingly took hours, based upon the number of them and their curious and unfathomable complexity. Finally, when the limits of his blood loss had been reached, he succumbed, collapsing in front of the fireplace. His head had been too close to the flames, and the hair was singed off, and the skin of his face and scalp blackened and blistered – but by then he had been beyond any pain.

Lestrade had stopped by on other business the day after Nicky Armilus was discovered, and had casually mentioned the facts of the case, relating some aspects that hadn't been reported in the press. He seemed to question whether Holmes had any interest in helping to establish a solution, knowing as he did my friend's interest in all things *outrè*, but Holmes shut that notion down quickly. "I've heard far too many stories of the Armilus family from a few of my acquaintances in the State," he said. "Their offences against a few of the Vanderbilts, for instance, are unforgiveable. I have no interest whatsoever in becoming that agent who clears this affair up. Justice, however brutal, has been served."

"Fair enough," Lestrade nodded. "I wish that I had the luxury to take the same tack," he added, and then we moved on to other topics.

But now this curiously plain house seemed to have made an attack on yet another victim, this time one that didn't deserve it, and there was no question that Holmes would offer his assistance. Of course, mine was available as well, although I could never pretend to be as helpful or useful as Sherlock Holmes.

We made our way inside and up the stairs to the seemingly cursed study on the second floor. A grim constable was standing in the hallway beside the open door, and we passed him with a nod.

It was a fair-sized room, and with a curious open feeling, as there was very little furniture – a desk, a modest bookshelf, a couple of smaller chairs, and one big chair near the fireplace. There were a few small tables placed beside the three chairs. The two beside the smaller chairs were bare, but the one by the big chair had a book lying on it, and an ashtray.

The room was well-lit, with several gaslights spaced on both sides – two over the fireplace, and another pair near the door to the hall, which was the only entrance. There were several table lamps, all lit. Conspicuously, another was lying on the floor, broken. A bit of lamp oil had seeped out onto the rug, its smell tinging the atmosphere of the room. I suspected that this was the source of that which had soaked Riley's clothing.

The wallpaper was a light tan with a small pattern that initially seemed innocuous, but upon further inspection appeared to suggest a much more subtle and objectionable image. I was unexpectedly reminded of the Ripper murders of a decade before.

There were two other aspects of the room that demanded one's attention. The first were the collected sketches in blood that filled every available space along the walls, and even some spots of the great rug that covered most of the floor. They were vile, and one had to wonder about what Nicky Armilus had seen in his life that could provide him such with fodder. In a few places above the desk, where he had stood during his artistic frenzy, Nicky had painted similar subjects on the ceiling. As a physician, I'm aware that a just a small measure of blood can seem like a great deal, and that the human body can stand to lose a sizeable quantity of it before expiration, but the amounts that had been used to decorate the room were simply astounding. It was now dried to a crust brown colour, but the coppery scent was still in the air, and I could only imagine how it must have looked when it was fresh, red, and wet and shining in the gaslight.

While Holmes immediately commenced his investigation of the room, Lestrade and I stood to one side, conversing softly.

"We were told that Nicky Armilus had brought a number of important documents with him from New York, and that someone from America is coming immediately to take charge. I assume that these are the papers that are there in the desk. I glanced through them, but it's more than I can decipher. In any case, we don't know yet what had happened here, so we've been leaving a man on duty. Riley's shift started last night at sunset. We've had men on similar duty since the last death, and no one has reported any problems. I wonder," he added, "why Riley chose to sit in here, rather than on a chair in the hallway. I'd hate to spend a moment more than I had to in this charnel room."

He drifted into silence and shifted his gaze to Holmes, now standing at the desk, and paying careful attention to the tobacco jar on one corner. It was a tall thing, white Delft porcelain, with the word *Tabac* written on the side in complex and twining script. Decorating the jar alongside the word was a pudgy representation of the god Mercury, a rather sheepish smile on his face. I wondered just what he had to do with tobacco.

Holmes noticed me watching. "Watson, can you examine the book on the table? Lestrade, see what you can determine from the shelves."

The inspector and I separated, and I walked to the big chair near the fire. Examining the slim volume, I saw that it was covered with a thin layer of dust. Picking it up, I determined that it was written in French. My limited knowledge of the language revealed that it was of questionable nature – not surprising, considering whose house we were in. "Did Riley speak French?" I asked.

Lestrade, bent down at the bookcase to look at the titles, said, "No. Why?"

"This book is written in French, although I don't think that he was reading it. The dust indicates that it hasn't been handled in several days. No doubt it was something that Nicky was enjoying before his death."

Lestrade grunted. "There's an empty space here – probably where it was shelved." He straightened. "I couldn't recommend any of these books, although I'm not surprised at their titles. The rich are interested in the most deviant sorts of things."

I glanced at Holmes to see that he'd moved from the desk to join me at the big chair, and that he was looking at the table before us. At first, I thought that he was also looking at the book, but then he reached into the ashtray beside it, plucking something from it and putting it into one of the small envelopes that he habitually carries for the collection of evidence. Placing it in his pocket, he asked, "Did Riley smoke?"

Lestrade nodded. "He rolled his own."

"How many other men have stood guard here since Nicky Armilus died?"

Lestrade thought for a moment. "Two. Eckstien and Templeton. Riley was the third."

"Do either of those men smoke?"

"No, they don't. Why?"

"I have an idea about what has happened here, but there is more that must be determined. Can we speak to the man and woman who make up the household staff?"

"Certainly. I'll get them up here."

"No, perhaps downstairs would be better. I think you'll agree that this room is rather off-putting."

We moved downstairs to the large kitchen, located in the basement. Holmes indicated that he wished to speak first with the housekeeper. Her name was Lila Ring, a big woman with long, dark, and unbound hair. She watched with a grim eye as we settled around the table. "This house is cursed," she began, without prompting. "From the time the fat father arrived, I knew that he was doomed."

Lestrade raised an eyebrow. "If you knew, why didn't you do something to prevent it?"

"Why prevent it?" she countered. "A man like that – a family like that – they deserve to reap all that they have sown."

"Be careful, my girl," said the inspector. "That kind of talk will land you in chokey. It isn't just the father and son now. One of our own has been afflicted as well."

"I am truly sorry to hear that," she said. "They said that he set himself on fire and then threw himself out of the window."

"That seems to be the case."

"I warned him not to go in that room. He could have done his duty from downstairs, or if he had to be that close, he could have sat in a chair in the hallway. But when I went by last night, he was in there, sitting in the master's chair. Is it any wonder that he fell victim as well?"

"Fell victim to what?" I interjected.

"The curse. The evil that men do follows them like a cloud and getting too close can destroy even a good man. And your constable seems like a good man. Will he live?"

"We're not sure," I answered evasively.

"Aye," she nodded. "I have that sense as well. My vision of his future is vague and uncertain."

"So, you think that you have The Sight?" scoffed Lestrade. "If so, why didn't you see this coming?"

"Did I not say that I warned him? But he ignored me. There is only so much that I can do. Can I save all of them who has set their feet on a path to destruction? Should I? The threads of fate are woven already. They were fixed for the master and his son long before they arrived here, and well-deserved too. I'm sorry that your constable was caught up in that same net. I tried to warn him, but it was his own path to choose and follow."

Throughout this exchange, Holmes had been silent. Now he spoke. "You are from originally from America, I believe."

She nodded, warily. "But not since I was a wee child. How did you know?"

"Certain aspects in the tonality of your speech. You have been in England for much of your life, but certain qualities of your American background are unmistakable. You were initially raised in one of the southern states."

She nodded. "My family was from Shooting Creek, in the mountains along the North Carolina and Georgia border, not far from Tennessee. We'd lived there since coming over from England in the early 1600's. I'm named for my ancestor, ten generations back, who came over then with a large party and settled in the wilderness. She was a wise woman who was originally from Anglesey, of the Blood of Nial."

Welsh. That, I thought, explained her colouring and notable visage.

"Druids," said Holmes.

"She had The Gift," explained Lila Ring. "As do I."

"We're more interested in down-to-earth explanations," countered Holmes, and the woman scowled.

"You should have a care as well, Mr. Holmes," she said. "You also choose to walk a dangerous path."

Holmes ignored the warning. "Has your family in America ever have any dealings with Donald Armilus, or his children?"

She shook her head. "How would I know that? My parents came back to England years ago, and we lost track of our American kin. I'd never heard of Donald Armilus or his son until I was hired by the master's agent last year, when the master decided to move to England. After his madness, his living death, it seemed as if no one thought to close up the house or sell it, and so I simply stayed, continuing to receive my pay for keeping the place liveable."

"And the agent continued to fund the upkeep of the house? To pay for the coal and the gas, and any other maintenance?"

"He did."

"What about food and tobacco, and other daily staples?"

"We still receive an allowance for all of it – the food, and the laundry as well. Not tobacco, though. No need for that. Bill Kilbride – he's the caretaker – doesn't smoke, and neither do I. We both thought that at some point it would be realised that we were still here, keeping up an otherwise empty house, but we didn't want to disrupt a comfortable arrangement before we had to, and so we didn't say anything to anyone. Then, a few days ago, the agent came by, and it turned out that he hadn't forgotten about us after all. He knew all along that we were taking their money for doing practically nothing. That's when he told us that the son would be staying here soon. He made sure that the house was in good shape – which it was! – and soon after, the son arrived. He was as much of a devil as his father."

"In what way?"

"It was obvious by the way he talked and the things that he said."

"Do you have any idea what happened to them both – the father and son – and now the constable, to cause such a result?" asked Holmes.

She shook her head decisively. Lestrade looked impatient, and Holmes, seeming to have heard all that he needed, stood and thanked her for her help. As she walked out, he asked for her to have Kilbride sent in.

Normally at this time, Lestrade would have asked several questions, but he seemed strangely subdued, as if putting the matter completely in Holmes's hands. We remained in silence for the short time until Bill Kilbride entered the room.

He was a small man, about Lestrade's size, with the same lean, quick energy about him. He had a full head of hair that was more salt than pepper, cut rather short. Whitish whiskers gave an ashy look to his face. He walked with a rather rolling gait as he crossed the room. When he was closer, I could see that his skin had a leathery tanned look, and his hands were rough, with enlarged knuckles. There were several old scars across the backs of his fingers, and a faded blue-black tattoo peeked from underneath his cuff, although I couldn't see what it depicted. He nodded and took the seat across from us that was indicated by the inspector.

"Mr. Kilbride," said Holmes, "I suspect that you've been interviewed by the police extensively following the death last year of Donald Armilus, and then again after his son's peculiar demise a few days ago."

The man nodded and swallowed. "No doubt about that. But I couldn't tell them anything that seemed useful." He glanced at Lestrade. "Isn't that right, Inspector?"

Lestrade grimaced. "We're still considering it."

"Were you aware of Mrs. Ring's ideas that these men were under some sort of curse?" I asked.

Kilbride shook his head, smiling fondly. "She talks a great deal of that sort of thing – dark visions, and terrible destinies. She's warned me before, a time or two, and yet here I sit. Let the grocer forget to include an item in the weekly delivery and she's ready with a pronouncement of his doom. And yet," he added, as the smile drained from his features, "she has been right on several occasions – when old Mr. Whitaker on the next street died, she'd told me a week before – privately, you understand – that his time was nearly up, and that was just from the two of them having a passing conversation. The same for Lydia Striker on the next street – her with child, and Mrs. Ring knew when the girl's husband went to sea, that he wouldn't be coming back."

"And the Armilus men?" asked Holmes. "How close to the mark were her predictions in those cases?"

"Well," Kilbride replied, leaning back a bit, "she said they'd come to no good end, right from when we met them, but that's no surprise, is it? I thought the same thing, and I don't have any special gifts."

"I know that you were interviewed after the events last year, and again the other day," said Holmes. "Do you have any new theories considering last night's tragedy, and what happened to the unfortunate constable?"

Kilbride shook his head. "None at all. Mrs. Ring said it's because he insisted on going into that cursed room on the second floor. I know that I've stayed out of it since then, but not just because of that. Since the younger Armilus died so peculiarly, the police have been here, keeping an eye on the papers, until someone from America can arrive to take charge. The local agent didn't want the responsibility, I'm told, and it was him that summoned the police to watch the place. I was told not to leave, or to make any plans about a new billet."

"It's been a pretty nice one for you so far," said Holmes. "All told, the Armilus family probably didn't live here much more than a week during the entire time that you've been employed."

"That's right. It was much more normal for the place to be quiet as a tomb, with Mrs. Ring going about her own business, and me mine."

"And what is your business?" asked Holmes.

"Well, it doesn't take much to keep up the house, as you can imagine. With most of it standing empty, I hardly ever go upstairs at all."

"Not even to relax in the sitting room, for instance – smoking the master's cigars, or using his tobacco or brandy?"

Kilbride shook his head, a touch of anger apparent in the emphatic way that he did it. "We kept to the downstairs, Mrs. Ring and me. When my daily duties are finished, such as they are, I read, or take walks, or visit museums – I'm trying to better myself, you see. I went to sea when I was younger, and it was enough to convince me that I could do better. I returned to London late last year and happened upon this job, not knowing who was going to be living here. I thought that I was incredibly fortunate when I was hired – that is, until soon after, when Mr. Armilus moved in. I've never met a more objectionable piece of work – at least, until his son arrived. I'm not sure who was worse."

Lestrade started to say something, but then he shut his mouth and again deferred to Holmes, who asked, "During those times when the house was yours, so to speak, did you ever have visitors? Did your friends stop by? What about the tradesmen?"

Kilbride frowned. "I like to pursue my own thoughts, and I don't really cultivate many acquaintances. I suppose Steven Mullingar is the closest thing to a friend that I have."

"Oh? And who is he?"

"He works around the corner, at MacLean's, the tobacconist."

"Indeed. And how often does he visit?"

"Not all that often. I don't smoke, you see, so I suppose it's curious that we ever became friends. But he's a very smart man, and I enjoy our conversations."

"And how did you meet him?"

"Why, he delivered the tobacco that was originally ordered for Mr. Armilus when he moved in late last year."

"The tobacco that's upstairs in the jar on his desk?"

"Yes."

"And did the son, Nicky, smoke as well?"

"He did. Like a chimney."

"Was the old tobacco from last year replaced when he moved in?"

Kilbride's eyes widened in surprise. "No, it wasn't. We should have replaced it, I suppose, as I understand that tobacco gets old and dry, but I just never thought of it. You don't think – "

"I'm not sure what to think right now, Mr. Kilbride," said Holmes, "but you would do well to keep any speculation to yourself, even from Mrs. Ring. Do you understand?"

Kilbride nodded enthusiastically. "I do. Anything that I can do to help, sirs."

Holmes informed him that he was finished for now, and the man stood and left, pulling the door shut behind him.

"I would have thought," said Lestrade, "that there might be some vulgar intrigue going on below stairs between those two, disrupted by the arrivals of the Armilus clan."

"An affair between Mrs. Ring and Kilbride is actually quite likely," concurred Holmes, "but I don't think that they would need to murder the Americans to sustain it, or because it was somehow disrupted. After all, what happened to Donald Armilus last year should have resulted in the immediate closing of the house, ending their association with it, and likely each other as well. The same factors make it unlikely that they killed the son."

"But what if either Donald or Nicky Armilus advanced some sort of objectionable action toward the housekeeper?"

"What if, indeed? Did it need to result in such a drastic action as that which happened to each of them – father and son, both driven mad, in different ways, and to different but no less terrible ends? And that doesn't explain Constable Riley's fate."

"The tobacco," I said. "You showed an interest in it upstairs, and it was on the edge of your questioning just now."

"Very good, Watson," nodded Holmes, reaching into his pocket. He withdrew a couple of the envelopes wherein he stored evidence. "This," he said, "is a sample from the jar containing the year-old tobacco. Do you notice anything?"

He handed it to me, and I held it so that Lestrade could also take a look. At first it appeared to simply be typical tobacco of some rich mixture, its dryness indicating that it had indeed been lying around unused for quite a while. I put my nose close to the envelope and sniffed it, perceiving a slight sourness. As I had done, Lestrade did the same, and commented aloud confirming the observation. Holmes nodded. "Look closer," he said.

I did, and then saw what he meant. Mixed in with the various grains of tobacco were a number of smaller pieces of something else, each dark brown, also of the same dark colour.

"It looks like some sort of seed," I indicated.

"Now," added Holmes, "look at this sample from the ashtray." And he handed us the other envelope.

Within were the remains of a rolled cigarette, some unburned tobacco, and an equal amount of ashes. I pushed it around with my finger, showing that the seeds were also in the unburned tobacco, and a few burned seed husks were mixed into the ashes. I smelled it and perceived the same sourness, mixed with the burned smell of an old cigarette.

"The inference," explained Holmes, "is that Constable Riley sat in the study during his shift, and at some point rolled a cigarette, using the tobacco from the jar on Armilus's desk – the same tobacco that has been in there for a year, and was there when both father and son went mad."

"So the tobacco has been poisoned," I concluded.

"As a starting hypothesis, yes. But there is still much that still needs to be answered before we can consider the matter closed. Lestrade, what can you tell us about Kilbride and Mrs. Ring. I assume that you've already investigated them in relation to the two previous incidents."

"We have. Kilbride is what he told us he was – a former sailor, originally from Manchester, who came ashore late last year and happened to hear about this job. He has a sister who works for the agent, and she recommended him. It suited him, as he wanted to pursue his 'studies', which seems to mean reading books and visiting museums. I wish someone would pay me to do the same."

"And what about the agent, of whom we have frequently heard?"

"He's a man named Dennehy, long established in this type of work. He has connections with similar businesses in the United States, obtaining lodgings or offices for Americans who are coming over here without any previous associations. From what we learned a year ago, from our questioning of him and examining his correspondence, the man has no other connection to Armilus than being instructed to find this house and manage its upkeep. He pays the bills from an account funded by Armilus's New York office, and forwards the invoices, such as they are, back to America like clockwork."

"And Mrs. Ring? What is her story?"

"Well, she's actually never been married. Like most housekeepers, the 'Missus' is an assumed title to maintain authority. But in this case there's no one to maintain, as there is no other staff. Her family moved here from where she said, not long after the American Civil War, when she was very small, and she's worked in domestic service since her teenage years. Like Kilbride, she found this job through Dennehy's office, as she had worked for one of his previous clients, also an American, who moved here for a time several years ago. The files at Dennehy's noted that she had a sterling character from her previous employer. Neither she nor Kilbride have ever shown a speck of dishonesty."

"In any case," I interjected, "I suspect that the question about the tobacco will lead us to MacLean's."

"Indeed," replied Holmes. "Perhaps we can determine if the two caretakers, both seemingly without a blot upon their respective copybooks, were responsible for the curious addition to the tobacco, or if instead it occurred at the tobacconists – either from the efforts of Mr. MacLean, or possibly Kilbride's friend, Steven Mullingar."

Lestrade announced that he would reopen the investigation into the caretakers' pasts, looking for some clue or connection that had been missed before, and that he would discreetly see what could be learned about MacLean and Mullingar of the tobacco shop. In the meantime, Holmes announced that we intended to visit there in person.

MacLean's shop wasn't far, and both Holmes and I had previously stopped there upon before, although it wasn't our usual vendor of choice. It had always seemed to be a respectable and well-maintained little business, and I wondered about its possible association with the terrible events within the Dorset Square house.

Recalling the seeds, I asked, "Do you suspect ergot poisoning?"

Holmes nodded, but said, "Not entirely. Those were clearly something that very much resembled rye seeds. Their darker colouring could simply be from absorbing the moistures of the tobacco. But these symptoms – a man screaming until he dies, another painting with his own blood until his heart no longer has enough blood to beat, and now a third who has set himself on fire and then leapt from a window – are much too drastic for the symptoms of typical ergot poisoning, as bad as that can be. No, something else happened here."

By then we had reached the doorway to MacLean's little shop, which had seemingly just resumed operations for the day, as the owner himself was in the process of turning a sign in the window from "*Closed*" to "*Open*".

MacLean was a dour Scot, but friendly enough in his own way. He greeted us by name and asked what he could do for us. Of course, Holmes made no reference to the events relating to Constable Riley, or the connections between the tobacco from MacLean's shop and that found in Armilus's study. Rather, he went through some complicated story about having tried a tobacco blend, shared with him by a friend, that had many positive points. It had come from MacLean's shop, but he didn't recall the name. Could the owner help him?

MacLean nodded. I knew that he'd long coveted Holmes's custom, and I felt bad that my friend's attempts to gain information did not necessarily mean that he was on the way to becoming a regular customer.

MacLean showed us to a shelf where several jars were lined up, each with curious and intriguing names. "I don't recognize many of these," I said. "Are they special to your shop?"

MacLean nodded. "I have an assistant – originally trained as a chemist – who has created a number of unique mixtures."

"Indeed?" said Holmes. "And why haven't we heard of this before?"

"Well, he's only been in my employ for slightly over a year, and it took him some time to convince me to sell the results of his experiments. Only now is word starting to spread of 'MacLean's Special Blends', as I like to call them."

"And where is this Sorcerer's Apprentice of Tobacco?" Holmes asked. "I'd like to meet him."

"Alas, he's on a delivery. He's in and out all day long. He'll be sorry that he missed you both, I'm sure."

"Oh well. We shall certainly have another chance. Can I see some of his other blends?" And he turned away, back toward the rows of jars.

Having worked with Holmes for many years by that point, I recognized when he signalled that he needed a moment to investigate without MacLean's attention. I was only glad that he hadn't chosen to upset a whole shelf of jars – and this had happened before – in order to slip away while MacLean and I tried to clean up the mess.

Following Holmes's implied instruction, I walked to the other side of the shop, calling MacLean after me to ask about a few of the pipes that were for sale on a rack there. Out of the corner of my eye, behind MacLean's back, I could see Holmes slip behind the counter and into the rear of the shop.

I became truly interested in one of the pipes, and MacLean's enthusiasm joined mine as I convinced myself that I wished to buy it. When the topic could no longer be stretched any further, and the time had come for me to make my payment, I was relieved to see Holmes standing innocently by the opposite counter, having successfully completed his researches. I paid for my new pipe, then Holmes requested a few ounces of three of the different blends, saying that he wished to compare them, and then he'd be back. MacLean had a satisfied expression as he led us to the door, following our transactions, and he wished us well before closing the door behind us.

We walked for a hundred feet or so before Holmes hailed a cab. In moments we were making our way through the awakening city to Barts, where Holmes still maintained privileges in the laboratories, when he encountered something that was beyond the facilities of his own small chemical corner.

"I found where Mullingar carries out his tobacco alchemy," he explained. "Most tobacconists blend different strains – Virginia, Burley, or Oriental – and they add their own secret ingredients. I knew a man who added orange peel, for instance. But Mr. Mullingar has a chemical set-up that looks more like something one would find in the research laboratories at Woolwich Arsenal. I cannot tell if he synthesizes the various powders and liquids as additives to the tobacco, or if he's up to something with far more sinister implications. But I did find a jar, hidden beneath the work counter, containing the rye-seed-impregnated tobacco, along with an adjacent bottle of clear liquid. As they were the only items secreted there, the implication that there is a connection cannot be ignored. I took another sample of the rye-tobacco, as well as pouring myself some of the clear liquid into one of the little empty bottles that he had stacked nearby.

"When we arrive at Barts, you would do me a great service by researching what you can find about ergot poisoning and lysergic acid in the medical library. Meanwhile, I'll make my way upstairs and attempt to determine what exactly Mr. Mullingar is keeping in that bottle, and what he's done to the tobacco, if anything."

Not long after, we were dropped outside the hospital, and we passed through the Henry VIII Gate before bearing right and through the inner court. Soon we reached the door which would lead to both the laboratory and the medical library. As always whenever I entered through that doorway, with its sign overhead proclaiming, "*Whatsoever Thy Hand Findeth To Do, Do It With Thy Might*", I recalled all the other times that I'd read it beforehand, both as a student and young doctor, and on that New Year's Day in 1881 just before I was introduced to Sherlock Holmes, and then, on so many other later occasions as well. They were good words and seeing them yet again was always a comfort.

While Holmes proceeded upstairs, I entered the familiar and comfortable medical library. I didn't recall my way around with quite the same familiarity that I'd had as a student, but with the aid of a very knowledgeable and helpful medical librarian, I found what I sought rather quickly. My quick examination of the books didn't reveal anything new. Ergot poisoning is the result of a fungus that grows on rye, producing lysergic acid. Its hallucinogenic effects can have a profound effect upon humans, and while I had identified several case histories, nothing was recorded to the degree of what had occurred in the Dorset Square house.

After gathering several volumes from the library stacks, I wandered out and up the stone steps to the laboratory, where Holmes already had a complex system of piping in place. Always a careful scientist, he had a notebook open beside him, and he diligently made note after note concerning his findings.

I approached and set the library books nearby, with the relevant articles marked. He made no acknowledgement besides a short nod, and I turned to go. With no other task at hand, I planned to return to Baker Street.

I tarried a moment in the hall outside to share pleasantries with our friend Dr Dickinson. He seemed to wish to draw me into a discussion about his latest research into the characteristics of blood, always a fascination for him, but I managed to extricate myself without offending him and then trod the familiar path down and out to the street. Not long after, I was in a hansom and on my way.

Considering that I was quite exhausted, having spent the previous day and into the evening assisting Holmes in his pursuit of the Watership Down killer, and then having had no sleep upon our return to London, I should have returned to Baker Street immediately. However, as I was out and about, I decided to carry out some errands. By mid-day I found myself near Charing Cross, and I impulsively entered the station, procuring a meat pie and a glass of cider from a little vendor, set up in the eastern corner of the station, which I had discovered during one of Holmes's investigations. After that was finished, I ambled north to Charing Cross Road and examined the bookshops there, where I was fortunate enough to find a particular volume which I had long sought. Feeling that I had accomplished a great deal indeed, I hailed a cab and settled back for the slow early afternoon journey to Baker Street.

I awoke with a start when the cabbie announced that we had arrived. Amused that I had fallen into a nap, and trying to recall exactly when it had occurred, I let myself in and went upstairs in something of a dream-like haze, having given myself over to the idea that as soon as I could gain my chair by the fireplace, I would resume my slumbers.

The house was quiet, and the sun, now in the west, had left the sitting room in shadows. I set my purchases down on the dining table and noticed that a package was already there, addressed to Holmes. Curiously, it had a label which read: *MacLean's Fine Tobaccos,* pasted upon it.

I found that I was no longer sleepy, pondering just how it had come to rest there. Even as I was considering calling Mrs. Hudson and questioning her about it, I heard the sound of a vehicle halting outside, followed by the opening and closing of the front door, and then Holmes's confident and energetic steps, as he climbed the stairs.

He immediately glanced past me to the package. "From MacLean's," I said, as he crossed the room. He leaned over the table, resting his hands on either side of the box, looking this way and that, and muttering to himself as he recorded various facts. Then, having seen all that he found useful, he walked to the chemical corner, retrieved a small knife, and returned, leaning over to cut the string. In moments, the contents were revealed – a package of tobacco, with an unsigned card that said *"With our compliments..."*

I didn't need to be Sherlock Holmes to spot the darkened seeds that were interspersed throughout the blend. "Steven Mullingar must have heard about our visit this morning," I said.

"Now, Watson," said Holmes. "Perhaps you're slandering the poor fellow. Mr. MacLean himself could have brought this, although it's unlikely. But I expect that you're right, and that we can probably piece together what has happened. For some reason, Mullingar has adulterated the tobacco with his own concoction. This was aimed at the Armilus men but caused the innocent Constable Riley to suffer the same effects when he used the old tobacco. No doubt Mullingar has heard about the incident and the constable's injuries, and then our involvement. The fact that we then showed up at MacLean's not long after, our innocent story fooling him not one iota, forced him into this clumsy attempt to stop our investigation."

He stepped to the door and called for Mrs. Hudson to come up. In the meantime, I went to my own desk, in order to obtain some of my own tobacco. "I shouldn't if I were you," said Holmes, suddenly quite serious. At that moment, Mrs. Hudson entered.

When questioned, she explained, "I had gone round the corner, to the butcher's." She was suddenly concerned. "When I returned, the tobacco man was at the door, and he offered to take it up, as my hands were full."

"Did you see him leave?" asked Holmes. She hadn't.

"Was the page boy out as well?" I added.

"He was. His sister has just had a baby, and I let him go round to see her."

"Ah, well," mused Holmes. "He has had a few minutes alone, then. Thank you, Mrs. Hudson." She nodded, frowned, and departed.

I understood then why Holmes had stopped me from using my own tobacco. "I suppose we'll have to get rid of all of it," I said ruefully.

"And any bottled items as well," he added. "My research indicates that Mr. Mullingar has produced an extremely strong variant of lysergic acid. Apparently, he discovered a way to add an amide group with two ethyl substituents to the original lysergic acid compound, greatly increasing the hallucinogenic aspects. It was present in the augmented tobacco in the seeds, and also in its pure form, poured into the leaves, matching the sample of liquid that I obtained. If Mr. Mullingar broke in to leave the tainted tobacco. It is not too difficult to speculate that he also poured some of the fluid in our existing tobacco, or onto our cigars, or into our alcohol. For that matter, the liquid is easily dissolved in sugar, and likely in other substances."

"I would advise," I said, "that we wash down our pipes as well, along with the silver and dishes, and anything else that might enter our bodies." A thought occurred to me. "Mrs. Hudson didn't see when he left. He was in the house alone – the *entire* house, and not just up here. Our food stocks downstairs might also be contaminated! I must notify her."

I turned quickly, but not before seeing Holmes' expression as he pictured our usually very-patient landlady being told that she would have to throw out anything that might remotely have had a chance of being poisoned.

Later, when Mrs. Hudson had been mollified and promised reimbursement for the loss of most of the contents of her pantry, we summoned Lestrade for a council of war. It was then that I learned that he already knew just enough, by way of a telegram from Holmes before he'd arrived home, to have placed Mullingar under surveillance. He explained that the report showed Mullingar travelling from the tobacco shop on a number of deliveries, and that among them was a stop at our rooms in Baker Street. The officer who had compiled the report, clearly a man of no imagination or gumption who recorded what he saw without further thought, had believed 221 to be simply another rooming house of no consequence. The constable had watched Mullingar disappear inside before returning a few minutes later, whereupon he completed his other deliveries, before going back to MacLean's. Soon after, seemingly done for the day, he'd gone to his home in nearby Edward Street. "He's there now," added Lestrade, "if we want to pick him up."

"There's no reason to wait," agreed Holmes. "There's still a chance that he's innocent, but regardless, he has a story to tell us."

We found a cab and set off to obtain reinforcements. Along the way, Lestrade mentioned a curious fact. "I had a message from your brother, Mr. Holmes. About this case."

Holmes raised an eyebrow. "Indeed? And what is his interest?"

"He didn't reveal a great deal, but he asked to be informed of any developments."

"And have you related any of the specifics to him yet? About Mr. Mullingar's involvement, for instance."

"No, not so far. I didn't feel that we had enough to tell him. It's only now, after our conversation, that I have more of a sense of what's happening."

Holmes didn't respond, other than to nod and then sank into his own thoughts. We stopped at a police station to gather several other officers and then, in a few minutes, we found ourselves in narrow Edward Street. Men were dispatched to watch the various exits while we and a couple of brawny constables walked up the four flights, and so to Mullingar's room.

Holmes knocked and, when a muffled voice from within questioned who it was, he replied that he had a telegram. Mullingar opened the door to find Holmes facing him. The man's eyes widened, and then, seeing the rest of us, he seemed to sag a bit upon realizing that he had been discovered. He submitted quietly when the handcuffs were placed upon his wrists, and he made no comments as our growler carried us south to Scotland

Yard. Only when we were in one of the offices and his interrogation had begun did he say, with a half-smile and shake of his head, that perhaps trying to poison Holmes and me had been a bit too much.

"That's the least of your worries," snapped Lestrade.

"Yes," replied Mullingar. "I can see that you're upset about the constable, and for that I'm truly sorry. I had thought that I was remiss in not retrieving my special blend sooner, after it delivered justice on Donald Armilus. Still, I knew that Kilbride and Mrs. Ring didn't smoke, and I thought that it was safe enough. Time passed, and then, a year later, when Armilus's cursed son arrived, I could see that there had been a purpose in my leaving it in the house, for his punishment was enacted as well. Afterwards, with the police presence, I never had the chance to slip into the house and carry away the evidence."

"You refer to justice," said Holmes. "Then you feel that Armilus and his son needed punishment, and you were the hand of vengeance to carry it out?"

Mullingar nodded. "I never thought that I'd have the chance. But then, a year ago, the newspapers reported how Armilus had moved to England to escape the investigations overtaking his American enterprises, and that he was going to be living nearby. I took it upon myself to fix up my special blend and take it around, as if it had been arranged beforehand. I met Kilbride then, and he accepted delivery, along with all the other items that were arriving then to stock the house. It only took a few days for justice to be enacted, although I was uncertain as to what form it might take."

"I take it that you speak of the uncertain nature of the chemical that you've derived from the lysergic acid."

"That's right," replied Mullingar. "Reactions can manifest themselves in many ways, all hallucinatory, but not necessarily unpleasant. However, I made sure that what I added to the Armilus tobacco, both the poisoned seeds and the fluid, was guaranteed to result in a terror-filled death. Sadly, Donald Armilus didn't actually die, but what is left of him must be in a living hell, until his soul goes to the real place."

I stared at the man. "What did the Armilus family do to you that you hate them so much?"

Mullingar gave a sad smile. "Long ago, when I was a young man, I studied chemistry at a New York university. I was brilliant and had an incredible future before me. One night, I was attending a reception to honour the various New York elite who had contributed in one way or another to the school, and Armilus was there, along with his daughter."

"Daughter?" said Lestrade. "I hadn't heard that he had a daughter."

"I suppose that it's little known now," replied Mullingar. "She was beautiful, but truth be told, she was just as scheming and devious as her father. However, I didn't see it then, and it didn't matter in any case – I would have sold my soul for her. In fact, I suppose that I have. We talked that night, just for a few moments, and my fate was sealed. She began to find ways to pay little attentions to me, although it was just a distraction for her, and those crumbs were enough to make me realize that I'd been starving before I met her, my life empty in ways that I'd never before realized.

"I was foolish enough to believe that we had a future – that *she* was *my* future – but I was nothing to her, although I didn't realize it then. I began to speak as if we were making plans, and she let me, for I suppose that it was amusing. I became bolder in my attentions, and soon there was a mention of the two of us in one of the New York newspapers, as if we were truly a couple. That brought it to the attention of Armilus and his sons. They had other plans for this girl, and clearly, I needed to be discouraged. One night, thinking that I'd been summoned to meet with my love, I instead found myself facing Armilus and his sons, along with several of his bullyboys. The latter proceeded to beat me within an inch of my life. Only when I had been broken, literally and spiritually, did Armilus and his sons step forward to get in their weak licks as well, as I no longer presented any danger or possibility of response.

"As I healed, I became aware that a number of my friends would no longer associate with me. After I could get about, I learned that Armilus had gone to great lengths to destroy my reputation in various ways, all vile and irredeemable. I was dismissed from school, and suddenly my bright future was extinguished. A few weeks later, Armilus announced that his daughter was to be married to the son of a Russian nobleman of very dark reputation to fulfil some business ambition. I never saw her again, and as I understand it, she was carried away to Russia, where she later died under mysterious circumstances.

"I made my way after that as best as I could, but wherever I went, it seemed that the long reach of the Armilus family was still there to destroy me. By then, my association with his daughter was long in the past, but it looks as if they took sport in constantly finding new ways to cause me harm. Finally, I left America entirely and set myself up anew. Mullingar is not my real name, and my former identity isn't important anymore. I was prepared to live out my dull life here, without further incident – and then, I saw that Armilus was moving to London.

"As I said, I fixed up some of my special blend, made with one of the substances that I had discovered years before, and delivered it to the house, not knowing exactly what form the punishment would take. It seems that whatever horrors are in that evil man's mind have been released, to haunt him until he dies. Afterwards, I was satisfied, and seeing no urgent need to retrieve the tainted tobacco, I let it be. Then, as if it were a sign from the heavens, the son arrived as well. I knew that it was just a matter of time until the punishment would also fall upon him, and in fact it took less than a day. I'm only sorry that I wasn't able to destroy the other Armilus sons, and that the constable was injured before I could take away the tobacco."

"And yet," said Lestrade, "you had no hesitation in trying to do the same to these two men that you had done to Armilus and his son. They had never wronged you."

Mullingar shrugged. "I suppose that it was simply a reaction to the knowledge that my involvement was known. In an effort to preserve my life, I thoughtlessly attempted to shore up all the places where my plan was starting to collapse." He looked at Holmes, and then me. "Gentleman, I apologise."

At that moment, the door opened, and a grim-faced constable entered, handing Lestrade a note. He read it and then angrily threw it on the table. "Constable Riley has died of his injuries."

Mullingar suddenly looked pained, and a haunted look entered his eyes. "I am truly sorry." And then he lowered his head, refusing to speak any further, before eventually being led from the room. He was found later that day in his cell, hanged by a noose fashioned out of his own shirt.

We offered our condolences to Lestrade and indicated that we'd be available later if he needed any further information. Then we stepped outside, where Holmes hailed a cab. I expected that we'd return to Baker Street, but instead he urged the cabbie to get us to MacLean's shop with all possible speed. I wanted to ask what was so urgent, but the expression on his face indicated that he wasn't in a mood to converse.

When we arrived, Holmes was already out of the cab and in the door before I could disembark and ask the cabbie to wait for us. Stepping inside, I found MacLean looking shocked while Holmes disappeared into the back room. "Tell him, Watson!" he cried.

Not knowing how much to reveal, I simply stated that MacLean's brilliant assistant had been arrested for murder. The Scot was speechless, clearly wanting to ask questions, but not knowing where to begin. Before he could order his thoughts, Holmes had returned, carrying a large jar of tobacco, as well as another of a clear liquid. "Evidence!" he snapped to MacLean. "I'll be back later to tell you more." And then he was out the door, leaving me to apologise and follow.

Back at our rooms, Holmes asked the cab to wait, although he gave no indication to me for what purpose. We entered 221b to discover Mrs. Hudson, tidying the sitting room, her lips tight, obviously still peeved at having to re-stock her larder from scratch because of some activity related to one of Holmes's cases. She left without speaking, pulling the door shut firmly behind her. Holmes, typically oblivious to her mood, crossed the room and placed both the tobacco and the container of clear liquid on his chemical table.

"We'll need to be careful how we dispose of it," I said. "We can't burn it here, as the fumes would likely drive us mad, and the neighbours as well. We can't just toss it, as some vagrant would doubtless retrieve it and come to a bad end."

"I agree," said Holmes. "Perhaps a trip to the Thames later today, where we'll sprinkle it in, a few handfuls at a time – although I fear that a fish might eat it and then end up in some poor soul's frying pan. But first . ... ."

He was still wearing his Inverness and, from a deep side pocket, he pulled out a notebook – the same that he had been using to make notes in the laboratory at Barts. Stepping to the fireplace, he opened it, looked at one of the pages for a long moment as if committing something to memory, and then carefully tore out the sheet. Leaning down, he tossed it upon the fire.

"You heard Lestrade," he said. "My brother Mycroft is interested in this case. He has somehow dimly perceived what is going on, and I fear that he wishes to obtain this augmented lysergic acid for some devious purpose. I would trust Mycroft with my life, but the government not so much. One can only hope that Mullingar will keep the process to himself. I'll return momentarily to his rooms in Edward Street, and then again to the tobacco shop, in order to see if he kept any notes. But in the meantime, this tobacco, the fluid, and my own notes where I derived the formula as well, must be removed from the board before Mycroft can appropriate them."

We watched as the sheet with Holmes's notes browned and curled before bursting into flame. Then, with an instruction to hide the poisoned tobacco and dangerous liquid until he returned, Holmes departed. He returned several hours later, with news that he had thoroughly searched both Mullingar's rooms and MacLean's shop, after explaining to the owner exactly what had occurred. The tobacconist indicated that no one had been by the shop since our previous visit who'd shown any interest in Mullingar or his experiments. Holmes had been unable to find any notes relating to the experiments at either location, and he hoped that the formula was now only known to himself and

Mullingar. As he finished saying this, the doorbell rang, and in a few minutes the page boy delivered a note from Lestrade, telling us of Mullingar's suicide.

We never heard a word from Mycroft about whether he felt vexed upon being denied further knowledge of the dangerous substance, and of course Holmes was careful never to bring up the subject. Later that afternoon, we hailed a cabbie that we knew and made our way to Limehouse. There, after walking down a narrow and slimy alley, we stepped along the narrow shore. The tide was low, and we were able to make our way to one of the nearby sewer entrances, where a vile and malodorous flow steadily joined the river. I was tasked with pouring out Mullingar's concoction, while Holmes, wearing old gloves, scattered handful after handful of the tainted tobacco onto the surface of the greasy waters. We watched it drift away and gradually sink. After a few moments, we turned and made our way back to the street, and thence to our usual tobacconist. Then, once more in Baker Street, we warily lit our pipes and smoked in our comfortable chairs before the fireplace, each lost in our own thoughts for the rest of the day.

About the Author

David Marcum plays The Game with deadly seriousness. He first discovered Sherlock Holmes in 1975 at the age of ten, and since that time, he has collected, read, and chronologized literally thousands of traditional Holmes pastiches. He is the author of over fifty Sherlockian pastiches, some published in anthologies, others collected in his own books, 'The Papers of Sherlock Holmes,' 'Sherlock Holmes and A Quantity of Debt,' and 'Sherlock Holmes – Tangled Skeins.' He has edited nearly fifty Sherlockian anthologies, including the ongoing series 'The MX Book of New Sherlock Holmes Stories,' which he created in 2015. This collection is now up to 18 volumes, with several more in preparation. He is now doing the same for the adventures of Dr Thorndyke and Solar Pons. He has contributed numerous essays to various publications and is a member of several Sherlockian groups. He is a licensed Civil Engineer, living in Tennessee with his wife and son. His Sherlockian blog, 'A Seventeen Step Program' can be found at http://17stepprogram.blogspot.com/ Since the age of nineteen, he has worn a deerstalker as his regular-and-only hat from autumn to spring, and often in summer. In 2013, he and his deerstalker were finally able to make his first, trip-of-a-lifetime, Holmes Pilgrimage to England, with return Pilgrimages in 2015 and 2016. If you ever run into him and his deerstalker, out and about, feel free to say hello!

A CANONICAL PIPE CONCORDANCE

Being a compilation of pipe references in the Sherlock Holmes Stories

By Kelvin I Jones

'Then he took down from the rack the old and oily clay pipe, which was to him as a counsellor, and, having lit it, he leaned back in his chair...'

A Study in Scarlet

'You remind me of Edgar Allan Poe's Dupin. I had no idea that such individuals did exist outside of stories.' Sherlock Holmes rose and lit his pipe. 'No doubt you think that you are complimenting me in comparing me to Dupin,' he observed. 'Now, in my opinion, Dupin was a very inferior fellow.

There was no need for him to ask me to wait up for him, for I felt that sleep was impossible until I heard the result of his adventure. It was close upon nine when he set out. I had no idea how long he might be, but I sat stolidly puffing at my pipe and skipping over the pages of Henri Murger's Vie de Bohème. Ten o'clock passed, and I heard the footsteps of the maid as they pattered off to bed. Eleven, and the more stately tread of the landlady passed my door, bound for the same destination.

'There was no name appended to this message.'

'And there was nothing else?' Holmes asked. 'Nothing of any importance. The man's novel, with which he had read himself to sleep, was lying upon the bed, and his pipe was on a chair beside him. There was a glass of water on the table, and on the window-sill a small chip ointment box containing a couple of pills.'

Sherlock Holmes sprang from his chair with an exclamation of delight.

The Sign of Four

I made no remark, however, but sat nursing my wounded leg. I had had a Jezail bullet through it sometime before, and, though it did not prevent me from walking, it ached wearily at every change of the weather.

'My practice has extended recently to the Continent,' said Holmes, after a while, filling up his old briar-root pipe.

'I was consulted last week by François le Villard, who, as you probably know, has come rather to the front lately in the French detective service. He has all the Celtic power of quick intuition, but he is deficient in the wide range of exact knowledge which is essential to the higher developments of his art.

'They are all upon technical subjects. Here, for example, is one "Upon the Distinction Between the Ashes of the Various Tobaccos." In it I enumerate a hundred and forty forms of cigar, cigarette, and pipe tobacco, with coloured plates illustrating the difference in the ash. It is a point which is continually turning up in criminal trials, and which is sometimes of supreme importance as a clue. If you can say definitely, for example, that some murder had been done by a man who was smoking an Indian lunkah, it obviously narrows your field of search.'

'But you spoke just now of observation and deduction. Surely the one to some extent implies the other.'

'Why, hardly,' he answered, leaning back luxuriously in his armchair, and sending up thick blue wreaths from his pipe. 'For example, observation shows me that you have been to the Wigmore Street Post Office this morning, but deduction lets me know that when there you dispatched a telegram.'

'Right!' said I.

Standing at the window, I watched her walking briskly down the street, until the grey turban and white feather were but a speck in the sombre crowd.
'What a very attractive woman!' I exclaimed, turning to my companion.
He had lit his pipe again, and was leaning back with drooping eyelids.

'Is she?' he said, languidly; 'I did not observe.'

'You really are an automaton - a calculating machine,' I cried.

As I glanced at him I could not but think how, on that very day, he had complained bitterly of the commonplaceness of life. Here at least was a problem which would tax his sagacity to the utmost. Mr. Thaddeus Sholto looked from one to the other of us with an obvious pride at the effect which his story had produced, and then continued, between the puffs of his overgrown pipe....

Holmes was standing on the doorstep, with his hands in his pockets, smoking his pipe. 'Ah, you have him there!' said he. 'Good dog, then!'

'Now, off you go!'

He handed them a shilling each, and away they buzzed down the stairs, and I saw them a moment later streaming down the street. 'If the launch is above water they will find her,' said Holmes, as he rose from the table and lit his pipe. 'They can go everywhere, see everything, overhear everyone. I expect to hear before evening that they have spotted her.'

It was evening before I left Camberwell, and quite dark by the time I reached home. My companion's book and pipe lay by his chair, but he had disappeared. I looked about in the hope of seeing a note, but there was none. 'I suppose that Mr. Sherlock Holmes has gone out?' I said to Mrs. Hudson as she came up to lower the blinds.

Mr. Abel White was a kind man, and he would often drop into my little shanty and smoke a pipe with me, for white folk out there feel their hearts warm to each other as they never do here at home.

I tried again and again to make my Sikhs talk, but without much success. At two in the morning the rounds passed, and broke for a moment the weariness of the night. Finding that my companions would not be led into conversation, I took out my pipe, and laid down my musket to strike a match. In an instant the two Sikhs were upon me.

A Case of Identity

Sherlock Holmes sat silent for a few minutes with his fingertips still pressed together, his legs stretched out in front of him, and his gaze directed upwards to the ceiling. Then he took down from the rack the old and oily clay pipe, which was to him as a counsellor, and, having lit it, he leaned back in his chair, with the thick blue cloud-wreaths spinning up from him, and a look of infinite languor in his face.

'Quite an interesting study, that maiden,' he observed.

I left him then, still puffing at his black clay pipe, with the conviction that when I came again on the next evening I would find that he held in his hands all the clues which would lead up to the identity of the disappearing bride-groom of Miss Mary Sutherland....

The Red-Headed League

'What are you going to do then?' I asked.

'To smoke,' he answered. 'It is quite a three pipe problem and I beg that you will not speak to me for fifty minutes.' He curled himself up in his chair, with his thin knees drawn up to his hawk-like nose, and there he sat with his eyes closed and his black clay pipe thrusting out like the bill of some strange bird. I had come to the conclusion that he had dropped asleep, and indeed was nodding myself, when he suddenly sprang out of his chair with the gesture of a man who had made up his mind and put his pipe down upon the mantelpiece.

The Boscombe Valley Mystery

'He had even smoked there. I found the ash of a cigar, which my special knowledge of tobacco ashes enabled me to pronounce as an Indian cigar. I have, as you know, devoted some attention to this, and written a little monograph on the ashes of 140 different varieties of pipe, cigar, and cigarette tobacco. Having found the ash, I then looked round and discovered the stump among the moss where he had tossed it. It was an Indian cigar, of the variety which are rolled in Rotterdam.'

The Five Orange Pips

Sherlock Holmes sat for some time in silence with his head sunk forward, and his eyes bent upon the red glow of the fire. Then he lit his pipe and leaning back in his chair, he watched the blue smoke rings as they chased each other up to the ceiling.

'I think, Watson,' he remarked at last, 'that of all our cases we have had none more fantastic than this.'

'Save, perhaps, the Sign of Four.'

The Man with the Twisted Lip

Ordering my cab to wait, I passed down the steps, worn hollow in the centre by the ceaseless tread of drunken feet, and by the light of a flickering oil lamp above the door I found the latch and made my way into a long, low room, thick and heavy with the brown opium smoke, and terraced with wooden berths, like the forecastle of an emigrant ship. Through the gloom one could dimly catch a glimpse of bodies lying in strange fantastic poses, bowed shoulders, bent knees, heads thrown back and chins pointing upwards, with here and there a dark, lack-lustre eye turned upon the newcomer. Out of the black shadows there glimmered little red circles of light, now bright, now faint, as the burning poison waxed or waned in the bowls of the metal pipes. The most lay silent, but some muttered to themselves, and others talked together in a strange, low, monotonous voice, their conversation coming in gushes, and then suddenly tailing off into silence, each mumbling out his own thoughts, and paying little heed to the words of his neighbour. At the further end was a small brazier of burning charcoal, beside which on a three-legged wooden stool there sat a tall, thin old man, with his jaw resting upon his two fists, and his elbows upon his knees, staring into the fire.

'You should be ashamed of yourself!'

'So I am. But you've got mixed, Watson, for I have only been here a few hours, three pipes, four pipes - I forget how many.'

The words fell quite distinctly upon my ear. I glanced down. They could only have come from the old man at my side, and yet he sat now as absorbed as ever, very thin, very wrinkled, bent with age, an opium pipe dangling down from between his knees, as though it had dropped in sheer lassitude from his fingers. I took two steps forward and looked back. It took all my self-control to prevent me from breaking out into a cry of astonishment.

A dull wrack was drifting slowly across the sky, and a star or two twinkled dimly here and there through the rifts of the clouds. Holmes drove in silence, with his head sunk upon his breast, and the air of a man who is lost in thought, whilst I sat beside him curious to learn what this new quest might be which seemed to tax his powers so sorely, and yet afraid to break in upon the current of his thoughts. We had driven several miles, and were beginning to get to the fringe of the belt of suburban villas, when he shook himself, shrugged his shoulders, and lit up his pipe with the air of a man who has satisfied himself that he is acting for the best. 'You have a grand gift of silence, Watson,' said he. 'It makes you quite invaluable as a companion.

He took off his coat and waistcoat, put on a large blue dressing-gown, and then wandered about the room collecting pillows from his bed, and cushions from the sofa and armchairs. With these he constructed a sort of Eastern divan, upon which he perched himself cross-legged, with an ounce of shag - tobacco and a box of matches laid out in front of him. In the dim light of the lamp I saw him sitting there, an old brier pipe between his lips, his eyes fixed vacantly upon the corner of the ceiling, the blue smoke curling up from him, silent, motionless, with the light shining upon his strong-set aquiline features. So he sat as I dropped off to sleep, and so he sat when a sudden ejaculation caused me to wake up, and I found the summer sun shining into the apartment. The pipe was still between his lips, the smoke still curled upwards, and the room was full of a dense tobacco haze, but nothing remained of the heap of shag which I had seen.

The Blue Carbuncle

I had called upon my friend Sherlock Holmes upon the second morning after Christmas, with the intention of wishing him the compliments of the season. He was lounging upon the sofa in a purple dressing-gown, a pipe-rack within his reach upon the right, and a pile of crumpled morning papers, evidently newly studied, near at hand....

'...I came to the Brixton Road. My sister asked me what was the matter, and why I was so pale; but I told her that I had been upset by the jewel robbery at the hotel. Then I went into the back yard, and smoked a pipe, and wondered what it would be best to do.

There was a rush, a clatter upon the stairs, the bang of a door, and the crisp rattle of running footfalls from the street. 'After all, Watson,' said Holmes, reaching up his hand for his clay pipe, 'I am not retained by the police to supply their deficiencies. If Horner were in danger it would be another thing, but this fellow will not appear against him, and the case must collapse. I suppose that I am commuting a felony, but it is just possible that I am saving a soul.'

The Speckled Band

'Palmer and Pritchard were among the heads of their profession. 494 This man strikes even deeper, but I think, Watson, that we shall be able to strike deeper still. But we shall have horrors enough before the night is over: for goodness' sake let us have a quiet pipe and turn our minds for a few hours to something more cheerful.'

The Engineer's Thumb

'Then my servant will call a cab, and I shall be with you in an instant.' I rushed upstairs, explained the matter shortly to my wife, and in five minutes was inside a hansom, driving with my new acquaintance to Baker Street. Sherlock Holmes was, as I expected, lounging about his sitting-room in his dressing-gown, reading the agony column of The Times, and smoking his before-breakfast pipe, which was composed of all the plugs and dottles left from his smokes of the day before, all carefully dried and collected on the corner of the mantelpiece.

The Copper Beeches

'You have erred, perhaps,' he observed, taking up a glowing cinder with the tongs, and lighting with it the long cherrywood pipe which was wont to replace his clay when he was in a disputatious rather than a meditative mood - 'you have erred, perhaps, in attempting to put colour and life into each of your statements, instead of confining yourself to the task of placing upon record that severe reasoning from cause to effect which is really the only notable feature about the thing.'...

'At the same time,' he remarked, after a pause, during which he had sat puffing at his long pipe and gazing down Into the fire, 'you can hardly be open to a charge of sensationalism, for out of these cases which you have been so kind as to interest yourself in, a fair proportion do not treat of crime, in its legal sense, at all.'

Silver Blaze

For a whole day my companion had rambled about the room with his chin upon his chest and his brows knitted, charging and re-charging his pipe with the strongest black tobacco, and absolutely deaf to any of my questions or remarks. Fresh editions of every paper had been sent up by our newsagent only to be glanced over and tossed down into a corner. Yet, silent as he was, I knew perfectly well what it was over which he was brooding.

We all filed into the front room, and sat round the central table, while the Inspector unlocked a square tin box and laid a small heap of things before us. There was a box of vestas, two inches of tallow candle, an A.D.P. briar-root pipe, a pouch of sealskin with half an ounce of long-cut cavendish, a silver watch with a gold chain, five sovereigns in gold, an aluminium pencil-case, a few papers, and an ivory-handled knife with a very delicate inflexible blade marked Weiss & Co., London....

The Yellow Face

'It's very annoying though, Watson. I was badly in need of a case, and this looks, from the man's impatience, as if it were of importance. Hullo! that's not your pipe on the table! He must have left his behind him. A nice old briar, with a good long stem of what the tobacconists call amber. Some people think a fly in it is a sign. Why, it is quite a branch of trade, the putting of sham flies into the sham amber. Well, he must have been disturbed in his mind to leave a pipe behind him which he evidently values highly.'

'How do you know that he values it highly?' I asked.

'Well, I should put the original cost of the pipe at seven-and-sixpence. Now it has, you see, been twice mended: once in the wooden stem and once in the amber. Each of these mends, done, as you observe, with silver bands, must have cost more than the pipe did originally. The man must value the pipe highly when he prefers to patch it up rather than buy a new one with the same money.'

'Anything else?' I asked, for Holmes was turning the pipe about in his hand and staring at it in his peculiar, pensive way.

He held it up and tapped on it with his long, thin fore-finger as a professor might who was lecturing on a bone'

'Pipes are occasionally of extraordinary interest,' said he. 'Nothing has more individuality save, perhaps, watches and bootlaces. The indications here, however, are neither very marked nor very important. The owner is obviously a muscular man, left-handed, with an excellent set of teeth, careless in his habits, and with no need to practise economy.'

My friend threw out the information in a very off-hand way, but I saw that he cocked his eye at me to see if I had followed his reasoning.

'You think a man must be well-to-do if he smokes a seven-shilling pipe?' said I.

'This is Grosvenor mixture at eightpence an ounce,' Holmes answered, knocking a little out on his palm.

'As he might get an excellent smoke for half the price, he has no need to practise economy.'
'And the other points?'

'He has been in the habit of lighting his pipe at lamps and gas-jets. You can see that it is quite charred all down one side. Of course, a match could not have done that. Why should a man hold a match to the side of his pipe? But you cannot light it at a lamp without getting the bowl charred. And it is all on the right side of the pipe. From that I gather that he is a left-handed man. You hold your own pipe to the lamp, and see how naturally you, being right-handed, hold the left side to the flame. You might do it once the other way, but not as a constancy. This has always been held so. Then he has bitten through his amber. 66 It takes a muscular, energetic fellow, and one with a good set of teeth to do that. But if I am not mistaken I hear him upon the stair, so we shall have something more interesting than his pipe to study.'

The 'Gloria Scott'

Now he sat forward in his armchair and spread out the documents upon his knees. Then he lit his pipe and sat for some time smoking and turning them over. 'You never heard me talk of Victor Trevor?' he asked. 'He was the only friend I made during the two years that I was at college.'

The Reigate Squires

Mr Cunningham saw him from the bedroom window, and Mr Alec Cunningham saw him from the back passage. It was a quarter to twelve when the alarm broke out. Mr Cunningham had just got into bed, and Mister Alec was smoking a pipe in his dressing-gown.

The Crooked Man

One summer night, a few months after my marriage, I was seated by my own hearth smoking a last pipe and nodding over a novel, for my day's work had been an exhausting one. My wife had already gone up stairs, and the sound of the locking of the hall door some time before told me that the servants had also retired. I had risen from my seat and was knocking out the ashes of my pipe, when I suddenly heard the clang of the bell.

'Ah! He has left two nail marks from his boot upon your linoleum just where the light strikes it. No, thank you, I had some supper at Waterloo, but I'll smoke a pipe with you with pleasure.' I handed him my pouch, and he seated himself opposite to me, and smoked for some time in silence.

'Having gathered these facts, Watson, I smoked several pipes over them, trying to separate those which were crucial from others which were merely incidental. There could be no question that the most distinctive and suggestive point in the case was the singular disappearance of the door. A most careful search had failed to discover it in the room.'

The Resident Patient

'This, however, is beside the question, Mr Sherlock Holmes, and I quite appreciate how valuable your time is. The fact is that a very singular train of events has occurred recently at my house in Brook Street, and to-night they came to such a head that I felt it was quite impossible for me to wait another hour before asking for your advice and assistance.'

Sherlock Holmes sat down and lit his pipe. 'You are very welcome to both,' said he. 'Pray let me have a detailed account of what the circumstances are which have disturbed you.'

Sherlock Holmes had listened to this long narrative with an intentness which showed me that his interest was keenly aroused. His face was as impassive as ever, but his lids had drooped more heavily over his eyes, and his smoke had curled up more thickly from his pipe to emphasize each curious episode in the doctor's tale. As our visitor concluded Holmes sprang up without a word, handed me my hat, picked up his own from the table, and followed Dr Trevelyan to the door.

'You come at a crisis, Watson,' said he.

'I have not the heart to interrupt your breakfast any further, and yet I am dying to know how you got it and where it was.'

Sherlock Holmes swallowed a cup of coffee and turned his attention to the ham and eggs. Then he rose, lit his pipe, and settled himself down into his chair.
'I'll tell you what I did first, and how I came to do it afterwards,' he said...

The Hound of the Baskervilles

My first impression as I opened the door was that a fire had broken out, for the room was so filled with smoke that the light of the lamp upon the table was blurred by it. As I entered, however, my fears were set at rest, for it was the acrid fumes of strong, coarse tobacco, which took me by the throat and set me coughing. Through the haze I had a vague vision of Holmes in his dressing-gown coiled up in an armchair with his black clay pipe between his lips. Several rolls of paper lay around him. 'Caught cold, Watson? said he.

The Empty House

There were the chemical corner and the acid-stained deal-topped table. There upon a shelf was the row of formidable scrapbooks and books of reference which many of our fellow citizens would have been so glad to burn. The diagrams, the violin-case, and the pipe-rack - even the Persian slipper which contained the tobacco - all met my eye as I glanced round me. There were two occupants of the room-one Mrs. Hudson, who beamed upon us both as we entered; the other, the strange dummy which had played so important a part in the evening's adventures.

The Solitary Cyclist

'It is part of the settled order of Nature that such a girl should have followers,' said Holmes, as he pulled at his meditative pipe, 'but for choice not on bicycles in lonely country roads. Some secretive lover, beyond all doubt. But there are curious and suggestive details about the case, Watson.'

The Priory School

Sherlock Holmes left the house alone, and only returned after eleven. He had obtained a large ordnance map of the neighbourhood, and this he brought into my room, where he laid it out on the bed, and, having balanced the lamp in the middle of it, he began to smoke over it, and occasionally to point out objects of interest with the reeking amber of his pipe.

'This case grows upon me, Watson,' said he. 'There are decidedly some points of interest in connection with it.

As we approached the forbidding and squalid inn, with the sign of a gamecock above the door, Holmes gave a sudden groan and clutched me by the shoulder to save himself from falling. He had had one of those violent strains of the ankle which leave a man helpless. With difficulty he limped up to the door, where a squat, dark, elderly man was smoking a black clay pipe.

'How are you, Mr Reuben Hayes?' said Holmes.

'Who are you, and how do you get my name so pat?' the countryman answered, with a suspicious flash of a pair of cunning eyes.

Black Peter

His initials were inside it. And it was of sealskin - and he was an old sealer.'

'But he had no pipe.

'No, sir, we could find no pipe; indeed, he smoked very little. And yet he might have kept some tobacco for his friends.'

'I saw these advertisements about harpooners and high wages, so I went to the shipping agents, and they sent me here. That's all I know, and I say again that if I killed Black Peter, the law should give me thanks, for I saved them the price of a hempen rope.'

'A very clear statement,' said Holmes, rising and fighting his pipe. 'I think, Hopkins, that you should lose no time in conveying your prisoner to a place of safety.

'But all I heard pointed in the one direction. The amazing strength, the skill in the use of the harpoon, the rum and water, the seal-skin tobacco-pouch, with the coarse tobacco - all these pointed to a seaman, and one who had been a whaler. I was convinced that the initials "PC" upon the pouch were a coincidence, and not those of Peter Carey, since he seldom smoked, and no pipe was found in his cabin. You remember that I asked whether whisky and brandy were in the cabin. You said they were.'

Charles Augustus Milverton

For half an hour he was silent and still. Then, with the gesture of a man who has taken his decision, he sprang to his feet and passed into his bedroom. A little later a rakish young workman with a goatee beard and a swagger lit his clay pipe at the lamp before descending into the street. 'I'll be back some time, Watson,' said he, and vanished into the night.

We had breakfasted and were smoking our morning pipe, on the day after the remarkable experience which I have recorded, when Mr Lestrade, of Scotland Yard, very solemn and impressive, was ushered into our modest sitting-room.
'Good morning, Mr Holmes,' said he - 'good morning. May I ask if you are very busy just now?'

The Missing Three-Quarter

These few inquiries proved, however, to be a more lengthy proceeding than Holmes had imagined, for he did not return to the inn until nearly nine o'clock. He was pale and dejected, stained with dust, and exhausted with hunger and fatigue. A cold supper was ready upon the table, and when his needs were satisfied and his pipe alight he was ready to take that half-comic and wholly philosophic view which was natural to him when his affairs were going awry. The sound of carriage wheels caused him to rise and glance out of the window.

The Abbey Grange

'Well, good-bye, and let us know how you get on.'

Dinner was over and the table cleared before Holmes alluded to the matter again. He had lit his pipe and held his slippered feet to the cheerful blaze of the fire. Suddenly he looked at his watch.

'I expect developments, Watson.'

The Second Stain

When our illustrious visitors had departed, Holmes lit his pipe in silence, and sat for some time lost in the deepest thought. I had opened the morning paper and was immersed in a sensational crime which had occurred in London the night before, when my friend gave an exclamation, sprang to his feet, and laid his pipe down upon the mantelpiece.

'Yes,' said he, 'there is no better way of approaching it. The situation is desperate, but not hopeless.'

Wisteria Lodge

I find it recorded in my notebook that it was a bleak and windy day towards the end of March in the year 1892. Holmes had received a telegram whilst we sat at our lunch, and he had scribbled a reply. He made no remark, but the matter remained in his thoughts, for he stood in front of the fire afterwards with a thoughtful face, smoking his pipe, and casting an occasional glance at the message. Suddenly he turned upon me with a mischievous twinkle in his eyes.

'I suppose, Watson, we must look upon you as a man of letters,' said he.

A good deal of clothing with the stamp of Marx and Co., High Holborn, had been left behind. Telegraphic inquiries had been already made which showed that Marx knew nothing of his customer save that he was a good payer. Odds and ends, some pipes, a few novels, two of them in Spanish, an old-fashioned pin-fire revolver, and a guitar were amongst the personal property.

Inspector Baynes visited us at Baker Street with a printed description of the dark face of the secretary, and of the masterful features, the magnetic black eyes, and the tufted brows of his master. We could not doubt that justice, if belated, had come at last. 'A chaotic case, my dear Watson,' said Holmes, over an evening pipe.

The Bruce-Partington Plans

'Yes, yes, here he is, sure enough! Cadogan West was the young man who was found dead on the Underground on Tuesday morning.'

Holmes sat up at attention, his pipe half-way to his lips.

'This must be serious, Watson. A death which has caused my brother to alter his habits can be no ordinary one.'

The Devil's Foot

'It is the most unheard-of business. We can only regard it as a special Providence that you should chance to be here at the time, for in all England you are the one man we need.'

I glared at the intrusive vicar with no very friendly eyes, but Holmes took his pipe from his lips and sat up in his chair like an old hound who hears the view-hallo. He waved his hand to the sofa, and our palpitating visitor with his agitated companion sat side by side upon it.... It was not until long after we were back in Poldhu Cottage that Holmes broke his complete and absorbed silence. He sat coiled in his armchair, his haggard and ascetic face hardly visible amid the blue swirl of his tobacco smoke, his black brows drawn down, his forehead contracted, his eyes vacant and far away. Finally, he laid down his pipe and sprang to his feet.
'It won't do, Watson!' said he, with a laugh. 'Let us walk along the cliffs together and search for flint arrows.

(Holmes): 'I, at least, am not prepared to prevent you.'

Dr Sterndale raised his giant figure, bowed gravely, and walked from the arbour. Holmes lit his pipe and handed me his pouch.

'Some fumes which are not poisonous would be a welcome change,' said he. 'I think you must agree, Watson, that it is not a case in which we are called upon to interfere.'

The Red Circle

'The matches have, of course, been used to light cigarettes. That is obvious from the shortness of the burnt end. Half the match is consumed in fighting a pipe or cigar. But, dear me! This cigarette stub is certainly remarkable.'

The Dying Detective

Then, unable to settle down to reading, I walked slowly round the room, examining the pictures of celebrated criminals with which every wall was adorned. Finally, in my aimless perambulation, I came to the mantelpiece. A litter of pipes, tobacco-pouches, syringes, penknives, revolver cartridges, and other debris was scattered over it. In the midst of these was a small black and white ivory box with a sliding lid.

The Valley of Fear

Sherlock Holmes had pushed away his untasted breakfast and lit the unsavoury pipe which was the companion of his deepest meditations.

'I wonder!' said he, leaning back and staring at the ceiling. 'Perhaps there are points which have escaped your Machiavellian intellect.'

He appeared to be a man of considerable wealth, and was reputed to be a bachelor. In age he was rather younger than Douglas, forty-five at the most, a tall, straight, broad-chested fellow, with a clean-shaven, prize fighter face, thick, strong, black eyebrows, and a pair of masterful black eyes which might, even without the aid of his very capable hands, clear a way for him through a hostile crowd. He neither rode nor shot, but spent his days in wandering round the old village with his pipe in bis mouth, or in driving with his host, or in his absence with his hostess, over the beautiful countryside...

He sat with his mouth full of toast and his eyes sparkling with mischief, watching my intellectual entanglement. The mere sight of his excellent appetite was an assurance of success, for I had very clear recollections of days and nights without a thought of food, when his baffled mind had chafed before some problem whilst his thin, eager features became more attenuated with the asceticism of complete mental concentration. Finally, he lit his pipe and, sitting in the inglenook of the old village inn, he talked slowly and at random about his case, rather as one thinks aloud than as one who makes a considered statement...

'You think, then, definitely, that Barker and Mrs Douglas are guilty of the murder?'

'There is an appalling directness about your questions, Watson,' said Holmes, shaking his pipe at me. 'They come at me like bullets. If you put it that Mrs Douglas and Barker know the truth about the murder and are conspiring to conceal it, then I can give you a whole-souled answer.'

Below, it stated that a guard of Coal and Iron Police, armed with Winchester rifles, had been requisitioned for the defence of the office. McMurdo had laid down the paper and was lighting his pipe with a hand which was shaky from the excesses of the previous evening, when there was a knock outside, and his landlady brought to him a note which had just been handed in by a lad. It was unsigned, and ran thus:

'I should wish to speak to you but had rather not do so in your house.'

The Mazarin Stone

It was pleasant to Dr Watson to find himself once more in the untidy room of the first floor in Baker Street which had been the starting point of so many remarkable adventures. He looked round him at the scientific charts upon the wall, the acid-charred bench of chemicals, the violin-case leaning in the corner, the coal scuttle, which contained of old the pipes and tobacco...

'The gasogene and cigars are in the old place. Let me see you once more in the customary armchair. 'You have not, I hope, learned to despise my pipe and my lamentable tobacco?'

'It has to take the place of food these days.'

'But why not eat?'

Thor Bridge

'There you have it,' said Sherlock Holmes, knocking out the ashes of his after-breakfast pipe and slowly refilling it. 'That is the gentleman I await. As to the story, you have hardly time to master all these papers, so I must give it to you in a nutshell if you are to take an intellectual interest in the proceedings.'

'Well, I was trying to express it as delicately as I could, but if you insist upon the word I will not contradict you.'

I sprang to my feet, for the expression upon the millionaire's face was fiendish in its intensity, and he had raised his great knotted fist. Holmes smiled languidly, and reached his hand out for his pipe.

Late that evening, as we sat together smoking our pipes in the village inn, Holmes gave me a brief review of what had passed. 'I fear, Watson,' said he, 'that you will not improve any reputation which I may have acquired by adding the Case of the Thor Bridge Mystery to your annals...'

The Creeping Man

The relations between us in those latter days were peculiar. He was a man of habits, narrow and concentrated habits, and I had become one of them. As an institution I was like the violin, the shag tobacco, the old black pipe, the index books, and others perhaps less excusable. When it was a case of active work and a comrade was needed upon whose nerve he could place some reliance, my rôle was obvious. But apart from this I had uses.

When I arrived at Baker Street I found him huddled up in his arm-chair with updrawn knees, his pipe in his mouth and his brow furrowed with thought. It was clear that he was in the throes of some vexatious problem. With a wave of his hand he indicated my old armchair, but otherwise for half an hour he gave no sign that he was aware of my presence.

I shook my head. 'Surely, Holmes, this is a little farfetched,' said I.

He had refilled his pipe and resumed his seat, taking no notice of my comment.

'The practical application of what I have said is very close to the problem which I am investigating. It is a tangled skein, you understand, and I am looking for a loose end.'

The Three Garridebs

'I reckon you will hear within a day or two.' With this assurance our American bowed and departed.

Holmes had lit his pipe, and he sat for some time with a curious smile upon his face.

'Well?' I asked at last. 'I am wondering, Watson - just wondering!'

'At what?'

Holmes took his pipe from his lips.

'I am wondering, Watson, what on earth could be the object of this man in telling us such a rigmarole of lies.'

The Illustrious Client

'I have had several opponents to whom that flattering term has been applied,' said Holmes, with a smile. 'Don't you smoke? Then you will excuse me if I light my pipe. If your man is more dangerous than the late Professor Moriarty, or than the living Colonel Sebastian Moran, then he is indeed worth meeting. 'May I ask his name?'

'I'll go now. 'Anything more?

'Put my pipe on the table - and the tobacco-slipper. Right! Come in each morning and we will plan our campaign.'

The Three Gables

I had not seen Holmes for some days, and had no idea of the new channel into which his activities had been directed. He was in a chatty mood that morning, however, and had just settled me into the well-worn low armchair on one side of the fire, while he had curled down with his pipe in his mouth upon the opposite chair, when our visitor arrived. If I had said that a mad bull had arrived, it would give a clearer impression of what occurred.

The door had flown open and a huge negro had burst into the room.

Without waiting for any further questioning, our visitor bolted out of the room almost as precipitately as he had entered. Holmes knocked out the ashes of his pipe with a quiet chuckle.

'I am glad you were not forced to break his woolly head, Watson. I observed your manoeuvres with the poker.

The Blanched Soldier

The greatest martinet in the Army in his day, and it was a day of rough language, too. I couldn't have stuck the Colonel if it had not been for Godfrey's sake.'

I lit my pipe and leaned back in my chair.

'Perhaps you will explain what you are talking.about.'
My client grinned mischievously. It was a cheery place enough, a bright lamp and a blazing fire. Opposite to me was seated the little man whom I had seen in the morning. He was smoking a pipe and reading a paper.

"What paper?' I asked.

My client seemed annoyed at the interruption of his narrative.

The Retired Colourman

It was late that evening before I returned to Baker Street and gave an account of my mission. Holmes lay with his gaunt figure stretched in his deep chair, his pipe curling forth slow wreaths of acrid tobacco, while his eyelids drooped over his eyes so lazily that he might almost have been asleep were it not that at any halt or questionable passage of my narrative they half lifted, and two grey eyes, as bright and keen as rapiers, transfixed me with their searching glance.

'The Haven is the name of Mr Josiah Amberley's house,' I explained. 'I think it would interest you, Holmes.

The Veiled Lodger

A smart lad that! He was sent later to Allahabad. That was how I came into the matter, for he dropped in and smoked a pipe or two over it.'

'A thin, yellow-haired man?'

'Exactly.'

Shoscombe Old Place

'Then he gave it to Sandy Bain, the jockey, and told him to take the dog to old Barnes at the "Green Dragon", for he never wished to see it again.'

Holmes sat for some time in silent thought. He had lit the oldest and foulest of his pipes. 'I am not clear yet what you want me to do in this matter, Mr Mason,' he said at last. 'Can't you make it more definite?'

The Field Bazaar (although not strictly Canonical! – ed.)

Now I looked across at him to find his eyes fastened upon me with the half-amused, half-questioning expression which he usually assumed when he felt he had made an intellectual point.

'Do what?' I asked.

He smiled as he took his slipper from the mantelpiece and drew from it enough shag tobacco to fill the old clay pipe with which he invariably rounded off his breakfast.

'A most characteristic question of yours, Watson,' said he. 'You will not, I am sure, be offended if I say that any reputation for sharpness which I may possess has been entirely gained by the admirable foil which you have made for me.

HOLMES, WATSON and TOBACCO

By Colonel R.D. Sherbrooke-Walker

'It is quite a three pipe problem...'
Sherlock Holmes, The Red Headed League

In introducing this paper at the March (1952) meeting of The Sherlock Holmes Society of London. Col. Sherbrooke-Walker mentioned that there were about 160 references to tobacco in some form or another, in the Sacred Writings.

Every student knows that Holmes had a vast and instructed knowledge of tobacco. This speaks for itself throughout the records. His monograph on cigar ash - ("I have made a special study of cigar ashes. I flatter myself that I can distinguish at a glance the ash of any known brand either of cigar or of tobacco.") To say nothing of - "Upon the Distinction Between the Ashes of the Various Tobaccos" with coloured plates - produced, no doubt, in those halcyon days, at his publisher's expense. But while Mr. Vaughan-Thomas showed us that Holmes had a nice taste in wine (we shall not easily forget the Montrachet), we must come irresistibly to the conclusion that he had no palate for tobacco.

Smoking to Holmes was merely a habit and a drug. "Your evidence?" you ask. *The shag, Mr Chairman, the shag!*

I appeal to those who have had the terrifying experience of making the tenth man in what Holmes would have called, a carriageful of workmen returning home", and what, I suppose, our Civil Service would call a compartment occupied to optimum capacity by personnel – (manual operatives) proceeding in the return direction to their accommodation units. Anyway, we know what we *mean* and can we accept the contention that any smoker of shag tobacco has a palate? Further, could any man have been a gourmet of tobacco who not only smoked disgusting shag but carefully saved up yesterday's plugs and dottles for his pre-breakfast pipe? And this, when Grosvenor Mixture (evidently the Dunhill equivalent of the day) was 8d. an ounce; and we have Holmes's own word that you could get an excellent smoke for half the price! We cannot believe that poverty drove him to this sordid practice.

Then how did Holmes smoke? A leisurely inhalation of the fumes? No! Witness again The Red Headed League:

"It is quite a three pipe problem and I beg that you won't speak to me for 50 minutes."

Three pipes of shag in 50 minutes. It was not a feat - it was a monstrous abuse of the membrane of the mouth and throat! How poor Watson must have suffered, too!

Let us conjure up in all its stark horror that repulsive scene in Mrs. St. Clair's spare bedroom during the running down of "The Man with the Twisted Lip". The large comfortable double-bedded room, a tired Watson quickly between the sheets. Holmes in his dressing gown turning round and round, like a dog before settling on his pile of pillows and cushions; the ounce of shag (seven pipefuls, mark you), the box of matches, the old briar pipe between his lips. The light fades and Watson sleeps. The hours pass. Suddenly the awakening; the summer sun shining in. "The pipe was still between his lips, the smoke still curled upwards and the room was full of a dense tobacco haze, but nothing remained of the heap of shag which I had seen upon the previous night". Black Peter's cabin "droning like a harmonium with the flies and bluebottles and the floor and wall like a slaughter-house," must yield place to the horrible atmosphere which must have greeted Watson on his return to consciousness, with, we can only conclude, a split- ting head and a mouth like the bottom of a birdcage.

Poor old Watson!

Holmes, as we know, also smoked cigars and cigarettes, and took snuff, although Thaddeus Sholto does not seem to have been able to induce him to take to a hookah, but it is as the avid inhaler of the fumes of strong, coarse tobacco that we shall always think of him.

Now let us turn to the accessories of Holmes's smoking. A briar pipe - probably a dirty one as we hear no mention of pipe cleaners, of conventional pattern, or otherwise. A cherrywood - well, even that could hardly have defiled the bouquet of the shag. The old and oily clay A rigorous examination of this point soon demolishes the contention that it was probably a meerschaum. Even Watson would have recognised a meerschaum.

What did Holmes keep his pipes in? We are told he had a pipe rack, but it can hardly have borne his college arms, or the vexed question of Oxford v Cambridge would have been settled long since. It was probably carved from the skull of an Andaman Islander!

Now for a more important matter. What did he keep his tobacco in? There is no need to remind any student of the Persian slipper. Would any smoker who respected his tobacco have kept it exposed to the air and dust in the toe end of a slipper - Persian or Northampton? And where did he keep the slipper? We have it from Watson that Holmes's cigars lived in the coal scuttle, from which we may well argue that his shag tobacco can hardly have found a more exalted resting place. From the Apocrypha, we learn that on occasion Holmes would fire his pistol three times into the coal box - a sure sign that he was pleased. If this be true, we can only hope that he did not puncture the slipper and add coal dust to the mixture!

Strange to say, there is no mention of any other form of pouch. Holmes surely did not carry the slipper around with him. What was his travelling pouch? Was it a plain moleskin? Or a matter of silk and oilskin, executed in the colours of the Baker Street Irregulars? Was it fashioned from the skin of the soft under-belly of the Giant Rat of Sumatra?

There remain the other containers to be considered. First, Holmes's cigar case. Let us assume that this, at any rate, was of an orthodox pattern and material, but we cannot forget that at his reunion with the benign Watson over the Irene Adler case be "threw across his case of cigars" - a smoker's act of desecration, comparable with that of a wine drinker warming up his *Chateau Lafite* in an aluminium saucepan. And, moreover, be threw the case to Watson, who he must have classified long before as a butterfingers. Altogether this cigar business does Holmes little credit.

As we come to cigarettes, the scene lightens for a moment before a dark cloud looms up and sets us creeping fearfully down an avenue of dreadful supposition.

Cigarettes! Some of us, perhaps, have never quite been able to associate Sherlock Holmes with this effeminate form of smoking. Expert opinion says that they would almost certainly have been Turkish or Egyptian, and that Holmes probably smoked them after coffee, as a concession to the social convention of his time. In view of the incident in Professor Coram's bedroom, we can accept the Turkish or Egyptian, but we are not convinced that Holmes treated cigarettes with any more restraint or delicacy than his tobacco. When Watson came down to breakfast one morning at the height of 'The Norwood Builder' investigation, his stomach must have been turned yet again, when be found Holmes sitting up pale and harassed, and he noticed that "the carpet round his chair was littered with cigarette ends." And what did the patient Mrs. Hudson think in that pre-Hoover era?

However, we can acquit Holmes of one sin. He was no packet smoker. He never joined the ranks of those reprehensible people, too idle or too inordinate in their smoking to carry a cigarette case, who subsist from hand to mouth on the contents of squashed packets. Holmes had a silver case, we learn, from Watson's discovery, after the struggle above the Reichenbach Fall.

Can we accept this? Holmes with a mere silver cigarette case! Surely it would have been an affair of platinum and gold, heavily encrusted with rubies, presented to him by a grateful South American republic after he had cleared up the notable case of ex-

President Murillo?

Now Watson's discovery after, (as he thought,) Holmes had plunged to his death over the Reichenbach Falls, raises a strange and frightening discrepancy. Watson records that be found a cigarette case ('the gleam of something bright caught my eye") but Holmes, when clearing it all up three years later refers to his cigarette box, left with his stick and the note on a rock beside the path. Is it not probable that Watson's untrained memory was at fault, and that Holmes, as usual, was right, and that it was a box? If so, it can have been no ordinary box - bulk supplies, we feel sure, would have been carried by his faithful henchman. What box would Holmes, with his macabre sense of humour, have used? Can it be that Miss Susan Cushing, stricken after the event with the realisation that she had failed to show proper appreciation of Holmes's services in clearing up her grim mystery (or perhaps, by way of a fee - in defiance of the Truck Acts) had sent him the Cardboard Box as a memento and that in this ghastly receptacle (a half-pound honeydew box, be it noted), Holmes was pleased to carry his cigarettes? We do not know. We shall never know.

Let us now turn to lighter matters - to Doctor Watson, that son of Zebedee, as Watson père must surely have been named since, apparently, he fathered both James and John.

We know little of interest about Watson's smoking but we can assume his complete ignorance of the scientific side of tobacco, We are on more certain ground, however, in maintaining that, like Holmes, his palate was undistinguished, although clearly less vitiated than that of his senior partner. Watson never speaks of any personal pleasure in his smoking, of the delight of the after-breakfast pipe, or of the fragrance of his cigar. He smoked a pipe of an unspecified kind, and also, cigars and cigarettes; and Holmes's rebuke: "What with your eternal tobacco, Watson," shows that even Holmes considered him a heavy smoker. Whether, like Holmes, he could blow smoke rings, we do not gather, but I have an odd feeling that this might well have been one of the few things Watson could do with distinction. At any rate, Holmes spotted that he favoured Arcadia Mixture ("there is no· mistaking that fluffy ash upon your coat.") This makes us suspect that Watson was being more polite than truthful when, in reply to Holmes's early inquiry: "You don't mind the smell of strong tobacco, I hope?", Watson says: "I always smoke 'Ships' myself," in his desire to be affable to his future stable companion. Poor Watson little knew what he was letting himself in for.

As for Watson's cigarettes, it is from The Hound of the Baskervilles that we remember Holmes's remark outside the prehistoric hut on Dartmoor: "If you seriously desire to deceive me you must change your tobacconists; for when I see the stub of a cigarette marked Bradley, Oxford Street, I know that my friend Watson is in the neighbourhood." This shop, Bradley, in Oxford Street - is not now to be found but the search has opened up a curious question.

To sum up our conclusions – Holmes knew everything about tobacco - except how really to enjoy it. He possessed neither palate nor restraint, and yet he criticised what be deemed Watson's excesses. Watson knew nothing of tobacco scientifically, and smoked heavily, but retained at least his olfactory sense. He censured Holmes as a self-poisoner by tobacco. The pot and the kettle, with Watson was, for once, a little brighter than Holmes.

And there we will leave them, the master and his disciple, on either side of their fire at 221B, Baker Street, while the wind screams outside and the rain beats on the windows. Holmes is cross-indexing his records of crime, the old and oily clay between his teeth, while the acrid fumes of strong coarse tobacco swirl around him Watson, the Pink 'Un at his elbow, is planning the expenditure of half the next instalment of his wound pension, puffing at his cigar - and we would not have them otherwise.

A peaceful scene, but one we fear inevitably will be disturbed within the hour by the long grind of a wheel as it rasps against the kerb in the street below.

(This essay first appeared in March 1952 in 'The Sherlock Holmes Journal' and is reprinted here with kind permission by the editor.)

THE CURIOUS CASE OF THE OPIUM DEN

By Kelvin I Jones

'Isa Whitney, brother of the late Elias Whitney, D.D., Principal of the Theological College of St. George's, was much addicted to opium. The habit grew upon him, as I understand, from some foolish freak when he was at college; for having read De Quincey's description of his dreams and sensations, he had drenched his tobacco with laudanum, in an attempt to produce the same effects. He found, as so many more have done, that the practice is easier to attain than to get rid of, and for many years he continued to be a slave to the drug, an object of mingled horror and pity to his friends and relatives. I can see him now, with yellow, pasty face, drooping lids, and pin-point pupils, all huddled in a chair, the wreck and ruin of a noble man.'

So begins Watson's account of The Adventure of 'The Man with The Twisted Lip.' The questions we Sherlockians must face are: was Isa Whitney a purely fictional invention, did Holmes smoke it and was Sherlock Holmes addicted to opium?

Who exactly was Whitney? At first glance, he was the brother of an ecclesiastical cleric. Was Whitney also a student of theology? Most likely. But why did he become so deeply influenced by the works of De Quincey?

De Quincey, who was well known to Conan Doyle, and who, similarly, lived for some years in Edinburgh, was alienated from his solid, prosperous mercantile family by his sensitivity and precocity. At the age of 17 he ran away to Wales and then lived incognito in London (1802–03). There he formed a friendship with a young prostitute named Ann, who made a lasting impression on him.

Reconciled to his family in 1803, he entered Worcester College, Oxford, where he conceived the ambition of becoming, in his words. 'the intellectual benefactor of mankind.' He became widely read in many subjects and eventually would write essays on such subjects as history, biography, economics, psychology, and German philosophy. While he was still at college in 1804, he took his first dose of opium in the form of tincture of laudanum to relieve the pain of facial neuralgia. By 1813 he had become "a regular and confirmed opium-eater" (i.e., an opium addict), keeping a decanter of laudanum (tincture of opium) by his elbow and steadily increasing the dose; he remained an addict for the rest of his life.

De Quincey was an early admirer of the Lakeland poets, and in 1807 he became a close associate of its authors, Wordsworth and Coleridge. He rented Wordsworth's former home, Dove Cottage, on and off from 1809 to 1833. In 1817 De Quincey married Margaret Simpson, who had already borne him a son. Though he wrote extensively, he published almost nothing at all. His financial position as head of a large family worsened, until the appearance of 'Confessions' (1821), in 'London Magazine' made him famous. It was reprinted as a book in 1822. Sadly, he later revised the work, adding what can only be described as a great deal of discursive and pedantic flim – flam. De Quincey's rambling and often self-congratulatory style is often intensely irritating, and the secret of his book's success is almost certainly due to the fact that no one in the Western world had bothered to make an accurate record of the drug and its side effects.

In the original version of the book, De Quincey, in the later stages of the drug, and where his usage has significantly increased, begins to experience hallucinations. He compares his phantoms to the ghosts that children sometimes claim to see. He has some control over his hallucinations; he can consciously think of a particular topic, and it will then manifest itself in the apparitions he sees in the darkness. However, these conscious hallucinations often reappear in his dreams in more sinister forms. The tone of De Quincey's nightmares becomes more depressing and melancholic, and this often affects his mood during the day as well, so that he feels 'suicidal despondency.' The opium also distorts the proportions of the things he sees and seemingly, makes time pass more slowly. Insignificant incidents from his past that he had forgotten about, come back to haunt him in his dreams.

De Quincey explains that "The Pains of Opium" will be the memoir's most impressionistic and disorganized section, but it remains the most structurally rigid part of the text. De Quincey relates his thoughts in numbered lists, and clearly says, at the beginning of each new anecdote, what the anecdote is about and what its broader significance is. Unlike in the early parts of the memoir, which read similarly to fiction, "The Pains of Opium" uses the rhetorical conventions of the classical essay.

De Quincey presents individual anecdotes as examples of broader changes in his lifestyle. He often dreamt of lakes and became worried this was a sign that his brain had dropsy. In the May of 1818, De Quincey dreamt about the Malay. The dream is set in China, and in it, De Quincey is terrified of the intimidating foreign culture. A year later, he dreamt of visiting a child's grave and of seeing Ann sitting on a stone. The setting changed to where he was walking with Ann through their old haunt, London's Oxford Street. The most recent dream, from 1820, was a nightmare, in which De Quincey is surrounded by a chorus of loud music that evokes the "caves of hell" and "everlasting farewells". Shortly after this, De Quincey realized that he would die if he did not decrease his opium use, and he did so despite very painful symptoms.

The opium den, with all its mystery, danger and intrigue, appeared in many Victorian novels, poems and contemporary newspapers, and fuelled the public's imagination. Here are two examples, one of which was written at the period, some while after TWIS appeared in the Strand Magazine.

"There were opium dens where one could buy oblivion, dens of horror where the memory of old sins could be destroyed by the madness of sins that were new."

Oscar Wilde in his novel, 'The Picture of Dorian Gray' (1891) conveys this melodramatic picture:

"It is a wretched hole... so low that we are unable to stand upright.

Lying pell-mell on a mattress placed on the ground are Chinamen, Lascars, and a few English blackguards who have imbibed a taste for opium."

So reported the French journal 'Figaro', describing an opium den in Whitechapel in 1868. The first of these descriptions is by Wilde, who had written his novel as a response to an invitation both he and Conan Doyle had received from the agent who subsequently printed their work in Lippincott's Magazine. Intriguingly, Wilde chose to write about the gradual erosion of the self, experienced by his protagonist through the use of drugs and a libidinous lifestyle.

'The Sign of Four,' which Doyle submitted, is also much preoccupied with drugs and drug taking. Indeed, the first chapter of Watson's narrative is almost entirely devoted to Homes' explanation of why he uses cocaine and morphine. Readers at the time would have regarded both Dorian Gray and Holmes as 'Bohemians', a widely used concept which had connotations of decadence, self – indulgence, 'art for art's sake' and 'fin de siècle.' Wilde himself believed that he was witnessing the end of civilization, and that it was a period of decadence, much like the latter days of the Roman Empire. Apart from drugs and art, what else was there to enjoy during those declining days of an Empire which had grown gluttonous and terminally exploitative?

The public must have shuddered at these descriptions and imagined areas such as London's docklands, and the East End, to be opium-drenched, exotic and dangerous places.

In the 1800s a small Chinese community had settled in the established slum of Limehouse in London's docklands, an area of backstreet pubs, brothels and opium dens. These dens catered mainly for seamen who had become addicted to the drug when overseas. Despite the lurid accounts of opium dens in the press and fiction, in reality, there were very few outside of London and the ports, where opium was landed alongside other cargo from all over the British Empire.

The den visited by Holmes and Watson was situated in Upper Swandam Lane, in Rotherhithe. As a youth, I often cycled from my home in Lewisham to Rotherhithe, which was still then a place of gaunt red brick warehouses, interspersed with small public houses and residential buildings. Here I discovered several likely contenders for the opium den of TWIS, with a basement and upper floor at the back of which doors opened to convey goods onto barges.

What puzzled me at the time when I first read Dr Watson's account, and what still intrigues me now, is Holmes' comment to his chronicler about his familiarity with the opium den: 'Had I been recognised in that den my life would not have been worth an hour's purchase; for I have used it before now for my own purposes, and the rascally Lascar who runs it has sworn to have vengeance upon me. There is a trap door at the back of that building, near the corner of Paul's Wharf, which could tell some strange tales of what has passed through it upon the moonless nights.'

Exactly what does Holmes mean by telling Watson that he has used the place 'before now for my own purposes'? Does it mean that he has used the den for recreational opium smoking? Or is he referring to some undercover work which in the past has necessitated his visiting the den in a disguise? Both would imply that he stayed on the premises, smoking amounts of opium unspecified.

Even more curious is the fact that in the June 1891 edition of the, then relatively new, illustrated Strand Magazine. an entire article appeared, graphically illustrated, and entitled 'A Night in An Opium Den.' The anonymous author describes in some detail the sordid den he visited in the Ratcliffe Highway.

Here, with the Ratcliffe Highway murders, we come full circle with De Quincey once more. As Nick Louras points out in his intriguing and scholarly article about De Quincey and Doyle, (BSJ Vol 69, No 3): 'De Quincey wrote at length about the Ratcliffe Highway Murders which occurred in Wapping East London.' The Ratcliffe Highway Murders are mentioned in 'A Study In Scarlet' where they are compared to the Brixton Road murder.

Referred to in the newspaper report in STUD, Ratcliffe Highway is a road in the London borough of Stepney, subsequently renamed St. George's Street. Holmes, it will be recalled, sent "a couple of messages" to "Sumner, shipping Agent" in BLAC. Several murders took place here in the early 19th century.

On December 7, 1811, a family known as the Marrs were found brutally murdered in their East End shop. In less than a fortnight another massacre occurred. This time the victims were the landlord and his wife in a pub in Gravel Lane. Four days later an Irish sailor was arrested on suspicion of the murders. His name was Williams. At first, the evidence was hardly convincing. Fresh evidence, collected from witnesses who knew the publican, was only circumstantial (for instance, a laundress, who washed William's linen, stated he had given her a shirt to wash which was torn and bloodstained.) While the inquiry was still in progress, Williams hanged himself in his cell at Coldbath Fields prison. Although Williams' and Marrs' pasts were connected, no real motive for the murders of the victims was satisfactorily established.

We return now to the mention of the Ratcliffe Highway murder in the Strand article. In the opening paragraphs of the article, the name of De Quincey is mentioned twice. The author claims that his efforts to describe the effects of the drug are not as effective as those literary descriptions of Coleridge or De Quincey. The den hosts several Chinese operatives and, like the Swandam Lane establishment which has a 'Lascar' in charge of operations, – an East Indian sailor, army servant, or artillery trooper during the era of European colonialism in Asia). The Ratcliffe Highway den also has an obligatory 'Malay – a person from the east Sumatran peninsula. In the Strand account, the Chinaman in charge is described in grotesque and caricatured terms:

'The smile became even more rigid, when I explained that I was anxious to smoke a pipe of opium. The way in which he turned his face upon me was...for all the world like the turning on by a policeman of a bull's eye lantern. With a final grin which threatened to permanently distort his features, he bade us follow him...'

In a similar article to the 'Strand Magazine' piece, published in

'Tit-Bits' on 31st October 1891, the anonymous author describes a visit to an opium den near the East India Docks, 'within the sound of the big bell of St Paul's (cathedral), where the author explains how 'we turn(ed) down a dreary side street, at the corners of which are loafing some rather ugly customers of the Lascar type' and then reach 'what appears to be a shop. Within lies the kitchen with a tin pan on a fire of coke and coal in which the opium is prepared; a staircase leads up to a pair of rooms' where the customers 'wander through scenes which none but a De Quincey can portray.'

The close resemblance of the Ratcliffe Highway den to the one in Upper Swandam Lane poses the question: in writing up the narrative of TWIS, did Watson simply reinvent the former location, basing it upon these contemporaneous accounts? If so, one is led to the conclusion that Watson never actually visited an opium den and that the opium den episode is simply a poetic elaboration, a piece of sensationalism designed to intrigue and entertain readers of the Strand when the story appeared in its pages in the latter part of that year.

If that assumption is correct, why the mention of opium at all? We already know that Holmes injected himself with morphine, by his own admission (SIGN). Would it therefore be quite logical and inevitable that he also took opium on a regular basis? If so his 'undercover' operations would seem even more impressive to the Malay or Lascar.

The links between De Quincey and Conan Doyle are intriguing. As both Nick Louras, (q.v.) and Michael Harrison in his 'A Study In Surmise' suggest, Doyle had read De Quincey closely and the De Quincey book also comes up in a non Holmes story entitled 'The Silver Hatchet.' Harrison notes in his book that there was an 1888 edition of the De Quincey book in Doyle's house at 1 Bush Villas, Southsea, where he conceived many of the initial Holmes tales.

The use of opium as a powerful narcotic and as a substance which could be used in a criminal context occurs elsewhere in the Canon. For example, the victim of the assumed attack in 'Silver Blaze' – John Straker – has the remains of his supper analysed.

However, '...an analysis has shown that the remains (of his supper,) left by the stable lad, contained an appreciable quantity of powdered opium, while the people of the house partook of the same dish on the same night without any ill effect.' Holmes then conjectures: 'Powdered opium is by no means tasteless. The flavour is not disagreeable, but it is perceptible. Were it mixed with any ordinary dish, the eater would undoubtedly detect it, and would probably eat no more.'

Elsewhere, in the case of 'Wisteria Lodge,' the victim has been drugged with opium to render her helpless. 'She bore upon her aquiline and emaciated face the traces of some recent tragedy. Her head hung listlessly upon her breast, but as she raised it and turned her dull eyes upon us, I saw that her pupils were dark dots in the centre of the broad grey iris. She was drugged with opium.' Finally, in the 'Lion's Mane,' the unwitting victim of an attack by a deadly jellyfish asks for opium to ease his terrible pain:

'He pushed himself up on one arm and swung his coat off his shoulders. 'For God's sake! oil, opium, morphia!' he cried. 'Anything to ease this infernal agony!' The Inspector and I cried out at the sight.'

There was nothing remarkable about Holmes' taking opium, or indeed about administering it to patients or oneself. In a letter written to the BMJ in September 1879, Conan Doyle comments on his researches into the effects of gelsemium: 'The system may learn to tolerate gelsemium as it may opium.'

As we have seen, opium smoking was highly popular among the 'Bohemian' set. Opium and other narcotic drugs played an important part in Victorian life. Shocking though it might be to us in the 21st century, in Victorian times it was entirely possible to walk into a chemist and buy, without prescription, laudanum, cocaine and even arsenic, as long as the recipient of such drugs signed for them. Opium preparations were sold quite freely in towns and country markets and were often obtainable from market stalls run by 'quacks.' Indeed, the consumption of opium was just as popular in the country as it was in urban areas.

The most popular preparation was laudanum, an alcoholic herbal mixture containing 10% opium. Called the 'aspirin of the nineteenth century,' Laudanum was a popular painkiller and relaxant, recommended for all sorts of ailments including coughs, rheumatism, 'women's troubles' and also, perhaps most disturbingly, as a soporific for babies and young children. As we know, Samuel Taylor Coleridge became addicted to laudanum after he took it on a regular basis to quell the pain of his rheumatism. As twenty or twenty-five drops of laudanum could be bought for just a penny, it was also very affordable. Laudanum addicts would enjoy highs of euphoria followed by deep lows of depression, along with slurred speech and restlessness. Withdrawal symptoms included aches and cramps, nausea, vomiting and diarrhoea but even so, it was not until the early 20th century that it was recognised as addictive.

Many notable Victorians are known to have used laudanum as an effective painkiller. Authors, poets and writers such as Charles Dickens, Elizabeth Barrett Browning, Elizabeth Gaskell and George Eliot were users of laudanum. Anne Bronte is believed to have modelled the character of Lord Lowborough in 'The Tenant of Wildfell Hall' on her brother Branwell, who was a laudanum addict. The poet Percy Bysshe Shelley suffered terrible laudanum-induced hallucinations and Robert Clive, 'Clive of India', used laudanum to ease gallstone pain and depression.

Many of the opium-based preparations were targeted at women. Marketed as 'women's friends'. These were widely prescribed by doctors for problems with menstruation and childbirth, and even for fashionable female maladies of the day, such as 'the vapours', which included hysteria, depression and fainting fits. In the Sherlock Holmes Canon, there are numerous examples of people experiencing fainting fits. Watson incorrectly assumes that brandy is the antidote to such fits (see the fainting fit by Ryder, the hotel attendant in BLUE), but as Doyle would have known, laudanum would have sufficed, though he does not use it.

Children were also given opiates. To keep them quiet, children were often spoon-fed Godfrey's Cordial (also known as Mother's Friend), consisting of opium, water and treacle and recommended for colic, hiccups and coughs. Overuse of this dangerous concoction is known to have resulted in the severe illness or death of many children. The Victorians had an ambivalent attitude to laudanum. They were censorious about the working class taking it, which they regarded as a misuse of the drug whereas the middleclass users of the narcotic were above reproach.

The Victorians had an ambivalent attitude to laudanum. They were censorious about the working class taking it, which they regarded as a misuse of the drug whereas the middle - class users of the narcotic were above reproach.

But what of Holmes? I believe that he was a regular user of opium; that as a typical 'Decadent' of his time he indulged in a number of substances which heightened consciousness. He abhorred the dull routine of everyday existence and, like the 1890s poets, who similarly used absinthe to escape from the ennui of their urban existence, Holmes, the self - poisoner by tobacco, the morphine and cocaine user, also smoked opium, but when Watson came to write up the Neville St Clair case, Holmes instructed his companion and amanuensis to slightly bend the truth.

(Note: a shorter version of this essay appears in the author's revised edition of 'Sherlock And Porlock: Literary Influences in the Sherlock Holmes Stories'.)

Made in the USA
Columbia, SC
14 February 2021